THE RISE AND FALL OF THE EAGLE

An Assessment of the Liberal World Order

THE RISE AND FALL OF THE EAGLE

An Assessment of the Liberal World Order

Çağatay Özdemir

AAP APPLE ACADEMIC PRESS

First edition published 2024

Apple Academic Press Inc.
1265 Goldenrod Circle, NE,
Palm Bay, FL 32905 USA

760 Laurentian Drive, Unit 19,
Burlington, ON L7N 0A4, CANADA

CRC Press
2385 NW Executive Center Drive,
Suite 320, Boca Raton FL 33431

4 Park Square, Miiton Park,
Abingdon, Oxon, OX14 4RN UK

Library and Archives Canada Cataloguing in Publication

Title: The rise and fall of the eagle : an assessment of the liberal world order / Çağatay Özdemir, PhD.
Names: Özdemir, M. Çağatay, author.
Description: First edition. | Includes bibliographical references and index.
Identifiers: Canadiana (print) 20230555071 | Canadiana (ebook) 20230555144 | ISBN 9781774917251 (hardcover) | ISBN 9781774917268 (softcover) | ISBN 9781032701370 (ebook)
Subjects: LCSH: United States—Foreign relations—20th century. | LCSH: United States—Foreign relations—21st century. | LCSH: International relations—History—20th century. | LCSH: International relations—History—21st century.
Classification: LCC E744 .O93 2024 | DDC 327.73—dc23

Library of Congress Cataloging-in-Publication Data

....

CIP data on file with US Library of Congress

....

ISBN: 978-1-77491-725-1 (hbk)
ISBN: 978-1-77491-726-8 (pbk)
ISBN: 978-1-03270-137-0 (ebk)

About the Author

Çağatay Özdemir, PhD

Çağatay Özdemir, PhD, completed his doctorate studies at the Department of Political History and International Relations of the Middle East at the Marmara University, Institute of Middle East and Islamic Countries. He was granted the title of Associate Professor in International Relations with his academic studies on America, the Middle East, and Transatlantic Studies.

Özdemir, who has given various seminars and lectures in numerous universities on American grand strategy, diplomacy, and international relations in the globalizing world, is the author of the book *"American Grand Strategy: Obama's Middle East Legacy."*

Dr. Özdemir served at the Research Center for Foreign Policy in the Foundation for Political, Economic, and Social Research (SETA), has worked as an international board member of the Med-Or Leonardo Foundation in Italy and is currently a member of the advisory board of the Research Center of The Sea and Maritime Law (DEHUKAM) at Ankara University.

Dedication

This book is dedicated to
my beloved son
Eymen

Contents

Abbreviations

ADB	Asian Development Bank
AIIB	Asian Infrastructure Investment Bank
AoC	Alliance of Civilizations
CCP	Chinese Communist Party
CCTV	China Central Television
CIA	Central Intelligence Agency
CIS	Commonwealth of Independent Republics
Comecon	Council for Mutual Economic Assistance
CRA	Contingency Reserve Arrangement
CSCE	Conference on Security and Cooperation in Europe's
DFLP	Democratic Front for the Liberation of Palestine
EU	European Union
FBI	Federal Bureau of Investigation
FCIC	Financial Crisis Inquiry Commission
G7	Group of Seven
G20	Group of Twenty
GATT	General Agreement on Tariffs and Trade
GCC	Gulf Cooperation Council
GDP	Gross Domestic Product
GNA	Government of National Accord
GNC	General National Congress
GNP	Gross National Product
GUAM	Organization for Democracy and Economic Development
HOR	House of Representatives
ICC	International Criminal Court
IMF	International Monetary Fund
IP	Internet Protocol
ISAF	International Security Assistance Force
ISIS	Islamic State of Iraq and Syria
KLA	Kosovo Liberation Army
LNA	Libyan National Army
LPA	Libyan Political Accord
NAFTA	North American Free Trade Agreement

NATO	North Atlantic Treaty Organization
NDB	New Development Bank
NGO	Nongovernmental Organization
NPT	Nuclear Non-Proliferation Treaty
NSC	National Security Council
NSS	National Security Strategy
OAF	Operation Allied Force
OECD	Organization for Economic Co-operation and Development
OSCE	Organization for Security and Co-operation in Europe
PC	Presidential Council
PLA	People's Liberation Army
PLAN	People's Liberation Army Navy
PPP	Purchasing Power Parity
QDR	Quadrennial Defense Review
QRF	Quick Reaction Force
SCAF	Supreme Council of the Armed Forces
SEATO	Southeast Asia Treaty Organization
SOEs	State-Owned Enterprises
TPP	Trans-Pacific Partnership
UK	United Kingdom
UN	United Nations
UNDP	United Nations Development Program
UNHCR	United Nations High Commissioner for Refugees
UNITAF	Unified Task Force
UNOSOM	United Nations Operation in Somalia
UNPROFOR	United Nations protection force
UNSC	United Nations Security Council
US	United States
USAID	US Agency for International Development
USSR	Union of Soviet Socialist Republics
WHO	World Health Organization
WTO	World Trade Organization

Preface

Discussions regarding the global spread of the dominant state's power and ideology in the international system have been occurring for a very long time. Different ideological perspectives and international relations theories pertaining to the conjuncture, especially during periods of war and peace, form the center of these discussions. When we look at the past, especially during times when the power projection was determined according to a country or an alliance, we see that the ideology of the time also evolved in that direction. In other words, whichever center of power prevails in the international system, the ideology of that center becomes the determinant of the international system. For centuries, the sole goal of all states that have tried to establish hegemony in the international system has been to impose their basic ideologies on a global scale. However, this process introduces new challenges and raises discussions of sustainable hegemony as well as many other parameters.

One of the main problems for states that compete in the international system and create strategies for power maximization is how they will embellish their ideologies with these strategies and impose them on a global scale. In this respect, the state that becomes the most powerful in the international system can spread its set of ideological beliefs globally. The process in question emerges as a set of views that the dominant global power considers ideal, and those views continue to spread in direct proportion to the power of the dominant state in the international system. The aforementioned phenomenon contains some possibilities and dilemmas within itself. For instance, can a state that has become a global hegemony fully reflect its ideology while fortifying its power? Does this situation create stability, or does it fuel conflict? Does the ideological plane of the dominant state in the international system become an imposition? Although it sometimes creates paradoxes in the face of such questions, it is obvious that the state that strives to maximize its power at the global level tries every possible path. You can see this in the realist school of thought, as without power maximization, there is no other way to fully impose a systematic ideology. When we look at the past from this perspective, we can see strong state pressure behind every ideology that was believed to be correct in the international system. This pressure maximizes the global power of a state and forms the core of its goal to establish a sustainable hegemony.

There is a constant debate regarding the global system, from the emergence of state structure to the development and deepening of interstate relations, from traditional governments to monarchies, and from autocracies to democracies. The tension and wars between the Hittites and the Egyptians brought about an ideological debate, and the efforts of the Roman Empire to impose its existence and dominant ideology later on were the products of this debate. The empires, rulers, states, and governments that emerged throughout history all tried to gain acceptance in the international arena by reinforcing their power. The international system has become the primary domain in which states seek to demonstrate their power, causing it to undergo significant changes and transformations. It has been a stage for many states and different ideologies, witnessing their power struggles and efforts to gain ideological superiority for centuries. The struggle for the superiority of each state and ideological concept brought about a spiral of wars and methods of struggle, and a system has emerged where tension is maximized.

The book in your hands tackles the foreign policy choices of the United States (US), which has recently dominated the international system in terms of the aforementioned concept and the "liberal world order" that it has sought to establish through its foreign policy. This discussion itself is more than just a matter of cause and effect. Some international relations theorists claim that, based on the ideological imposition of the US, the international system has adopted the liberal values of the US on its own accord. However, the situation has many different dimensions because the US establishes its dominance and ideology in the international system through the use of military force. Since each international relations theory sees this situation differently, we may consider looking at it from a broader perspective. For example, while post-structuralists unsettle the ontological and epistemological roots of the international relations' theoretical framework and focus on non-state structures as the factors affecting the international system, constructivists reduce the matter to discussions of identity awareness and meta-ideological acceptance, liberals consider individuals and privately constituted groups as the main actors in international politics by favoring *international cooperation, human rights, and democracy*. Among all these different perspectives, the book in your hand addresses the hegemony debate in the international system on a realistic axis. At the core of this axis lies the maximization of power and the motto: "Sovereign is he who decides on the exception," as Carl Schmitt puts it.

The dominant actor of the international system in the 20th century has been the US. The White House has tried to establish its ideology of liberalism in the international system and exert it over other states. In this process, it has faced threats that any powerful state would face and has made various foreign policy choices. Since the day it was founded, the US has also experienced the process of making itself accepted at the international level, which has been experienced by every state throughout history. The rise of the US coincided with the end of the Cold War. The fact that the White House has become the dominant power of the unipolar world order has raised many debates, and it has developed policies to establish and maintain liberalism in the international system. Eventually, the US' set of values seemed to be accepted swiftly at the global level, especially in the Soviet geography after the Cold War. Although these value sets form an ideology based on liberal foundations, they ultimately prove to be an axis protecting US interests. However, the US' journey of maintaining power at a global level has severely eroded over the years and fueled the debate about the "rise and fall of the eagle." Even though the US maximized its power after the Cold War, end-of-history thesis thinkers like Fukuyama were in vain and extended to Huntington's "the clash of civilizations," but ultimately evolved to a point that should not be overlooked. Today, the White House's power in the international system is decreasing, putting the liberal world order in danger. The US and the liberal world order are further threatened by different actors and the ideological barriers that come to the fore more each day. An environment is emerging in which regional powers like China and Russia are threatening the balance of power in the world from different aspects.

This book looks at the "crisis in the liberal world system" from the framework of the crises that lie in the foreign policy of the US. Parallel to the US' decline in power, the liberal world order is also collapsing. The main purpose of this book is to present a perspective different from the leading figures of our time in the field of international relations, such as Mearsheimer, Walt, Waltz, and Gilpin, who all deal with the developments in the international system from different perspectives. To reach this goal, this book was written in an academic format and is based on a literature review, US laws, executive orders, primary sources, and the US foreign policy that is trying to protect the liberal world order.

I hope this book contributes to the academic world and the literature of international relations and becomes a source of reference for the liberal world order crisis, which the US is attempting to keep alive through its foreign policy. It should also be noted that a book is created based on an idea, and an idea is created based on concrete data and provable facts. I hope we never give up the search for truth. I wish you a pleasant reading!

Introduction

Following the end of the Second World War, the United States (US) and its allies established a new form of global governance centered on the principles of an open trade system, collaborative security, collective decision-making, democratic unity, and American hegemony. Regional and global institutions have been constituted to promote cooperation, uphold common norms, and foster social cohesion. The post-war era involved a heyday of economic development and social advancement throughout the industrial world. The liberal international order faced numerous difficulties during the Cold War, including the fear of nuclear war, the continuance of poverty, and inequality in many regions of the world. Despite these difficulties, the order managed to adapt and change with the times. This US-led liberal world order grew more widespread with the end of the Cold War and the dissolution of the Soviet Union. Thus, countries on the periphery of this order changed their political and economic systems to fit in. The ideological conflict between major powers was at its lowest level (Ikenberry, 2020, p. 2).

In this regard, the dissolution of the Soviet Union in 1991 represented a pivotal moment in global history. The bipolar global system that materialized after the Second World War, featuring the competition between the US and the Soviet Union, ultimately ended. It brought about significant alterations to the international system, which have had a lasting impact on global politics. Following the collapse of the Berlin Wall, a notable transformation in the global system was the ascension of the US as the sole superpower. After the dissolution of the Soviet Union, the US emerged as the preeminent global power in terms of both military and economic might. The aforementioned circumstance bestowed upon the US a notable degree of sway over worldwide matters and the capacity to mold the global framework in accordance with its preferences.

The ascent of the US as a sole superpower constituted a further transformation within the global system. The end of the Cold War ushered in a new epoch of economic amalgamation and the proliferation of capitalism on a global scale. The proliferation of global trade and investment has engendered new prospects for advancement and progress, albeit concomitantly posing fresh predicaments such as the exacerbation of income disparity and the erosion of domestic industries in certain nations. With the cessation of the Soviet Union's promotion of communism, the proliferation of democracy emerged as a viable objective for the US and other Western nations. The gradual dissemination of democratic principles and human rights has played a role in fostering a more stable and peaceful global system. The international system underwent a transformation marked by the emergence of new security challenges. Following the end of the Cold War, the potentiality of a nuclear conflict between the US and the Soviet Union was eliminated. Nevertheless, new security challenges have arisen, encompassing acts of terrorism, cyber assaults, and cross-border criminal activities. The emergence of new threats has necessitated different approaches to international security and cooperation, thereby posing challenges to conventional concepts of sovereignty and territorial integrity.

The role of international organizations has undergone a transformation in the context of the evolving nature of the international system. Although the United Nations (UN) has failed to prevent recent crises and conflicts, with the end of the Cold War, it assumed a more prominent role in the realm of global governance. The United Nations Security Council (UNSC), which was previously hindered by the competition between the US and the Soviet Union, has been able to assume a more proactive stance in preserving global peace and security. Furthermore, the proliferation of regional entities, such as the European Union (EU), has had an impact on the evolving character of the global system. Hence, the fall of the Soviet Union in 1991 had a significant effect on the global system, leading to the emergence of liberal internationalism as the dominant paradigm in international relations.

For the past two centuries, the overarching objective of liberal internationalism has been to establish a global system that is characterized by openness, a flexible framework of regulations, and a focus on advancing progressive ideals (Ikenberry, 2020, p. 1). The promotion and growth of the free international order have long been spearheaded by the US and have played a key role in fostering peace and economic development worldwide. The concept of liberal hegemony involves the pursuit of a global order that is liberal in nature, with the US serving as the guiding force behind its expansion and consolidation. The US has played a significant role in advancing the liberal world order by leading the establishment and sustenance of international organizations that uphold liberal principles. These institutions have significantly contributed to the promotion of free commerce, extending financial aid to emerging nations, and advocating for civil liberties and democratic principles globally.

A number of fundamental precepts or assumptions about the nature of world politics and the US position in the present international system serve as the foundation for liberal hegemony. Together, these ideas give the appearance of being both essential and compatible with fundamental American values, as well as being affordable and attainable. The significance attributed to US leadership for the expansion of liberal world order is indicative of the belief that the US held a distinctive position to disseminate democratic values and other liberal principles globally and that such an endeavor would be advantageous for all. Proponents of liberal hegemony held the view that its benefits would be readily discernible to a vast majority of individuals and that the virtuous objectives of the US would not be subject to skepticism (Walt, 2018a, pp. 75–78). The US leadership role was also emphasized by American politicians for many years. In his second inaugural address, President George W. Bush stated, "It is the policy of the US to seek and support the growth of democratic movements and institutions … with the ultimate goal of ending tyranny in our world … America's influence is not unlimited, but fortunately for the oppressed, America's influence is considerable, and we will use it confidently in freedom's cause" (President Bush's Second Inaugural Address, 2005).

However, after a brief concentration of power in the 1990s, the US hegemony faced a number of challenges. In other words, despite playing a leading role in advancing the liberal world order, the US has faced great difficulties in upholding and extending it. The complicated and continuous process of the US' relative decrease in power has led to noteworthy consequences for both the nation itself and the global community. The US, despite being the largest economy and military power globally, is facing challenges to its influence from other nations and global factors. Thus, recently, the US grand strategy has come under scrutiny, and there has been intense debate about the future of the liberal world order and the role that the US should play in shaping it.

Efforts to "turn back the clock of globalization," which have been manifested in the recent period with the rise of anti-globalization and anti-liberal nationalist tendencies, have now turned into a serious test in terms of the continuity and durability of the liberal international order. The perception that globalization and the liberal world order have not fulfilled their promises is a significant factor contributing to their opposition of them. Globalization has been associated with various advantages, including expanded trade, access to novel markets, and enhanced cultural interaction. However, it has also led to economic inequality and job losses, especially in developed nations. Thus, the liberal world order has faced criticism for its perceived emphasis on the interests of the elite and its alleged neglect of the other segments of the population.

In this regard, the current state of crisis in the global order can be attributed to various factors, such as the emergence of nationalism, populism, erosion of democratic norms, the spread of pandemics across international borders, and the challenges posed by globalization and technological advancements. These factors have collectively contributed to the destabilization of the foundations of the liberal world order.

Globalization has triggered effects on nationalism. The concept of nationalism is not a novel occurrence; however, it has experienced an upward trend in contemporary times. The phenomenon of globalization has resulted in a feeling of displacement and confusion among a significant number of individuals. There is a prevalent sentiment among individuals that they are experiencing a loss of agency in both their personal lives and the collective communities to which they belong. In a globalized world, nationalism serves as a means of providing individuals with a sense of identity and belonging. The ascendancy of protectionism is a notable consequence of nationalism's impact on the liberal global framework. Protectionism is a school of thought that advocates safeguarding a nation's industries and labor force by limiting the inflow of foreign goods and encouraging local manufacturing. Protectionist measures frequently run counter to the tenets of unrestricted commerce, which serve as a fundamental pillar of the liberal global system. Hence, nationalism threatens the foundations of the liberal world order.

The liberal international order that has dominated international relations since the end of the Second World War has also come under attack from populism, which has emerged as a powerful political force in recent years. As populist leaders and movements challenge the tenets of the liberal international order, the rise of populist movements has increased the sense of instability and unpredictability in the international system. Populist movements frequently espouse a political ideology that prioritizes the popular will over the rule of law and typically rejects the institutional mechanisms of checks and balances that are fundamental to liberal democracy. The denunciation of liberal democratic principles has the potential to erode the credibility of global institutions and standards that are founded upon these principles.

The impact of populism on the formation of public opinion regarding Brexit (the United Kingdom's (UK) withdrawal from the EU) was noteworthy. In other words, the influence of populism was a notable factor in determining the result of the Brexit referendum. The utilization of populist discourse was instrumental in galvanizing backing for the "Leave" campaign among individuals who perceived themselves to be marginalized by conventional politics. However, it also played a role in fostering a fragmented and contentious campaign that has had significant and enduring implications for British society. The vote for Brexit dealt a considerable setback to the liberal world order as it posed a challenge to the fundamental principles of international cooperation, openness, and interdependence that have served as the foundation of this system. The EU played a significant role in upholding the liberal world order by advocating for the principles of an open market, fundamental human rights, and democratic governance not only within the European continent but also in other parts of the world. In contrast, Brexit symbolized a repudiation of these principles and a withdrawal into domestic autonomy. The decision of the UK to withdraw from the EU has resulted in considerable ambiguity regarding the prospects of the Union and the wider global framework. This has led to speculation about the possibility of other nations emulating the UK's actions and pursuing exits from international organizations and accords. The enduring ramifications of Brexit are poised to be significant as both the UK and the EU grapple with the complexities of adapting to the altered terrain of global affairs. The task facing policymakers is to identify strategies for reinstating the fundamental values of collaboration, transparency, and mutual reliance that have served as the foundation of the liberal framework while simultaneously fostering stability and economic well-being in an ever more intricate and interrelated global landscape.

After the 2008 global financial crisis, while uncertainties persist regarding the future of global capitalism, the unexpected outbreak of a virus causing a pandemic has taken the world by storm. This development has made the future of the world order, facing a series of challenges, even more uncertain. The COVID-19 pandemic has brought to light the vulnerabilities of the liberal world order and has resulted in a decrease in confidence in liberal establishments. It has resulted in noteworthy ramifications in the realms of economics, politics, and society, ultimately contributing to the rise of nationalist and populist movements.

In addition, the liberal international order is encountering obstacles due to the economic and technological transformations that have been encouraged by globalization and new emerging technologies. The emergence of digital technology and the heightened interconnectivity of the worldwide economy have presented new obstacles for governance and regulation while concurrently endowing transnational corporations with substantial leverage over global affairs. The changes have also engendered new divisions between industrialized and emerging nations and have engendered a sense of exclusion among numerous individuals and communities vis-à-vis the worldwide economic framework.

Moreover, the global liberal world order is currently encountering a legitimacy crisis alongside these aforementioned challenges. There is a widespread sentiment among individuals globally that the present system is inadequate and is controlled by a limited group of elites who are disconnected from the necessities and apprehensions of the general populace. The present challenge to legitimacy has played a role in the emergence of populist movements and the gradual decline in confidence in democratic institutions and procedures. In general, various factors have played a role in fostering an international order that has been characterized by greater levels of uncertainty, fragmentation, and conflict throughout the past 10 years.

Over the past decade, numerous literary works and scholarly publications have stimulated discourse regarding the waning of American influence and the subsequent notion of the fall of the liberal world order. The phenomenon of the decline of American power and the fall of the liberal international order are multifaceted and complicated issues that have been the subject of analysis and discussion from diverse viewpoints. The US global standing to sustain the liberal world order is facing mounting challenges, which may be attributed to factors such as economic overextension, the ascent of China, political dysfunction, or cultural deterioration. The task for policymakers and individuals alike is to comprehend the factors behind this deterioration and strive toward a future that is both sustainable and prosperous.

Discussions have centered around the adequacy and appropriateness of the US global leadership, as well as the nature of the overarching approach the country should adopt during these unpredictable circumstances. Some commentators have contended that the deterioration of American culture constitutes a pivotal element in its diminishing influence. Christopher Lasch (1991) posits in his work, *The Culture of Narcissism*, that the emphasis on individualism and consumerism in America has resulted in the erosion of its collective sense of purpose and dedication to the common good. Robert Putnam (2001) claims in his work *Bowling Alone* that the deterioration of social capital in the US has had a detrimental impact on the country's capacity to address communal issues and uphold a shared sense of national identity. Some others have emphasized the role of political dysfunction in the decline of the US. George Packer (2014) suggests in his work *The Unwinding* that the political system in the US has experienced a rise in dysfunctionality, characterized by the concentration of power among the elites and the marginalization of the middle class. The aforementioned circumstances have resulted in a deterioration of communal unity and inadequate administration, ultimately undermining the international reputation of the US. Edward Luce's *The Retreat of Western Liberalism* is also a significant publication on the subject matter at hand. According to Luce (2017), the ascendance of populism and nationalism in Western democracies, in conjunction with the obstacles presented by globalization and technological advancements, is eroding the fundamental principles of the global liberal system. Luce (2017) also states that the US, which was previously at the forefront of this system, is experiencing a growing sense of seclusion and self-absorption, and the fate of democratic liberalism remains unclear. More recently, many scholars have identified the ascent of China as a significant contributor to the decline of the US-led liberal world order. According to Graham Allison, in his publication *Destined for War*, the US and China are headed toward a collision, and the present global order is inadequately prepared to confront this challenge (Allison, 2017). In his work titled *The End of the Asian Century*, Michael Auslin posits that the US' inability to adequately respond to China's ascension has eroded its standing in Asia and globally (Auslin, 2017).

In light of these discussions, this book presents a study of how and for what purpose the liberal world order was established, how it began to rise, its connection with the US hegemony, how it has been shaken by various practices, and whether it has been successful so far. The book will also elaborate on the underlying factors of the current crisis of the liberal international order. The positions and stances of the rising powers, which are assumed to have the potential to establish order, will be discussed. This study aims to provide a projection of the direction in which this crisis-stricken order will evolve and whether it will be able to continue in the future. Hence, this study contributes to the debate in the literature on the future of the US-led international liberal system. In this book, the existing literature on international system debates is analyzed, and primary sources that reflect the past and current state of the international order are scrutinized. In this regard, the book contributes to the literature by examining the national security strategies of the US, national security policy documents, executive orders, archives of the White House, interviews, and remarks by US presidents. Hence, the study ought to be regarded as a testament to the present state of affairs during the pivotal juncture in the history of the US and the world order.

Accordingly, the first chapter discusses the decisive victory of the liberal world order and the US. Following the end of the Cold War, the US assumed a position as the world's sole superpower, overseeing a unipolar global system that was distinguished by a new liberal framework. The fundamental principles of liberal world order served as the basis for the primary tenets of US foreign policy, which sought to advance democratic ideals, capitalist economic systems, and American values on a global scale. The US experienced a rise in global influence, prompting inquiries into the necessity or burden of its hegemonic stability within the international system. This inquiry has been evaluated in various instances of conflict, including but not limited to the Gulf War, operations in Somalia, the Bosnian War, and the Kosovo War.

In the second chapter, new actors and new challenges within the framework of the War on Terror, which began with the 9/11 attacks and the emergence of global terrorism, are addressed. The response of the US foreign policy to the aforementioned challenges, which encompassed the conflicts in Afghanistan and Iraq, generated controversy and additionally assessed the limits of American hegemony. The Great Recession had noteworthy consequences for the liberal world order, exposing the vulnerability of the worldwide economic structure and the necessity for its modification. The Great Recession of 2008 signaled a turning point in both the political and economic spheres of the world. The crisis revealed the shortcomings of post-Second World War economic policies and resulted in the fall of the liberal order that had supported the world economy. The crisis also exposed shifting global power dynamics and put the supremacy of the US and Western nations under scrutiny.

The third chapter focuses on a new world that started to take shape with the emergence of new players and new difficulties. While the Arab upheavals posed a threat to US Middle East foreign policy, China and Russia emerged as rising powers. The Arab uprisings had a tremendous impact on the international political system. The demonstrations exposed the boundaries of Western authority in the region and called into question the legitimacy of the principles of liberal world order, like democracy and human rights. The liberal world order has been significantly impacted by the rise of China and Russia. The ideas and standards that support the order have been contested by these nations, which has increased the sense of instability and unpredictability in the global system. The US foreign policy changed in response to these shifts, but ultimately the liberal world order gave way to a post-Second World War order in crisis.

In the final chapter, the crisis of the post-Second World War order is discussed. A new world, marked by the advent of new actors and new challenges, started to emerge as the liberal world order began to wane. Trump's foreign policies and the demise of the transatlantic order complicated the search for a new global order. The US' traditional approach to international relations was broken by Trump's foreign policy, particularly regarding the liberal international order. His advocacy of greater unilateralism and transnationalism in his views on alliances, China, international organizations, and diplomacy sparked doubts about the US ability to continue to lead the world. The US position in international organizations has also come under scrutiny. Concerns are raised regarding the viability of the global liberal order due to the US recent posture toward international institutions. Finally, recent challenges to the international system, including the COVID-19 pandemic, the Russia-Ukraine conflict, and cyber terrorism, posed various threats to the international order, causing many to speculate about its future.

CHAPTER 1

Decisive Victory of the Liberal World Order and the US

1.1 LIBERALISM AND THE US HEGEMONY

Political liberalism is an ideology that places a strong emphasis on protecting civil rights and liberties, such as the right to free speech and association. Throughout the 17th and 18th centuries, it evolved as a reaction to the absolutist monarchies that predominated in Europe during the period. Political liberalism has its roots in the Enlightenment, an intellectual and philosophical movement that began in Europe in the 18th century. According to Enlightenment philosophers like John Locke and Jean-Jacques Rousseau, people's inherent rights should be maintained by the state, and the government is required to get the consent of the citizens.

Political liberalism is based on the principle that people should be allowed to pursue their own interests and objectives without interference from the government or other people. For this, a government that is responsible to the people it rules, with a restricted scope of power is required. The rule of law is also crucial because it guarantees that everyone is bound by the same set of rules and that both the government and individuals are held accountable for their actions.

Political liberalism underlines the value of defending individual rights in addition to defending individual freedom. They include civic and political liberties like the right to free expression, the right to practice one's religion, and the right to vote in elections conducted in accordance with the law. Economic rights, such as the ability to trade and possess property, are also regarded as crucial for fostering individual liberty and prosperity.

The Rise and Fall of the Eagle: An Assessment of the Liberal World Order.
Çağatay Özdemir (Author)
© 2024 Apple Academic Press, Inc. Co-published with CRC Press (Taylor & Francis)

The philosophy of political liberalism is fundamentally an individual-istic one and individual rights are given precedence over communal rights. Political liberalism begins with the premise that people perceive the state of nature as a hazardous and sometimes fatal place, primarily because those people inevitably disagree on fundamental issues. Liberals address this issue by asserting that every person possesses unquestionable rights that should be upheld by others through advocating the standards of peaceful resolution of conflict and compassion (Mearsheimer, 2018, p. 211). Hence, liberalism supports that human beings are fundamentally free to construct a social contract as a group. Additionally, it assumes that people frequently disagree about fundamental concepts while having outstanding reasoning abilities. Since rights and tolerance alone cannot maintain peace in the state of nature, the person's life is still in danger. In this regard, a social contract, which results in a state that can uphold order, becomes a necessity (Mearsheimer, 2018, p. 211). Hence, one of the most important tasks is to design a political structure that can uphold order while simultaneously acknowledging the often profound and possibly challenging differences in opinion among individuals (Mearsheimer, 2021, p. 1).

Accordingly, the main tenet of political liberalism is that if it doesn't violate the rights of others, people are free to live any lifestyle they chose. This especially includes the "freedom of conscience," or the ability to practice one's religion, according to one's convictions. The goal of rights is to provide people with the most freedom possible in their daily lives (Mearsheimer, 2018, p. 82). As it is stated by Fukuyama (2022a, p. 7), it is possible to think of classical liberalism as an institutional response to the challenge of peacefully governing diversity in pluralistic communi-ties. Modern democracies have evolved significantly because of political liberalism. The constitutions of liberal democracies all over the world include many of the fundamental ideas of political liberalism, including the protection of individual rights and the rule of law. Thomas Paine, an early American liberal, one of the most influential writers during the American Revolution and founder of the modern concept of constitutions, proclaimed in 1791 that, "Monarchical sovereignty, the enemy of mankind, and the source of misery, is abolished; and the sovereignty itself is restored to its natural and original place, the Nation. Were this the case throughout Europe, the cause of wars would be taken away" (Paine, 1995, p. 342).

According to liberal theory, all people are entitled to their basic human rights universally and it is underlined by the introductory sentence of the

Declaration of Independence of the US (1776): "We hold these truths to be self-evident, that all men are created equal." The signatories of the Declaration of Independence committed themselves to a shared political goal, with the aim of establishing a government with restricted powers that would safeguard their entitlements and promote their interests. In 1821, Secretary of State John Quincy Adams stated that the Declaration "was the first solemn declaration by a nation of the only legitimate foundation of civil government. It was the cornerstone of a new fabric, destined to cover the surface of the globe" (as cited in Rose, 2019, p. 10).

The whole history of Western Europe was molded by these ideas. As a result, people rose in revolt against their monarchies and fought for their fundamental rights. The American Revolution (1773–1785) against the rule of Great Britain was one of the revolutions that occurred in the 18th century.

In this regard, the US was established as a liberal democracy. The American Revolution in 1775 was based on liberal values. It was built on the political liberal understanding of human nature and the appropriate relationship between a person and societal authority. The most popular phrase in the Declaration of Independence of the US (1776) simply expresses this fundamental tenet of political liberalism: "We hold these truths to be self-evident, that all men are created equal, that they are endowed by their Creator with certain unalienable rights, that among these are life, liberty and the pursuit of happiness."

Although Thomas Hobbes (1996, p. 88) was a monarchist and wrote during the English Civil War, he considered a strong state as a primary safeguard against a resumption of "every man against every man" warfare. Hence, preserving life was the state's foremost responsibility. In this regard, the phrase "life, liberty, and the pursuit of happiness" that appears in the US Declaration of Independence originated from this understanding.

In addition, political liberalism has been institutionalized in the foundational documents of the US, such as the Constitution and the Bill of Rights. The political structures and policies of the government also exhibit political liberalism in the US. The Constitution's established principle of the separation of powers between the executive, legislative, and judicial departments of government is meant to prevent the consolidation of power in the hands of any one branch or person. The federal form of governance in the US provides for more local autonomy and variety since authority is split between the federal government and the states.

The definition of liberalism has expanded over the years. In this regard, Fukuyama (2022, p. 5) argues that within years, the idea of three fundamental roles for liberal societies has advanced. First, liberalism is considered a means of controlling violence and enabling many populations to coexist in harmony. Second, liberalism upholds fundamental human rights, particularly personal autonomy, or the freedom to make decisions for oneself. Third, by defending property rights and the freedom to commerce, liberalism fosters economic growth and all the positive effects that are related to it.

Liberalism has a significant economic component that logically follows from its theory of individual rights. To be more specific, it is critical to establish free markets where people may seek their own self-interest and fulfill their liberties (Mearsheimer, 2021, p. 1). The state may step in at the market's periphery to stop fraud or dismantle monopolies, but protecting property rights and eliminating internal and external barriers to exchange should be its priority. The fundamental assumption is that egoistic behavior by individuals in the market eventually helps the whole community (Mearsheimer, 2021, p. 1).

Accordingly, there is a significant relationship between liberalism and economic growth. The power to buy, sell, and invest freely in a market economy was the most significant aspect of autonomy for many liberals in the 19th century. Property rights and contract enforcement through institutions that reduced the danger of commerce and investing with strangers were key components of the liberal agenda (Fukuyama, 2022a, p. 10). A robust legal framework that featured a system of independent courts, attorneys, and a state that could use its police authority to enforce judgments against private parties was required to uphold property rights. In this regard, Adam Smith (1776) revealed in his book *Wealth of Nations* how mercantilist trade prohibitions were incredibly ineffective. In addition, Smith was a proponent of the free-market system and the state's constrained involvement in economic concerns. He contended that the "invisible hands of the market" more effectively and efficiently distribute limited resources. In this regard, market forces ultimately result in development and peace (Smith, 1776).

In addition, it is said by proponents of this worldview that liberalism promotes economic success, which not only serves as a desirable goal in and of itself but also helps maintain peace and it is believed that promoting liberalism would lead to a safer, more peaceful, and wealthy world

(Mearsheimer, 2018, p. 237). For instance, President Theodore Roosevelt's Secretary of State and Secretary of War Elihu Root argued during the First World War that, "To be safe democracy must kill its enemy when it can and where it can. The world cannot be half democratic and half autocratic." In addition, Secretary of State Dean Rusk during the Vietnam War stated that the "United States cannot be secure until the total international environment is ideologically safe" (as cited in Layne, 1994, p. 46).

In this respect, liberal states are genuinely concerned about the rights of almost every person on the earth. At the time liberals contend that basic individual rights should not just be promoted and preserved in only one state but rather everywhere in the world, liberalism turns into a profoundly global philosophy. As it is argued by Mearsheimer, the power of reason, natural rights, and nonviolence are thereby highlighted by the universalist component of political liberalism (2018, p. 91). Hence, when a great power starts to promote individual rights at a global level by going beyond its national interests, the ideals of liberalism become a hegemonic goal.

As it is stated by Layne, hegemony is about hard power (2016, p. 11). Mearsheimer defines the military capacity of a hegemon as such that no other state has the resources to mount a significant defense against it (Mearsheimer, 2001, p. 40). In addition, according to Gilpin (1981, pp. 29–30), hegemony is about the goals of the ruling power. A hegemon operates in its self-interest to protect its political, economic, and security interests. Polarity is also important for hegemony. A hegemon represents the sole great power in the system, making it by definition unipolar because of its dominance over other states in terms of relative military and economic power (Mearsheimer, 2001, p. 40).

The definition of power becomes significant when hegemony is considered. According to Joseph Nye (2005), power is the ability to influence people to achieve one's goals. This may be done in three different ways: by force (sticks), by money (carrots), and by attractiveness or persuasion. Sticks and carrots are examples of hard power; attraction and persuasion are examples of soft power. Because these types of power are significant, the emergence of American hegemony cannot be understood just in terms of the economy (Nye, 2015, p. 394). For instance, when the US attained the position of having the largest economy at the close of the 19th century, it was not recognized as a significant player in the balance of power until Presidents Theodore Roosevelt and Woodrow Wilson decided to use some of that economic might to fund the military (Nye, 2015, pp. 394–395).

The US utilized its economic power to trade with other countries during the 19th century, but it had little impact on the balance of power in the world. With the risks of conflict in North America, the nation's founding mission, and the wars that broke out under the first President George Washington, the US kept its distance from international politics and was particularly remote from developments in Europe. Hence, the US had a minimal part in the balance of power because it followed George Washington's policy to avoid being entangled in alliances and adhered to isolationist policies and the Monroe Doctrine, which concentrated on the Western Hemisphere (Nye, 2015, p. 395).

In addition, the inability of the newly founded country to recover its military and economic strength deepened this attitude (Hooker, 2014, pp. 1–2). To take measures against these developments, the foundations of institutions of national security were laid during the George Washington and John Adams eras. During this period, institutions such as the Department of War in 1789 and the Department of the Navy in 1798 were established (Miller, 2012, p. 8).

As the US power increased, its foreign policy objectives began to change and it developed an expansionist approach, especially in North America. When Washington consolidated its power, it also broke away from the isolationist approach of avoiding confrontation with the great powers of Europe. Thus, in the early 1900s, Roosevelt adopted a grand strategy of dominance and developed policies to ensure global hegemony based on military power (Colucci, 2012, p. 74).

When looking at material capabilities, the US did have a position of overwhelming power by the end of the conflict. Not only in terms of overall aggregate economic and military terms but also in terms of the broad range of resources the US possessed at its disposal, there was a vast difference in resources and capabilities (Ikenberry, 1989, p. 380). On the eve of the First World War, the US had a larger proportion of global industrial production than either Britain or Germany, its closest industrial rivals, which made it the world's greatest industrial producer as early as 1900 (Ikenberry, 1989, p. 380). As a result of the war's destruction of the European economies' industrial foundation and the expansion of the American counterpart, this trend toward economic domination became increasingly obvious.

When Wilsonian idealism ruled international affairs in the first quarter of the 20th century, the search and struggle for a world order based on liberal principles and values began. President Woodrow Wilson's liberal vision, which was based on free trade, democratic governments, self-determination, and the possibility of progressive change, was accompanied by the establishment of the League of Nations as a global collective security apparatus (Özdemir, 2018, p. 41). However, this establishment of order, described by Ikenberry as "the first version of liberal internationalism" (liberal internationalism 1.0) failed to prevent the outbreak of the Second World War in the aftermath of the economic depression, and the rise of militarism and fascism (Ikenberry, 2009, pp. 71–72).

The focus changes from people to the relations of states when political liberalism is implemented in world politics. A vision of an open, rule-based system where states trade and cooperate to accomplish mutual goals is provided by liberal internationalism. Liberal democracy proposed a logical and practical plan for structuring international states with liberal democracy as their foundation. Liberal democracies faced both possibilities and risks as a result of the Industrial Revolution and the continuous increase of economic and security interdependence. The grand forces of modernity have been met by liberal internationalism in all of its many forms, which has provided models for collaboration (Ikenberry, 2018a, p. 10).

Accordingly, liberal democracy was a young and vulnerable political experiment at the beginning of the 19th century, a political gleam amid a larger universe of monarchy, autocracy, empire, and traditionalism (Ikenberry, 2018a, p. 11). It is difficult to discern clear or comprehensive liberal foreign policy goals in the 19th century. Such views were most prevalent at this time in international politics theories developed by philosophers and activists who were devoted to liberalism inside nations, including theories concerning trade liberalization, collective security, dispute resolution, and other topics (Ikenberry, 2018a, p. 13).

Liberal principles served as a major driving force behind American foreign policy. Throughout the past 200 years, links between domestic liberalism and liberal internationalism have developed and taken on new forms. It can be considered that a far more developed understanding of liberal internationalism, seen as a set of guidelines for structuring and changing the globe in a way that makes the pursuit of liberal democracy at home easier, arose in the 20th century. Starting with Woodrow Wilson in 1919, liberal internationalism arose as a plan for creating a certain order—a sort of "container" inside which liberal democracies might exist and survive (Ikenberry, 2018a, p. 13). Woodrow Wilson changed the tradition in 1917 and dispatched American troops to Europe for the first time. In addition, he suggested creating a League of Nations to coordinate worldwide collective defense (Nye, 2015, p. 396). As a result of these developments, the US grand strategy after the First World War was a mix of cooperative security and isolationism.

US political analyst Michael Lind (2014) states:

> In 1914 the American Century began ... A hundred years ago, World War I marked the emergence of the U.S. as the dominant world power. Already by the late nineteenth century, the U.S. had the world's biggest economy. But it took the First World War to catalyze the emergence of the U.S. as the most important player in geopolitics. The U.S. tipped the balance against Imperial Germany, first by loans to its enemies after 1914 and then by entering the war directly in 1917.

However, Nye argues that America "returned to normal" when the Senate rejected US participation in the League and the soldiers left (2015, p. 396). In this regard, the US became virulently isolationist in the 1930s, despite being a significant player in the balance of power in world politics at the time. Thus, it would be more correct to place the start of the American century at the start of the Second World War under Franklin D. Roosevelt.

As it is underlined by Ikenberry (2018a, p. 13), after 1945, liberal internationalism was used by Roosevelt and his generation to promote their mission of creating a global community where liberal democracies could be established and safeguarded. The liberal world order established after the Second World War, or as Ikenberry (2009, p. 76) calls it, "the second version of liberal internationalism" (liberal internationalism 2.0), was not a separate development from the establishment of American hegemony. The US, as the hegemonic leader of the capitalist Western bloc, undertook an order-building mission through the efforts of Roosevelt and emerged victorious from the war. The establishment of this liberal order was based on economic institutions and values such as freedom, democracy, and the rule of law (Ikenberry, 2017, p. 2).

The purpose of the post-war international order was to protect liberal democracies from the rising hazards of the economic and political upheavals brought on by modernity itself. Liberal internationalism provided a perspective of a controlled and reformatted Western order that would have the particular strategies, institutions, and capabilities to deal with the international disruptions and eventualities that pose a danger to the domestic pursuit of liberal democracy in this fashion (Ikenberry, 2018a, p. 13).

The state enhanced its power and the number of services it offered to citizens under the presidency of Roosevelt. Public spending that was driven by the state increased quickly and provided jobs for citizens (Mearsheimer, 2018, p. 69–74). The welfare state was established by the government, and John Maynard Keynes' theories were given precedence over those of traditional economists. However, due to the bipolar system in the post-Second World War era, it was not possible to implement these liberal hegemonic principles on a global scale. Yet as the Soviet empire fell apart in the late 1980s, there would be the chance to fulfill these hegemonic ambitions.

According to some scholars, the post-1945 era was characterized by an American-led hierarchical order with liberal traits, in which weaker states were granted the institutional opportunity to use American power, the US delivered public goods, and it continued to operate within a loose structure of multilateral rules and institutions (Nye, 2015, p. 398). According to John Ikenberry (2006, p. 14), "The US supplied global services—such as security protection and backing of free markets—which made other governments ready to cooperate with rather than fight American preeminence."

Since the end of the Second World War, the US has followed its interests by establishing and upholding the network of institutions, standards, and laws that make up the US-led liberal order. It is American-led since it is based on American hegemony: The US offers security assurances to its allies to stifle regional rivalry, and the US military maintains an open global common to permit unhindered commerce (Lind & Wohlforth, 2019, p. 71).

Throughout the Cold War, the US pursued a hybrid grand strategy of cooperative security and containment. The US leaders participated in the world's most comprehensive institution-building campaign between 1944 and 1951. After Roosevelt, Harry S. Truman advocated the continuation of international institutions to prevent threats of economic crisis, preserve the liberal economic order and prevent wars. Truman made choices after the war that resulted in a continued military presence abroad. Truman stated in a speech in 1947 that: "The free peoples of the world look to us for support in maintaining their freedoms. If we falter in our leadership, we may endanger the peace of the world -- and we shall surely endanger the welfare of our own nation" (Truman Doctrine, 1947). In this speech, Truman focused on the expansion of US power with its allies around the world. It is noteworthy that many steps were taken towards this goal.

Hence, by employing a containment strategy, the US aimed to stop communism from spreading beyond the Soviet Union's borders in the Cold War period. In addition, it offered financial and military support to nations under threat of communist danger. The rationale for this strategy was the conviction that if communism were allowed to advance, it would eventually endanger both American and global security. In this regard, in 1947, the US stepped in to support Greece and Türkiye when Britain was unable to. In 1948, Washington made significant investments in the Marshall Plan; in 1949, it established North Atlantic Treaty Organization (NATO); and in 1950, it served as the leader of a UN alliance that fought in Korea. These policies were a component of the containment strategy (Nye, 2015, p. 396). The outcome was a liberal hierarchical system based on a series of US political, economic, and security agreements with nations in Europe and East Asia (Ikenberry, 2011, p. 288).

Accordingly, a state that strives for liberal hegemony primarily focuses on defending individual rights and developing liberal democracy, but it also seeks two other significant goals: the development of international institutions and the advancement of economic cooperation among nations. These objectives arise as a result of the dual arguments that international organizations and economic interdependence support peace (Mearsheimer, 2018, p. 198). Hence, the US reinforced this order with a network of security and alliances, such as NATO, and the Southeast Asia Treaty Organization (SEATO), turning it into a "security community." The institutionalization of this liberal international order has been embodied by formal and informal global arrangements, as well as multilateral organizations, including the UN, the International Monetary Fund (IMF), the World Bank, the International Group of Seven (G7) and the General Agreement on Tariffs and Trade (GATT) (Glaser, 2019, p. 56).

In addition to attempting to contain communism, the US also aimed to advance liberal democracy globally. Many strategies were used to do this, including economic assistance, cultural exchanges, and propaganda. The US had the view that global democracy would increase wealth and security for all countries. Furthermore, the US deployed its military strength to advance liberal democracy. This was accomplished via operations where the US tried to install democratic administrations in support of its interests, such as in Vietnam and Afghanistan. Despite these interventions being contentious, they were seen to be essential in promoting liberalism and halting the growth of communism.

When international economic order in the post-war era was considered, it was based on a managed open world economy (Ikenberry, 2018a, p. 16). John Ruggie called this order "embedded liberalism." He argues that the main task of post-war institutional reconstruction was to maneuver between these two extremes and devise a framework that would safeguard and even aid the quest for domestic stability without, at the same time, triggering the mutually destructive external consequences that had plagued the interwar period (Ruggie, 1982, p. 393). In this regard, rules would be developed to support the welfare state while also allowing for nondiscrimination in commercial and financial relations (Ikenberry, 1989, p. 397). Accordingly, this novel way of thinking about how an open world economy should be run was inspired by the New Deal itself, and a medium ground between openness and stability was the idealistic objective. The kind of economic recovery and expansion needed to support centrist and progressive post-war political leadership in the US and Europe required free trade (Ikenberry, 2018a, p. 16). However, government initiatives to preserve economic stability, the security of employees, and the middle class would need to be balanced with trade and interchange. Hence, national security came to be associated with social and economic security (Ikenberry, 2018a, p. 16).

In addition, in the economic sphere, the US dollar's hegemonic domination was institutionalized by its use as a reserve currency in conjunction with the Bretton Woods system between 1944 and 1971, a recently developed international monetary framework (Bina, 2022, p. 48). In the Bretton Woods system, international agreements were developed to offer governments more power over how to control and manage economic openness so that it could be balanced with domestic economic stability and full employment objectives (Ruggie, 1982, pp. 393–394). Systemically, powerful US-backed international organizations like the World Bank and the IMF began to take the lead and shape the fundamental development plans that made it possible for the hegemonic rise of the whole system. Consent and the rule of law were imbued with dominance and hierarchy in this system. The provision of public good on rule-based collaboration and dispersed reciprocity exceptionally contributed to the liberal character of this order.

The world's power structure was defined as bipolar from 1945 to 1991, with two superpower nations dominating globally. Hence, in the Cold War period, the US considered itself the defender of liberty and democracy against the Soviet Union's totalitarianism. The US held the view that its political and economic systems were better than those of the Soviet Union and that the extension of liberal democracy was necessary for creating peace and stability around the globe. The Soviet Union and the US were ideological rivals, and Moscow was not a liberal democracy. There were two binding orders: one dominated by the US and mostly concerned with the West, and the other by the Soviet Union and primarily composed of the communist nations of the world. These orders were developed by the two superpowers to compete with one another over security (Mearsheimer, 2019, p. 18). To gain an edge in the non-aligned world, the US and the Soviet Union battled for bases of power and domains of influence. The two superpowers balanced each other's might through a nuclear arms race (Nye, 2015, p. 396). Nonetheless, the US triumphed as the sole superpower following the fall of the Berlin Wall in 1989 and the Soviet Union in 1991.

North America, Western Europe, and Japan were key locations in the US-centered system that emerged in the Cold War period. America's hegemonic position in the world, coupled with bipolar competition during the Cold War, also provided Washington with strategic incentives to forge alliances, integrate Germany and Japan, share the "spoils" of capitalism and modernization, and generally manage the system in ways that would be acceptable to all parties (Ikenberry, 2009, p. 77). The European states and Japan continued to be the principal US allies, despite the fact that the order extended significantly following the fall of the Soviet Union. The order's distinguishing characteristic is liberalism; to be a core participant in this order, a country must have a democratic political system and a market-based economy (Mastanduno, 2019, p. 50). In addition, containment policies against the expansion of Soviet communism and domestic regime type both fostered transatlantic and transpacific cooperation in the Cold War.

This US-centered liberal international order not only encouraged multilateral cooperation among states during the Cold War but also managed to prevent a war between the great powers in the system (Colgan & Keohane, 2017, p. 37). The quest for liberal hegemony has mostly been an endeavor to broaden the somewhat liberal system that the US established and maintained throughout the Cold War. American leaders drew a clear line between the democratic "free world" and the non-free world of Soviet-style communism from the beginning of that confrontation (Walt, 2018a, p. 74). Indeed, the post-war international system was not entirely liberal. The communist world was widely overlooked, and some important US allies did not even have democracies. The US disobeyed the rules at different times, and there was significant chaos in this system at various periods and locations (Walt, 2018a, p. 74). However, the Cold War liberal order served the interests of the US and its allies well, and their victory over the Soviet Union made the system appear particularly alluring to the nations that contributed to its creation.

With the end of the Cold War, the US held a dominant position, and the moment felt right to expand that order to encompass the whole world (Walt, 2018a, p. 74). As it is argued by Mearsheimer, when there is more than one big power in the system, it is not possible for a great power to achieve liberal hegemony. A strong state must behave realistically as long as the system is either bipolar or multipolar (2018, p. 202). Since the world is not safe, it is not feasible for it to prioritize defending individual rights over collective ones in its foreign policy. Hence, liberalism holds that opposing great powers have no choice but to vie for dominance to increase their chances of surviving in a dangerous world (Mearsheimer, 2018, p. 203). Accordingly, this liberal hegemonic order first appeared within the larger bipolar world order.

The relationship between liberalism and the US underwent a profound transformation when the Cold War ended. The US became the only super-power in the world with the fall of the Soviet Union. As a result, it was believed that liberal democracy had defeated communism and that the extension of democracy was no longer in question.

1.2 UNIPOLAR STRUCTURE OF THE INTERNATIONAL SYSTEM

A world where one superpower dominates all others in terms of economic, military, and political might is considered to be unipolar. In addition, William Wohlforth underlined the absence of a counterbalance by stating that "Unipolarity is a structure in which one state's capabilities are too great to be counterbalanced" (1999, p. 9). The international order became unipolar as a result of the Cold War when the US emerged as the only superpower in the globe. One of the significant features of a unipolar system is that there is a distinct hierarchy of power, with one country holding much more authority than any other state. The US maintained this position in the post-Cold War era, exerting unrivaled military, economic, and political power globally. Due to its dominance, the US was able to exercise its influence in a way that few other countries could. The dominant state's ability to define the agenda and control the discourse surrounding international affairs is one of the main effects of unipolarity. Due to its focus on advancing liberal democratic values and economic globalization in its foreign policy during the 1990s and early 2000s, the US was able to accomplish this. Additionally, the US took the lead in founding international organizations and standards that represented these principles.

After the Cold War ended, one of the most prominent aspects of the international system was the US dominance in the distribution of capabilities around the globe. The rapid fall of the Soviet Union and its alliance, slower economic development in Western Europe and Japan in the 1990s, and the excessive military spending of the US, all contributed to an American-led unipolar system. In establishing a liberal hegemonic system during the past century, the US has expanded to become the largest and most encompassing pole the world has ever seen. A unipolar international order has been made possible by the American political system and its power resources. In addition to a distinct distribution of material capabilities, unipolarity is established by the absence of other poles.

Wohlforth (1999, p. 7) defines unipolarity as "decisive preponderance in all the fundamental components of power: economic, military, technical, and geopolitical." The US is unipolar in many more ways than merely having disproportionately strong material capabilities. It is also a particularly significant hub, in that it serves as the administrative hub for a larger system of order. Other nations have established ties with the US, as well as with the larger institutions and laws that constitute the liberal international order (Ikenberry, 2011, p. 122). In this regard, the American-led order is "easy to join and hard to overturn" due to its liberal traits. This has made it more difficult for other powers to create competing poles, strengthening and maintaining unipolarity (Ikenberry, 2011, p. 122).

With the end of the Cold War, the general anticipation was that the US-led Western order would gradually disintegrate and shift toward a multipolar system that would be more competitive (Mastanduno, 1999, pp. 19–40). Most scholars had previously predicted multipolarity as the Cold War came to an end, both worldwide and in the crucial areas of Europe and Asia. Leading realists asserted that the world system was transitioning from bipolarity to multipolarity. Some urge states to acquire nuclear weapons because they believe a multipolar world will lead to increased violence (Lebow, 1994, p. 249). For example, American analyst John Mearsheimer predicted that Europe will "return to the future" by reigniting its great-power competition from before the Second World War. He even expressed a longing for the stability that the Cold War bipolar system provided (Mearsheimer, 1990, pp. 5–55). Mearsheimer also argued that, "Bipolarity will disappear with the passing of the Cold War, and multipolarity will emerge in the new international order" (Mearsheimer 1992, p. 227). Similarly, According to Kenneth Waltz, in the international system, nations tend to naturally establish a power balance; therefore, the emergence of a single dominant state after the Cold War would encourage the growth of other great powers or alliances of states to counterbalance it (Waltz, 2010, p. 121). Waltz argues, "The longest peace yet known has rested on two pillars: bipolarity and nuclear weapon" and asserts that the existence of nuclear weapons among the superpowers ensured that the lengthy peace would last (Waltz, 1993, pp. 44–45). Realists' central thesis is that attempts at hegemony fail because they are resisted by the counter-balanced actions of other states. Hence, for realists, aggressive balancing against the US would force the power structure of the international system to soon return to multipolarity after the conclusion of the Cold War (Layne, 2006, p. 10).

In this regard, unipolarity appears to be the least resilient international arrangement in the context of structural realist theory. According to Kenneth Waltz (2000, p. 23), there are two basic reasons for this. One is that dominating powers overextend themselves too much and end up weakening themselves over time. Another factor of the short period of unipolarity is that weaker nations will be concerned about the dominating power's future behavior even if it acts with restraint, moderation, and forbearance (Waltz, 2000, p. 23).

In contrast to the arguments of the structural realist theory, there hasn't been much of a reaction to counterbalance the rise of American unipolarity. The majority of the world's major powers chose to ally themselves with the US during the unipolar period. The US maintained and, in some cases, strengthened its relations with Japan and Western Europe. It has been challenging to observe systematic attempts by the other major powers to aggressively oppose the unipolar US, at least up to the crisis brought on by the US' military assault on Iraq in 2003 (Ikenberry, 2011, p. 360).

In the years following the Cold War, the unipolar-moment notion tremendously affected the scholarly discussion on international order.

Some American analysts were cautious not to take unipolarity for granted. According to Krauthammer, instead of being an era, unipolarity was to be a "moment" (Krauthammer, 1990/91, pp. 23–33). Another generation would be needed to achieve multipolarity. On the other hand, according to Wohlforth (1999, p. 8), unipolarity would be far more resilient. He was the major proponent of the "unipolar stability" school and contended that unipolarity might continue as long as bipolarity, which persisted for about 45 years. Another viewpoint developed that claimed unipolarity was an "illusion." Christopher Layne (1993, p. 7) argues that the power balance, or the propensity for states to unite in opposition to a hegemon, is both natural and unavoidable; it may even be considered a rule of international politics. It was just a matter of time before other big powers emerged to challenge the American supremacy.

In the existing literature, there are different explanations regarding the reasons for the absence of large-scale balancing against American unipo-larity. One reason is related to the absence of coordinated action (Wohl-forth,1999, p. 38). There is a propensity for "buck passing" (Mearsheimer, 2001, p. 393). In an ideal world, nations would prefer that other states handle the balance for them, saving them the expense of deploying force, forming alliances, and taking on the danger of reprisal from the unipolar state. In addition, coalition building against unipolarity is especially challenging since not all states face the same level of dominance threats. According to Wohlforth, states frequently consider local aspects of their security, hence systemwide balancing imperatives are unlikely to be as strongly felt by state leaders. Coalition balance is especially hazardous in these coalitions because of the loss of policy autonomy. It could poten-tially be harmful. When balancing attempts fail, the dominant state may take action to seek retribution (Wohlforth, 2002, pp. 98–108).

Another feature of an American-led unipolar world that prevents counterbalancing is the existence of a significant group of democratic superpowers. As opposed to the realist understanding of counterbalancing, democratic peace theorists argue that democracies are less likely to view one another as a danger to their security and interpret that as a reduced risk of conflicts (Doyle, 1983, pp. 213–215). As it is argued by Doyle, if two or more liberal states coexist in the same international system, liberal civilizations struggle to become prosperous, glorious, healthy, and cultur-ally advanced without anticipating that their rivalry will have to be settled by conflict (Doyle, 1997, p. 210).

The dominance of liberal states is one of the most noticeable aspects of the unipolar world. Advanced democratic nations that have close economic, political, and security ties to the US control the great majority of the world's wealth and military strength. 96 percent of the gross national product (GNP) was in the hands of great powers, including the US, France, Germany, Great Britain, and Japan in 1992 (Ikenberry, 2011, p. 130). On the other hand, Russia and China both had far lower economic capacities than the combined advanced democracies. Therefore, there was not a coalition of powerful states to put together a counterbalancing reaction against the US.

The presence of nuclear deterrence is another factor that contributes to the maintenance of the status quo international order led by the US. Since China and Russia have developed nuclear deterrents, they are no longer concerned about war and the hegemony of the dominant power. When compared to earlier ages, the necessity for great power balancing has decreased in the liberal international order. Similarly, the possibility of a countercoalition destabilizing the current system through conflict diminishes. Hence, the great power balance theory is undermined as a result of the overall situation (Ikenberry, 2011, p. 130). Unipolarity did not emerge as a result of war. As the Soviet Union collapsed and Western Europe and Japan evolved slower than the US while maintaining close ties to it, unipolarity gradually arose.

Growing power advantages for the leading state, brought about in part by the loss of a rival pole, are indicative of the growth of unipolarity. The leading state lacks any regional or international rivals. The unipolar state appears to have more negotiating power as a result of this change in power and polarity in a number of ways. Because it no longer has a security rival, the leading state has greater resources at its disposal. The power resources it has are the same as before but they are no longer constrained by bipolar security rivalry (Ikenberry, 2011, p. 130).

The dominant state is not being counterbalanced by other major states, which results in fewer external restrictions on its use of power. A competitor's great power is not actively using its might to resist and contain the dominant state, at least not on a global scale. There is no longer a way out for third, secondary, and weaker nations. The provision of security protection on a worldwide scale is almost monopolized by the lead state. Under these conditions of unipolarity, there is no way out of the hierarchy (Ikenberry, 2011, p. 138). The removal of geopolitical rivals and balancing restrictions opens up new possibilities for the unipolar power to "re-make the world in its own image, or rather in its intended self-image" (Jervis, 2009, p. 199).

In this regard, when a single state has an excessive amount of the system's politically significant resources, the system is said to be unipolar. Unipolarity indicates that the one superpower has no political rivals that are on an equal footing with them in terms of strength or influence (Walt, 2009, p. 91). The post-Cold War period was unipolar in the sense that the US maintained a constant military presence to prevent the rise of new great powers and to create the kind of regional stability required to support the existing order (Layne, 2006, p. 13).

1.3   A NEW LIBERAL ORDER: THE END OF HISTORY

In the years following the Second World War, as the Western countries worked to rebuild Europe and create a new international order, the concept of a new liberal order began to take shape. Democracy, capitalism, and the rule of law were regarded as the guiding principles of this order because they could be used to stop authoritarianism and war from returning. This order grew over time as more developing nations adopted liberal economic policies and political reform, joining the Western democracies as well as many other nations.

At the end of the Second World War, the US controlled roughly half of the world's manufacturing capacity, the bulk of its food supply, practically all of its capital reserves, and a military power unrivaled in human history. After 1945, American foreign policy makers wanted to leverage the country's new power to establish a global system of interdependent economies, conditional multilateralism, and networks of strategic alliances headed by the US (Stokes, 2018, p. 138). The military containment of Soviet expansionism was one goal of these networks, but they also served to prevent geopolitical rivalry with other global powers such as Japan and Western Europe.

The US' Cold War success can be attested to more than the defeat of just one nation by another. The fall of the Soviet Union symbolized liberalism's victory over the two opposing ideologies of the 20th century, communism and fascism. With the military defeat of Germany, Italy, and Japan during the Second World War, the threat of fascism was queled. With the fall of the Soviet Union and the transformation of Chinese communism into an economy heavily reliant on market forces, communism experienced a protracted death.

Francis Fukuyama (1989, p. 4) summarized the ebullient mood of the moment in his 1989 piece "The End of History": "What we may be witnessing is not just the end of the Cold War, or the passing of a particular period of history, but the end of history as such, that is, the end point of mankind's ideological evolution and the universalization of Western liberal democracy as the final form of government." President George H. W. Bush (1991) described his sense of triumphalism in a speech to a joint session of Congress: "We can see a new world coming into view, a world in which there is the very real prospect of a new world order, a world where the US—freed from Cold War stalemate—is poised to fulfill the historic vision of its founders; a world in which freedom and respect for human rights finds a home among all nations."

After the end of the Cold War, the US found itself in a position of global hegemon. It produced roughly 25 percent of the goods and services consumed worldwide in 1992, making it the largest and most developed economy in the world. As the unipolar period began, the US' relations with Russia were surprisingly warm since Russia accepted Western assistance in converting to a market economy and was keen to establish cooperative security arrangements as well.

According to some experts, the unipolar structure defined by the pre-eminence of the US might last even longer than bipolarity (Brooks and Wohlforth, 2008, p. 17). The US triumph in the Cold War revealed America's essential beliefs of individual liberty, free elections, and open markets. Due to its dominating position in the post-Cold War era, America encouraged other nations to defend fundamental human rights and assisted countries through democratic transitions in establishing the necessary legal framework and other components of civil society. With the end of the Cold War, political scientists had the common belief that great power politics were a thing of the past and that the world was slowly advancing toward a liberal peace (Fukuyama, 1992, p. 3).

Following the end of the Cold War and the fall of the Soviet Union, the US was by far the most powerful nation in the world. Security competition between great powers during the bipolar international system came to an end. The collapse of the Soviet Union brought a new opportunity to the US. The strategy of hegemony portrays the US as the "indispensable nation" that is particularly competent to propagate these political values, including "liberal principles of individual freedom, democratic governance, and a market-based economy" to other nations and to make other governments participate in a web of alliances and institutions created and directed by the US (Walt, 2018a, p. 24). Richard N. Haass (2002), former director of the State Department's Policy Planning Staff and later the president of the Council on Foreign Relations, stated one of the main aims of the US foreign policy as "integrating other states into arrangements that will sustain a world consistent with US interests and values, and thereby promote peace, prosperity, and justice as widely as possible."

Supporters of American hegemony believe that maintaining American supremacy and advancing a largely liberal world order is not only necessary for the security and prosperity of the US but that these goals are also beneficial to the rest of the world. According to Stephen Walt, the grand strategy of "liberal hegemony" was based on "an ambitious effort to use American power to reshape the world according to US preferences and political values" (Walt, 2018a, p. 72). Under the leadership of the US, the grand strategy of liberal hegemony aims to strengthen and broaden the liberal international order. Economic openness is a defining feature of the liberal international order, in which relations between nations are governed by law and organizations like the World Trade Organization (WTO) and NATO. International liberal hegemony was based on US domination and its priority to maintain, propagate and expand liberal values around the world. The proponents of liberal hegemony perceive a positive link between multilateralism and American hegemony since the US may compel allegiance and obedience from the weaker states through multilateral organizations by pledging not to threaten them or "use [its] power arbitrarily" (Ikenberry, 2001, p. 51).

The grand strategy of "liberal hegemony" was adopted by every administration of the US during the post-Cold War (Walt, 2018a, p. 24). George H. W. Bush (1990), who came into office just before the end of the Cold War, said in 1990, "Recent events have surely proven that there is no substitute for American leadership." Fundamentally, Bush and his White House successors were committed to establishing a new international order that was distinct from the Western system that had prevailed during the Cold War. In particular, they vowed to convert a confined realist order into a liberal international order (Mearsheimer, 2019, p. 22). Using American hegemony, this strategy aims to uphold and advance the historic liberal values of individual liberty and democratic government.

According to Mearsheimer (2019, p. 22), the establishment of a liberal international order included three significant tasks. First of all, it was crucial to create a web of international organizations with extensive membership that had a significant impact on how member states behaved. Secondly, it was necessary to constitute an open international economy that mainly targets free trade and capital markets. Thirdly, it was essential to actively promote liberal democracy throughout the world for both the US and its European allies. Building a strong, lasting liberal international order was seen by its founders as being equivalent to bringing about world peace. This ingrained conviction provided the US and its allies with a strong motivation to labor diligently to establish that new order.

When combined, the realist theory of anarchy and the concept of the balance of power make a significant contribution to the explanation of the nature and operation of the global order. It attracts attention to how the Westphalian system's great power relationships have changed through time, as well as the long-term changes in the way powerful nations have exploited and modified the mechanism of the balance of power regarding the creation and maintenance of the international order.

However, there are some problems in the realist concepts of anarchy and balance in terms of explaining the American-led liberal international order. Balancing and security competition that neorealist theory predicts is not present in the relationships among the nations in this sequence. Liberal democracies are united by elaborate and institutionalized mechanisms of collaboration. In the decades following the conclusion of the bipolar Cold War conflict, the stability of this American-led system is all the more remarkable. The order has stayed mostly consistent during these decades and has grown to include governments outside of its core Western nations. Other states in this order haven't attempted to balance against the US in response to unipolarity despite the problems that plague this American-led system. The balancing dynamic is not as simple as suggested by neorealist theory. The fact that the current international order is loosely hierarchical is perhaps the most significant. It is necessary to investigate how big powers establish themselves as poles and set up hierarchical relationships with weaker states if we are to comprehend the current system (Ikenberry, 2011, p. 55).

The liberal international order's power and authority informally assume hierarchical forms. The US is positioned at the top of the hierarchy, with variously arranged states below it acting as allies, partners, and customers.

The economic, military, and technological advantages of the US put it in a position of "command of the commons" (Posen, 2003). Barry Posen states that what distinguishes unipolar military strength from other forms of power is a leading state's capacity to militarily dominate the world's commons. Accordingly, he states that:

> Command of the commons is the key military enabler of the U.S. global power position. It allows the US to exploit more fully other sources of power, including its own economic and military might as well as the economic and military might of its allies. Command of the commons also helps the US to weaken its adversaries, by restricting their access to economic, military and political assistance. ... Command of the commons provides the US with more useful military potential for a hegemonic foreign policy than any other offshore power has ever had (Posen, 2003, p. 9).

As long as the leading state has the authority to uphold the norms and institutions of order, the hierarchical structure will continue to exist. The liberal international order starts to fall apart and disintegrate as hegemonic strength dwindles (Ikenberry, 2011, p. 55). According to the theory of power transitions, the international order starts to break down when the dominant power becomes weaker. A requirement for political change, according to Gilpin, is "a disjuncture between the existing social system and the redistribution of power toward those actors who would benefit most from a change in the system" (Gilpin, 1981, pp. 42–43). Power shifts result in geopolitical conflicts and security rivalries, which eventually lead to hegemonic war and the establishment of a new leading state that structures the global order based on a new system.

Despite its richness and diversity, liberal conceptions of order share a core set of assumptions and expectations. According to liberal theories, establishing a cooperative global order based on the concepts of reciprocity and the rule of law is in everyone's best interests (Ikenberry, 2011, p. 63). There is an assumption in liberal theories that states can overcome the constraints of a competitive and decentralized international system and cooperate to solve security dilemmas, pursue collective action, and create an open, stable system. Moreover, there is a presumption that big powers would wield their influence responsibly and find means of convincing other nations of their obligations.

According to liberal ideologies, commercial practices modernize and civilize states, counteracting illiberal tendencies and bolstering the foundation of the international community. Liberal theories also hold that democracies are especially capable and eager to function within an open, rule-based international order and collaborate for mutual benefit, as opposed to autocratic regimes. Liberals have also held the same belief that institutions and laws created by states encourage collaboration and group problem-solving. Governments and domestic players are motivated to trade, bargain, negotiate, and seek collaboration for mutual benefit by deep-seated social forces (Ikenberry, 2011, p. 63).

This liberal understanding of order draws concepts from a number of distinct theoretical bodies. According to Michael Doyle, there are three sources of liberal international theory. The first is commercial liberalism. Economic interconnectedness, shared benefits, common interests, and incentives for international collaboration are all developed by the growth of capitalism and markets. The second is democratic peace. Democratic political systems actively pursue alliances with one another. The third is liberal institutionalism. Liberal societies produce international law and organizations that constitute anticipations and duties based on rules between them (Doyle, 1997, p. 206).

One of the significant goals of establishing liberal international order was integrating China and Russia into it since the two countries were the next-most powerful powers in the system after the US. Similarly, since the US and its allies aimed to make the Western order a liberal international order, NATO expanded to Eastern Europe throughout the 1990s and early 2000s (Mearsheimer, 2014, p. 84).

In this regard, in 1995, Deputy Secretary of State Strobe Talbott stated, "Enlargement of NATO would be a force for the rule of law both within Europe's new democracies and among them … it would promote and consolidate democratic and free market values" (1995, pp. 27–28). In addition, during the post-Cold War era, the US foreign policy toward China was based on integrating China into the liberal international order that it was leading. For instance, Secretary of State Madeline K. Albright said in a 1997 Forrestal Lecture at the US Naval Academy that engaging China instead of attempting to contain it, as the US had done with the Soviet Union during the Cold War, is the key to maintaining a good relationship with a rising China. According to Albright (1997a), this policy of engagement would enable China to actively participate in some of the largest international organizations and help it become a part of the US-led economic order, all of which would ultimately contribute to China becoming a liberal democracy. Furthermore, the Bush administration proposed a liberal international order grounded in the US military and political power. Accordingly, it was claimed in the 2002 National Security Strategy (NSS) that, "The US would actively work to bring the hope of democracy, development, free markets, and free trade to every corner of the world" (Bush, 2002).

In this regard, the US has been a dominant global power since the end of the Second World War, and the country's foreign policy has played a significant role in shaping the international system. The US foreign policy in liberal international order had various features. It was mainly based on open multilateral trade. As part of its efforts to create institutions and alliances that would create a globally open order, the US opened up the international economy (Ikenberry, 2018a, p. 16). In addition, The US politicians had the goal of building order around a multinational governance structure. More than supranationalism, this was intergovernmentalism. Governments would continue to be the main authorities. However, governments would structure their interactions around enduring regional and international institutions (Ikenberry, 2018a, p. 16). Hence, it is significant to analyze the institutional framework of US foreign policy decision-making to understand the main dynamics and principles of the liberal international order.

1.4   MAIN PILLARS OF US FOREIGN POLICY IN THE LIBERAL WORLD ORDER

The end of the Cold War in 1991 concluded a conflict that had dominated global politics for close to 50 years. However, it did not make deciding on US foreign policy any easier. Contrarily, the years that followed saw the emergence of several transnational forces that led to racial conflict in some nations and democratic revolutions in others. As previous security pacts gave way to regional commercial blocs, diplomats faced the everyday problem of separating allies from enemies. Thousands of nongovernmental organizations (NGOs) put increased pressure on American officials to promote their agendas on topics such as human rights, climate change, and global poverty (Hook, 2016, p. 130). US foreign policy analysts and practitioners have vastly different perspectives on how the world works. Some people view the system of nation-states as a dangerous jungle. Others see it as a system that rewards collaboration over conflicts in the majority of foreign policy sectors, making it considerably more benign than this depressing image suggests.

US foreign policy decision-making is influenced by a number of dynamics (Redd & Mintz, 2013, pp. 11–37). When examining the sources of American foreign policy at the state level, structural realism offers a common starting point. Political leaders are seen by structural realists as rational decision-makers who analyze their alternatives in light of objective national interests, concrete indicators of power, and foreign dangers. According to this perspective, the relative benefits of various strategies for achieving foreign policy objectives are also self-evident. In addition, structural realists view countries as unified actors who speak with a unified voice when addressing global issues. Thus, these suppositions lend credence to the idea that rational decision-making underlies foreign policy (Bueno de Mesquita, 2009, p. 7).

Since the end of the Cold War, US foreign policy has expanded and involved many more domestic organizations that frequently participate in power struggles, or "turf wars." The most significant player with agenda-setting authority is the president. However, the Constitution is not as influential on his power as his political position with Congress and the general public. In addition, with each administration and the president's intentions, the vice president's duties change (Cameron, 2005, p. 35).

The US Constitution is the source of the institutional framework for American foreign policy. Given the institutions and the Constitution, foreign policy is the result of the interplay between three circles of decision-makers: the White House, the foreign policy bureaucracy, and Congress. The president is the most notable political figure in the US. The president is authorized as commander-in-chief of the armed forces by the Constitution, but he is not permitted to declare war on his own, send envoys abroad without the Senate's consent, or collect funds for foreign operations without the support of Congress (Cameron, p. 37).

The National Security Council (NSC) staff provides recommendations and briefings to the president. One of the important players in the US foreign policy apparatus is the national security adviser, and the NSC is crucial in organizing bureaucratic contributions to US foreign policy. While the State Department is legally the driving force behind US foreign policy, its sway fluctuates depending on the subject at hand and the relationship between the secretary of state and the president. During the 1990s, it received significantly less funding (Cameron, 2005, p. 35).

Furthermore, Congress possesses significant authority over US foreign policy, including the ability to control commerce, declare war, ratify treaties, and approve presidential candidates. In addition, all government spending must be approved by Congress (Cameron, 2005, p. 67). Congress's overall interest in foreign policy has decreased since 1992. Few members made the visits abroad. The major committees that oversee foreign policy are not very appealing to serve on. In response to lobby pressure, Congress frequently uses sanctions as an instrument for foreign policy. Over certain topics, individual legislators frequently demand ransom from the executive branch (Cameron, 2005, p. 67).

The domestic setting for US foreign policy in the country results from social influences as well as institutional arrangements and institutions put in place by the US Constitution. Several key factors make up the societal framework in which American foreign policy is created. Among these dimensions, democratic liberalism is the most important. Politically, American society is liberal, in that it places a strong emphasis on the individual and the rights and freedoms to which he or she is entitled. This commitment is especially seen in the nation's support of "individual liberty and the protection of private property; limited government, the rule of law, natural rights, the perfectibility of human institutions, and the possibility of human progress" (Dumbrell, 1997, p. 4). Therefore, democratic liberalism asks for a constrained, responsible government that is accountable to the people and is created with their input.

A sense of pragmatism or realism, or ad hoc problem solution, that forgoes overarching moral, ideological, or doctrinal aims in favor of a preoccupation with particular interests and an assessment standard based on results, is also supported by the constellation of social values in the US (Crabb, 1982). Even in foreign policy, values such as democracy, which stimulate free public discourse and pluralism, and inspire many organizations and people to collaborate to find mutually acceptable and ineluctably compromising solutions to their issues, tend to embrace pragmatism. Within the wider framework of American principles, the drive toward pragmatism entails a focus on immediate needs and interests, "case-by-case-ism," reactive strategies, and a short-term rather than long-term perspective (Rourke et al., 1996, pp. 111–113).

The foreign policy principle of the US was based on internationalism. Accordingly, to safeguard its interests and exercise essential leadership, the US should be fully involved in international politics. It involves the willingness to use force, interfere in international issues on a political, military, and economic level, assume a leadership role, and even export American institutions and ideals (Scott, 1998, p. 5).

Since the Vietnam and Watergate eras, it has been increasingly challenging for the president to effectively manage and guide the nation's foreign policy. The end of the Cold War has given the US foreign policy new options, but it has also made it more difficult for presidents to use their authority. Presidents are subject to what is known as the "paradox of power": on one hand, the president is a very potent actor, but on the other, concerning other members of the executive branch, society, and the wider environment, he faces numerous obstacles to effectively using his authority (Rosati & Twing, 1998, pp. 30–35).

It is common to characterize US foreign policy in the post-Cold War era as an unsuccessful search for a grand strategy to take the place of containment. Many experts see US foreign policy under the administrations of George H. W. Bush and Bill Clinton as a confused and sometimes awkward attempt to execute a number of mutually conflicting strategic alternatives all at once (Posen & Ross, p. 7). Accordingly, the foreign policy of the Bush administration has frequently been described as a "mixture of competence and drift, of tactical mastery set in a larger pattern of strategic indirection" (Debiel, 1991, p. 3). The Bush administration was often very timid and cautious when it came to topics that were outside of the Cold War, including the tremendous upheaval that was sweeping Europe and Russia, giving others the chance to lead on foreign policy. However, the Bush administration was ready to use a power politics approach that relied on the threat and use of force for crises more reminiscent of the Cold War era, such as the battle in the Persian Gulf.

It almost seemed as though the foreign policy of the Bush administration was pinned between the formidable legacy of the Cold War past and the tremendous uncertainty of a post-Cold War future (Rosati & Twing, 1998, p. 36). It has been said that Clinton conducted American foreign policy with a great deal of hesitation and vacillation. Early attempts to advance a more "multilateral-oriented" foreign policy were unsuccessful, particularly in Somalia. Despite resistance from the public and Congress, President Clinton did start a number of key foreign policy initiatives in

Haiti, Mexico, and Bosnia. However, it is widely believed that Clinton did not adopt a strong leadership stance or exerted much influence over American foreign policy. A post-Cold War president undoubtedly faces significant political limitations and concerns at home in addition to having to deal with a more complicated and unpredictable global situation.

In the end, the options of the US grand strategy may be reduced to assertiveness or restraint, or to a choice between starting the country's defense on the American side of the sea or the other side (Onea, 2013, p. 2). Since the end of the Cold War, the US has enjoyed a period of exceptional security and prestige since no other state can reasonably compete with it. Because of this, the US should have been able to reap the rewards of leadership exercised with lower costs, suggesting that the time was particularly favorable for implementing a policy of restraint. As it is stated by Robert Jervis: "The US should be then a very conservative state in its foreign relations; with its power and dominance thus assured, it should be the quintessential status quo power. It makes a puzzle of Washington's current behavior, which is anything but conservative" (Jervis, 2006, pp. 7–8). Therefore, it makes sense that the bulk of post-Cold War foreign policy studies have suggested that the US grand strategy should be guided by restraint (Posen, 2013, p. 123).

The US believed that other nations would automatically accord its prestige with the collapse of the Berlin Wall. As a result, it based its foreign policy from the Gulf War until the end of the ethnic conflict in Bosnia on the premise that restraint would prove to be the most successful tactic in fostering a more peaceful and cooperative global governance system while simultaneously defending American values and interests. That is not to claim that foreign policy during the administrations of George H. W. Bush and Bill Clinton was the most restrained strategy possible but rather moderate tactical decisions (Onea, 2013, p. 4). However, as the decade went on, unrest in Somalia, Bosnia, North Korea, Haiti, Rwanda, Kosovo, and Iraq disappointed American hopes that the world was going to become a more peaceful place.

In this regard, the US learned that it could not count on other states' enthusiastic backing for its political efforts. Hence, US policymakers determined that the prestige cost of the restraint experiment was too high. This growing discontent with restraint led to the implementation of an assertive approach, intended to reclaim reputation and penalize rivals. Hence, without the authority of the UNSC, the US' extensive military operations against Baghdad and Belgrade are good examples of this approach (Onea, 2013, p. 4).

1.5   INCREASING INFLUENCE OF THE US IN THE INTERNATIONAL SYSTEM

The US has dominated the global system, exerting tremendous power in a variety of economic, political, and military arenas. It has served as the supreme guarantor of global peace and regional power balances since 1945. Several nations that would otherwise be left to fend for themselves in anarchic international systems were provided security with the help of a forward-leaning military presence, a nuclear umbrella, and defense assurances from the US (Patrick, 2017a, p. 53). Relating to this, a complex and expansive international order centered on economic openness, multilateral institutions, security cooperation, and democratic solidarity was created after the Second World War by the US and its allies.

The US has had a tremendous influence on the international system due to its economic strength, which enables it to influence international trade and investment regulations and put pressure on other nations to support its objectives. Washington has also maintained a global network of military bases and alliances and has one of the highest military expenditures in the world. Few other countries can match the US' ability to project its influence throughout the globe and engage in conflicts and crises. Hence, the US, as the owner and protector of this order, enjoys several advantages that are both liberal and hierarchical (Ikenberry, 2009, p. 72).

During the Cold War, the US saw itself taking on responsibility for organizing and managing the system under the context of a weak Europe and a threatening Soviet Union, and as such the liberal hegemonic order began to take shape. To maintain a balance against Soviet dominance during the decades of bipolar struggle, the US supplied "system function" services and provided global security in bipolar conditions. The manner Washington used power was regulated and restrained by American might, which served the purposes of system stability and security (Ikenberry, 2009, p. 79). It increased American willingness to take on obligations on a global scale, to deliver public goods, and to support and participate in an institutional framework. The bipolar global power position of the US provided services and advantages to other nations. Both Washington and its allies needed each other. This served as the foundation for agreements and fostered motivations for collaboration in fields other than national security (Ikenberry, 2009, p. 79).

The US maintained its geopolitical interests in global stability after the Cold War. It continued to be interested in ensuring that no hostile nation controlled the continent of Europe or that European unrest did not create an unfavorable situation. In addition, the US had both economic and geopolitical interests in the Pacific. Asian states opposed to the remilitarization of Japan want the US to maintain its presence in the region since it is the only nation in the area with both economic and military power resources (Nye, 1992, p. 95).

The Soviet Union fell apart and descended into internal conflicts. China remained a rising power. Moreover, Japan did not possess military power and formed an alliance with the US following the Second World War. As a result, the unipolar global order gave the US the freedom to maintain a liberal foreign policy while ignoring the balance of power and politics. Hence, the US preferred worldwide dominance in the unipolar world instead of isolationist or containment policies.

Bipolarity in the Cold War ended, and liberal internationalism grew by expanding worldwide. After being liberated from the Cold War's constraints, the US quickly rose to prominence as the foundation for a developing global system of liberal democracy, markets, and complex interdependence (Ikenberry, 2018a, p. 9). A system controlled by a single state replaced a globe of contending great powers, which took the form of either Cold War bipolarity or a competitive multipolar system in prior times. Due to its unrivaled sea power and air power, the US has been the sole nation able to project its strength internationally since the fall of the Berlin Wall. It has even entertained the idea of simultaneous deployment in battle theaters located on separate continents (Onea, 2013, p. 20).

In this regard, along the process, the US developed as the "first citizen" of this system, exercising hegemonic leadership to establish alliances, stabilize the global economy, promote collaboration, and defend "free world" ideals (Ikenberry, 2018a, p. 7). This order grew more widespread following the end of the Cold War. East Asian, Eastern European, and Latin American states all underwent democratic reforms and integrated into the global economy. The post-war order's governing structures grew along with it. The WTO was established, NATO grew, and the G20 gained the main stage (Ikenberry, 2018a, p. 7).

The "inside" order turned into the "outside" order when the Cold War ended. With the fall of the Soviet Union, liberal internationalism's main foe was eliminated, and the American-led liberal order grew globally. Liberal internationalism went global once the Cold War ended. At first, this was celebrated as a victory for Western liberal democracies (Ikenberry, 2018a, p. 9). This was a significant transition in which the liberal international order's geography and influence were dramatically increased by the globalization of the world economy and the emergence of the developing world's economic expansion has pushed non-Western nations like China and India into the upper tiers of the global order for the first time in the contemporary period (Ikenberry, 2009, p. 80).

With the demise of a common external threat, the Soviet Union, it was expected that cooperation in the West would decline and NATO would weaken (McFaul & Goldgeier, 1992, p. 481). Yet, contrary to these expectations, the US became the main power in a unipolar system throughout the 1990s, rather than a return to a multipolar system of power distribution. The US built the Western order by prioritizing security and economic areas through expanding regional and global institutions. Accordingly, NATO underwent expansion by increasing its membership. Officials from the State Department outlined a series of institutional initiatives for ties with Europe, including the expansion of the Conference on Security and Cooperation in Europe's (CSCE) function to include associated connections with nations to the east (Ikenberry, 2011, p. 232).

Moreover, the US' growing influence was penetrated via the stabilization and integration of the new and growing market democracies into the Western democratic world. Hence, the US utilized international institutions as instruments. In a speech titled "From Containment to Growth" delivered on September 21, 1993 at the Johns Hopkins University in Washington, DC, National Security Advisor Anthony Lake (1993) unveiled the administration's new foreign policy strategy. Accordingly, he stated:

> First, we should strengthen the community of major market democracies -including our own—which constitutes the core from which enlargement is proceeding. Second, we should help foster and consolidate new democracies and market economies, where possible, especially in states of special significance and opportunity.

In addition, this plan of engagement and enlargement was officially stated by the Clinton administration, which also called for a multilateral solution to foreign policy issues:

> Whether the problem is nuclear proliferation, regional instability, the reversal of reform in the former Soviet empire, or unfair trade practices, the threats and challenges we face demand cooperative, multinational solutions. The only responsible US strategy is one that seeks to ensure US influence over and participation in collective decision making in a wide and growing range of circumstances (National Security Strategy, 1994, p. 6).

Accordingly, the US-led global liberal order had seen significant growth and consolidation by the end of the 1990s. Albright explained, stating that, "Our well-being depended on being integrated internationally" (as cited in Chollet & Goldgeier, 2008, p. 148). In this regard, Western order was carried out globally in terms of organizational principles of the Cold War era. NATO's initial cycle of expansion was successful in establishing the institutional foundation needed to stabilize and integrate new members into the Western system, enhancing security among allies and bolstering democratic and market institutions (Ikenberry, 2011, p. 234). The WTO, the successor of the GATT, represented a significant advancement in creating a judicial foundation for international trade law. Making sure that the US would not retrench its position as the world's undisputed leader was a key driving force behind the foreign policy initiatives of both the first Bush administration and the Clinton administration (Ikenberry, 2011, p. 235).

When a variety of international challenges such as terrorism, climate change, nuclear proliferation, and economic stability are considered in the post-Cold War era, the idea that the US is indispensable became a fact of the global scene. Few global issues could be resolved without the US' active support or engagement. This was particularly true when it came to a variety of international challenges like terrorism, climate change, nuclear proliferation, and economic stability (Chollet & Goldgeier, 2008, pp. 147–148). In the 1994 NSS of Engagement and Enlargement of the Clinton administration, it is stated that the US' "commitment to freedom, equality and human dignity continues to serve as a beacon of hope to peoples around the world" and "U.S. engagement is indispensable to the forging of stable political relations and open trade" (NSS, 1994, pp. i-ii).

The American-led international system experienced both expansion and depth in the global economy. While China and Russia were heading toward the US rather than away from it, Japan and Western Europe continued to be bound to it. The globe was not split into rival regional blocs or belligerent fighting groups 10 years after the conclusion of the Cold War. It was essentially a one-world system with the US and the institutional structure of the post-Cold War Western order at its core (Ikenberry, 2011, p. 236).

The increasing influence of the US in the international system reflects the country's economic, military, and political power strengths. The US military's might has allowed it to retain a sizable presence in many parts of the world and influence global security, while its economic might has allowed it to influence global economic policy and encourage the expansion of multinational firms. The US' overwhelming power position—advantages that allowed it to exercise hegemonic leadership—reinforced the stability and nature of the post-Cold War system. These power advantages came in a variety of forms. One was just its superiority in terms of global power capacities. At the start of the 1990s, the US had the biggest economy in the world, and it remained ahead of other developed nations' economies throughout the decade (Ikenberry, 2011, pp. 236–237). In addition, the US was the only power with a global military force, or the ability to project military strength anywhere in the globe. The US was responsible for 36 percent of all global military spending at the end of the 1990s (Ikenberry, 2011, p. 237). Therefore, the US had established itself as a unipolar force at the core of a free international order that was both stable and growing as the 20th century came to an end. The other traditional big powers did not have the capacity and motivation to aggressively oppose, much less overthrow, this unipolar system.

Global politics entered a period of unipolarity when the US was the only superpower. This moved the issue of American power to international politics itself. American leadership was less restricted by the unexpected appearance of unipolarity, and it did not serve the same system-functional purpose. In this regard, there have been discussions about the nature of American hegemonic power. What would limit American dominance? Was the US a de facto empire at this point? (Ikenberry, 2018a, p. 18). Hence, it became significant to revisit and interrogate the sustainability of the US-led liberal international order.

1.6   RETHINKING HEGEMONIC STABILITY IN THE LIBERAL WORLD ORDER: NECESSITY OR BURDEN?

The idea of hegemonic stability, which holds that a single dominant power can supply the stability required to preserve this international system, is fundamental to liberal world order. Political scientist Charles Kindleberger first proposed the theory of hegemonic stability, contending that the international system needs a dominant power to maintain peace and avert crises. Kindleberger argues that the hegemon offers security, open markets, stable currencies, and other public goods that benefit other states and support the liberal system (Kindleberger, 1981, p. 247). Pax Britannica and Pax Americana both refer to historical periods in which a hegemonic power was in charge and made use of its clout to maintain a stable and peaceful international order. In this respect, according to Robert Gilpin, "Great Britain and the US created and enforced the rules of a liberal international economic order" (1981, p. 145). The openness and stability of the global economic system likewise diminish when the influence of these hegemon nations becomes weaker. Accordingly, this thesis establishes strong conceptual connections between the rise and demise of states and the framework of international relations (Ikenberry, 1989, p. 377). For Kindleberger (1973), Britain's leadership was what maintained the pre-First World War international political economy stability, and the system in the inter-war period collapsed because of the lack of a hegemonic state.

Similar to Kindleberger, Gilpin (1981) created a theory of global leadership underlining the hegemonic nation's active involvement in establishing and maintaining the international political and economic order. Accordingly, Gilpin states that the emergence of a hegemonic nation "resolves the question of which state will govern the system, as well as what ideas and values will predominate, thereby determining the ethos of succeeding ages" (1981, p. 203). Hence, the hegemonic state controls the establishment of the rules and institutions governing international relations in a given era. Regarding the global political economy, hegemonic power is defined as having both strategic advantages in highly significant goods as well as control over raw materials, markets, and capital (Ikenberry, 1989, p. 378). In addition, the hegemon mainly uses coercion, inducements, or sanctions to exercise power.

At the end of the First World War, the US held an overwhelming position in terms of material capability. In terms of overall economic and military parameters as well as the vast range of resources the US had at its disposal, there was a significant gap in capacities and assets (Ikenberry, 1989, p. 380). The US was the world's top industrialized producer by 1900, and before the First World War, it had double the share of global industrial production of its closest industrial rivals, Britain, and Germany. The war itself, which damaged the industrial foundation of the European economy and boosted the American counterpart, made this tendency toward economic domination more obvious (Ikenberry, 1989, p. 380).

The US did use its resources to contribute to establishing the current political and economic world order, as the hegemonic narrative of the early post-war period claims. In the 1950s and 1960s, American oil reserves were used to cover worldwide shortfalls brought on by a string of crises and embargoes in the Middle East (Ikenberry, 1989, p. 381). Loans and lend-lease agreements were utilized to affect British commercial policies soon following the war (Krasner, 1982, p. 32). Throughout the 1950s, foreign aid was utilized to affect European monetary policy. Hence, the US' use of inducements and pressure, reinforced by its physical resource capabilities, had a significant impact and promoted a wide range of post-war regulatory and institution-building initiatives (Ikenberry, 1989, p. 381).

After the Second World War, the US dominated the international system. The liberal international order has been considered a set of institutions, standards, and laws that support international cooperation, free commerce, and democracy. It was obvious that the US was hegemonic, and it utilized its economic and military dominance to create the liberal international order in the post-war era. However, the exercise of coercion to maintain hegemonic order was less successful than was often thought (Ikenberry, 1989, p. 376).

The stability of the international system has been crucially maintained during this period thanks in large part to the US. The US offered public services like trade, financial stability, and security. The US has additionally utilized its authority to uphold international norms including the UN Charter and WTO agreements.

Despite being unprecedented, American power had its flaws. The US has played a hegemonic role since the end of the Second World War, but global events throughout the last decade of the 20th century have raised questions about the continued relevance of this concept. It was widely believed until the end of the Cold War that ethnicity and nationalism were old-fashioned ideas that primarily provided solutions to issues. The tendency appeared to show that the globe was shifting away from nationalism and toward internationalism on both sides of the Cold War. It was common to talk about the decrease in the number of ethnic and nationalist groups as a result of the threat of nuclear war, a strong focus on democracy and human rights, economic interdependence, and the adoption of universal ideals. However, a new cycle of ethnopolitical movements resurged with the end of the Cold War in many different regions of the world, including Central Asia, Africa, and Eastern Europe (particularly the Balkans). Nonetheless, it cannot be stated that the international community was well prepared for this trend. In addition, global powers were hesitant to assist, either out of concern for the law or to prevent possible losses, since internal conflicts often took place within the borders of states.

Accordingly, in the preface of the NSS, which bears President Bill Clinton's signature, it is stated:

> The end of the Cold War fundamentally changed America's security imperatives. The central security challenge of the past half century-the threat of communist expansion-is gone/ The dangers we face today are more diverse. Ethnic conflict is spreading and rogue states pose a serious danger to regional stability in many corners of the globe. The proliferation of weapons of mass destruction represents a major challenge to our security. Large scale environmental degradation, exacerbated by rapid population growth, threatens to undermine political stability in many countries and regions (NSS, 1994, p. 26).

Therefore, it is important to rethink hegemonic stability in the context of the changing global order. In this regard, it is conceivable to argue that liberal international order did not provide a favorable image when global crises and conflicts in the post-Cold War era are considered. Faced with problems, the practice of liberal world order is required to be questioned. Although the US-led liberal international order had some victories in the post-Cold War era, several major events in various parts of the world had tragic consequences that necessitated rethinking hegemonic stability in the liberal order. There have been many discussions regarding the future of the post-Cold War, and the US has tried to lead a coalition against rising instability in the third world.

One of the important concerns during this period is the Gulf War. When the war began, President George H. W. Bush spoke of "the new world order where the nations from different parts of the world come together to make international aspirations of humanity such as peace, freedom, security, and law sovereign the international community" having started (as cited in Chomsky, 1997, p. 19). In the Gulf War, the US was not the dominant power but rather a coalition of countries that took action to remove Iraq from Kuwait.

In addition, the operation in Somalia necessitated rethinking hegemonic stability in the liberal international order. The UN mission's narrow mandate, the absence of a functioning government, and the lack of resources and assistance all contributed to the failure in Somalia. The US intervention in Somalia tarnished the government's international image and called into question the core principles and practices of the liberal international order.

Another significant event that revealed the limits of the liberal international order's capacity to foster peace and avert violence was the Bosnian and Kosovo Wars. The US and its NATO allies took a long time to intervene and put an end to the conflicts in Bosnia and Herzegovina and Kosovo (Mearsheimer, 2019, p. 26). Muslims in Bosnia and Herzegovina and Kosovo were neglected and persecuted in Yugoslavia for a very long time. The war worsened and led to the worst tragedies seen in Europe since the Second World War, despite the efforts of the international community, including the UN, the EU, and NATO. The Kosovo War, which took place in 1999, also put the notion of hegemonic stability to the test. By passing the UN and operating without the Security Council's consent, the US and its NATO allies entered the Kosovo conflict. The US' inability to persuade other Security Council members to accept its activities undermined the conventional notion of the US as the hegemonic force. The Kosovo War also called into doubt the UN's and other international organizations' capacity to uphold security and order in the global system. This demonstrated that, despite having the ability to do so, the international community was unable to successfully intervene and end violence.

In this regard, the Gulf War, the operation in Somalia, the Bosnian War, and the Kosovo War challenged ingrained notions about the role of the US as a hegemon of the liberal international order and the capacity of international organizations to promote peace and security. This furthered the US' position as the world's dominant power, but it also highlighted concerns about the duties and responsibilities of a hegemon in preserving stability.

1.6.1   GULF WAR

The Gulf War, frequently known as the Persian Gulf War, was a battle between Iraq and a coalition of 35 countries led by the US that lasted from August 2, 1990, to February 28, 1991. The invasion of Kuwait by Iraq in August 1990, which prompted international disapproval and sanctions against Iraq, catalyzed the conflict. Due to its wide-ranging effects in the Middle East and beyond, the Gulf War was a pivotal moment in world history.

On August 2, 1990, Iraq invaded Kuwait, which it had long claimed as a part of its territory, starting the Gulf War. Iraq was led by Saddam Hussein at the time. The action was criticized by the whole community, and the UNSC adopted a resolution calling for Iraq's immediate and unconditional departure from Kuwait. A huge military action against Iraq known as Operation Desert Storm was initiated on January 17, 1991, after Iraq refused to abide by the resolution.

Iraq's invasion of oil-rich Kuwait caught everyone by surprise, including the US. The invasion put all the world's superpowers and oil-dependent developed economies at risk. Most international leaders were frightened by this act of war in a crucial region, especially Thatcher and Bush, who viewed it as a manifestation of "naked aggression" similar to that of Adolf Hitler in the 1930s (Mueller, 2004, p. 121). President Bush stated that it was crucial for safeguarding America's oil interests in the area. Saudi Arabia, which borders Kuwait, has a sixth of the world's known oil reserves and is a major supplier to the US, could have been the next country in line if the Iraqi invasion of Kuwait was ignored. On the other hand, Congress was doubtful of Bush's call for a military response from the US. Many others argued that applying sanctions would be an adequate reaction. Hence, only 52–47 senators voted in support of employing force in the Senate on that crucial occasion (Cameron, 2005, p. 15).

With the main goal of freeing Kuwait from Iraqi domination, the coalition's military campaign combined air and ground operations. The US, Britain, France, Saudi Arabia, and several other countries all had troops in the coalition forces (Finlan, 2005, pp. vi-viii). Despite having a larger force, the Iraqi army was no match for the coalition's cutting-edge equipment and superior training. Upon taking control of the skies, the coalition troops launched targeted airstrikes that destroyed Iraqi fortifications.

On February 24, 1991, the US and its allies launched a huge, armored attack that devastated the Iraqi army and signaled the start of the ground battle (Press, 2001, p. 12). Without adequate air defenses, the Iraqi soldiers were no match for the coalition's air power. The coalition largely destroyed Iraq's military infrastructure by the time the war was over, including its airfields, communication hubs, and command and control centers. On February 28, 1991, the coalition and Iraq reached a cease-fire, bringing the Gulf War to a conclusion. (Press, 2001, p. 24).

The US military, led by General Norman Schwarzkopf in the field and Colin Powell as chairman of the Joint Chiefs of Staff, were allowed to unleash a huge offensive attack against the Iraqi troops in February 1991. Bush's National Security Advisor Brent Scowcroft explained that, "The underlying premises for the president and me, probably for Baker, was to conduct this whole thing in a way that would set a useful pattern for the way to deal with crises in an area of cooperation" (as cited in Chollet & Goldgeier, 2008, pp. 49–50). Hence, the support of other states was crucial to the success of the US in the Gulf War.

The US got the support of a broad international coalition that included the Soviet Union. In just a few days, the US force, outfitted with the most advanced weapons and assisted by British and French contingents, decisively won "Operation Desert Storm" (Cameron, 2005, p. 15). America's action would have lacked legitimacy in the eyes of the rest of the world without international support. Although the Bush administration's tactics toward Iraq both before and after the Gulf War were unsuccessful, their organization of the multinational coalition that drove Iraq out of Kuwait suited the country's interests in a new world order. The government used both institutions to co-opt other states to share the burden and hard power, such as military strength, in its efforts. It might not have been conceivable for Saudi Arabia to admit troops or for other countries to send forces without the UN resolutions (Nye, 1992, p. 96). Hence, the Gulf War brought up several questions concerning the US' post-Cold War status.

The Gulf War was the first significant crisis following the collapse of the Berlin Wall. President George H. W. Bush stated that the conflict could be viewed as a "defining moment" since it was affected by the fundamental shifts in world politics and its growing nature was influenced by the precedents set (Freedman & Karsh, 1993, p. xxx). According to President Bush, the Gulf War was about "more than one small country; it is new world order," with "new ways of working nations ... peaceful settlement of disputes, solid aggression, reduced and controlled arsenals and just treatment of all peoples" (as cited in Nye, 1992, p. 83). Yet, soon after the war, Washington lost its enthusiasm for a new world order.

Significant repercussions of the Gulf War affected both Iraq and the larger Middle East. Many people were killed during the war, including soldiers and civilians, and extensive damage was done. The conflict badly damaged Iraq's infrastructure, especially in the oil industry, and destroyed its economy. The war also had political repercussions, strengthening Saddam Hussein's hold on power and serving as a battle cry for Arab nationalism. The Gulf War did not end in the way President Bush had hoped. He wanted Saddam's defeat to be clear-cut, considering he had called Saddam a monster and compared him to Adolf Hitler (Freedman, 2022, p. 275). However, he retreated and acknowledged that he had to stick to his goals of preserving the broadest international coalition possible (Alfonsi, 2006, pp. 154–162).

The US acknowledged its limitations in the Gulf. The Bush administration took significant financial risks in the Gulf War. Even though an economic slump was in progress, it took on the high expenditures of Desert Shield and an increase in the price of oil (Freedman, 1991, p. 198). The US assumed leadership in the Gulf, but its ability to act was based on cooperation from three different groups of states. Namely; those in the region threatened by Iraq; Western states sharing the risks and burdens of taking action against Iraq; and states reluctant to take direct action but who had significant power in affirming the UNSC's resolutions (with China and the Soviet Union being the most critical in this regard) (Freedman, 1991, p. 198).

After the Gulf War, a senior commander stated, "Desert Storm was the perfect war with the perfect enemy" (as cited in Klare, 1995, p. 67). The conflict resulted in the emergence of two civil wars, the collapse of Iraq's sanitary infrastructure, and a failure to overthrow the dictatorship that had been the root of the issue. These effects culminated in far more loss of civilian life than the actual battle itself (Mueller, 1995, p. 117).

In this regard, while the war ultimately resulted in the expulsion of Iraqi forces from Kuwait, it is not possible to consider the war a real success for the US. The early underestimating of the Iraqi military was a major contributing factor in the US' defeat in the Gulf War. As the Iraqi army had relatively inadequate weapons and training before the conflict, many in the American military thought that defeating them would be no challenge. The

Iraqi military's capabilities, however, proved to be more than first believed as the battle dragged on. One particularly well-equipped and well-trained section of the Iraqi military, the Republican Guard, proved to be a deadly foe for the US soldiers (Nowland, 2001, p. 62).

In addition, the choice to mainly rely on air power played a major role in the US' defeat in the Gulf War (Press, 2001, p. 9). The American Air Force was able to severely destroy Iraqi military and infrastructure targets, but it was unable to secure a clear victory on its own. This was partly because a lot of the military objectives in Iraq were well-defended and challenging to attack from the air. Furthermore, after just a few days, American forces were able to drive Iraqi troops from Kuwait, but they were unable to pursue them into Iraq and complete their offensive attack. This gave the Iraqi military a chance to rebuild and continue to threaten the area in the years to come.

The US' defeat in the Gulf War had important geopolitical repercussions as well. Although the US and its allies first perceived the fight as a win, it ultimately led to the spread of anti-American sentiment across the Middle East. This was partly caused by the idea that the US had only engaged in the area to further its own geopolitical goals, with little regard for the locals' welfare. The Gulf War also set the stage for the American military's continued presence in the Middle East, notably in Iraq. The US' inability to win the Gulf War decisively contributed to a sense of unfinished business in the area and prepared the ground for the 2003 US-led invasion of Iraq. Hence, several factors contributed to the US' defeat in the Gulf War. Although the US was ultimately successful in achieving its main goal of liberating Kuwait, its inability to defeat the Iraqi military and deal with the region's underlying geopolitical problems would have long-term effects on American foreign policy in the Middle East.

1.6.2 OPERATION IN SOMALIA

A civil war that had gripped the nation since 1991 led to the humanitarian catastrophe known as the Somalia Crisis of 1992 and 1993. The Siad Barre government was ousted, creating a power vacuum that was filled by numerous armed factions, which is when the crisis started. Widespread bloodshed, evictions, and famine resulted from these factions' acrimonious battle for dominance of the nation. A terrible drought that hit the area caused thousands of deaths due to malnutrition and disease compounded the crisis.

The US intervention in Somalia from 1993 to 1994, which was initiated by Bush and ended by Clinton, had a significant impact on American foreign policy. Over the majority of the Cold War, Somalia supported the Soviet Union while receiving little attention from the US (Cameron, 2005, p. 20). However, following the Ogaden War, in which the Soviet Union backed Ethiopia against Somalia, a US-Somali détente started in 1977, and resulted in a military access deal in 1980, which allowed the US to utilize naval ports and airfields in exchange for military and economic assistance (Cameron, 2005, p. 20).

Since 1991, interclan conflict in Somalia has decimated the country's already precarious economy. Before a UN-sponsored cease-fire could be negotiated in March 1992, approximately 50,000 Somalians had lost their lives in the country's civil war. By this point, a massive famine had been brought on by a drought, and there was no established authority to aid the suffering populace (Hook, 2016, p. 111). The Bush administration and senior officers frequently argued that any military engagement in Somalia would be extremely perilous due to the deeply rooted interclan rivalries that the nation was riddled with for most of 1992. The Joint Chiefs of Staff and senior White House staff's fundamental stance was that US soldiers would not be able to defend themselves or the distribution of humanitarian aid since the nature of the fight made it practically difficult to differentiate combatants from civilians or friends from enemies (Western, 2002, p. 112). However, President Bush eventually opted to launch a significant US military engagement in Somalia with the full backing of all of his top advisers in November 1992. The American public's frequent exposure to graphic images of malnourished children on daily news broadcasts is likely the most popular justification for American intervention. As a result of this moral outrage, the Bush administration was under political pressure to act swiftly to stop the widespread famine. In this regard, the US mission in Somalia was cited as a good example of "the CNN effect" and it forced the president to take action in Somalia (Western, 2002, p. 112).

Bush was making one final plea for international cooperation as he left the office, drawing on feelings of responsibility and compassion. He stated:

> The people of Somalia, especially the children of Somalia, need our help. We're able to ease their suffering. We must help them live.

We must give them hope. America must act. In taking this action, I want to emphasize that I understand the US alone cannot right the world's wrongs. But we also know that some crises in the world cannot be resolved without American involvement, that American action is often necessary as a catalyst for broader involvement of the community of nations (1992, p. 2175).

After Bush had been defeated by Clinton in the 1992 presidential election, the US' participation in "Operation Restore Hope" was formally announced by Bush in an address to the nation on the situation in Somalia. Bush (1992, p. 2175) stated:

Once we have created that secure environment, we will withdraw our troops, handing the security mission back to a regular UN peacekeeping force. Our mission has a limited objective – to open the supply routes, to get the food moving, and to prepare the way for a UN peacekeeping force to keep it moving. This operation is not open-ended. We will not stay longer than is absolutely necessary.

In his speech, Bush didn't bring up a crucial national interest. He had refrained from sending troops earlier in the year despite the severe famine that was taking place. In addition, Smith Hempstone, the US ambassador to Kenya, warned his State Department colleagues in a private communication that the US should consider "once, twice, and three times" before getting involved in Somalia. He warned that Somalis are "natural-born guerrillas who would engage in ambushes and hit and run attacks. They will not be able to stop the convoys from getting through. But they will inflict – and take – casualties" (as cited in Cameron, 2005, p. 20). The president was not prone to assist for humanitarian reasons abroad since he embraced a realist foreign policy; yet, his military advisors had ultimately concluded that they could reduce suffering at a reasonable price (Chollet & Goldgeier, 2008, p. 54).

The UNSC approved Operation Restore Hope (the sending of a peace-keeping force to Somalia). In the fall of 1992, the UN, which was already present in the nation as part of the United Nations Operation in Somalia (UNOSOM), called the US for assistance as a result of the threat of mass hunger (Onea, 2013, p. 55). The US served as the force's commander, and forces from numerous other nations, including Italy, Belgium, and Canada, also participated. The goal of the mission was to safeguard the supply of humanitarian relief to the Somalian people, uphold human rights, and bring about a return to peace and stability in the nation.

Before the deputies meeting on November 21, 1992, almost none of the officials in or outside of the administration had anticipated that President Bush or his top political and military advisers would endorse a significant US humanitarian mission to a struggling nation in the Horn of Africa. The Bush government, especially General Powell and the Joint Chiefs of Staff, had firmly been against calls for American humanitarian intervention in conflicts, in Somalia, Liberia, Bosnia, and other places. They claimed that these conflicts were not related to the country's core interests and that they were tragedies for humanity (Western, 2002, p. 112).

In December 1992, the need to support the idea of a new world order with action led the US to decide to send 25,000 troops to assist the UN in delivering food to the starving Somalians, known as the Unified Task Force (UNITAF) mission (Western, 2002, pp. 112–113). It was a massive military operation in a region that few Americans could locate on a map. The US and the UN had different objectives. The UN's aim was transformative in terms of bringing about Somalia's stabilization through nation-building and the disarmament of the warlords. In contrast, the objective for the Americans was simply humanitarian in the sense that US forces were sent only to make sure that food was delivered those in need, and they would have left once this was done (Tudor, 2013, p. 56).

The situation in Somalia worsened despite claims of progress as the conflict increased and US forces got more directly involved. The outcome was a classic conflict spiral in which Somali militias attacked, UN soldiers retaliated, and with each act of hostility, the need for greater weaponry increased (Chollet & Goldgeier, 2008, p. 73).

Most Americans were aware of the news out of Somalia as the Democrats assumed control, but few gave it high consideration. 52 percent of Americans reported that they were watching the operation very carefully in January, while 89 percent of Americans said they were monitoring developments in Somalia at least somewhat closely. Less than 0.5 percent of respondents who were asked to name the country's top issue did so in relation to Somalia (Chollet & Goldgeier, 2008, p. 57).

Although the Clinton administration consented to keep a minimal military presence in Somalia, primarily the Quick Reaction Force (QRF) to support the UN mission, he was then convinced to change his policy goals from one of providing humanitarian aid to one of "nation building or advancing democracy and political stability." Albright starts the article by arguing that, "More Americans may ask why we should care about the UN effort to restore that failed state," and also argues: "The decision we must make is whether to pull up stakes and allow Somalia to fall back into the abyss or to stay the course and help lift the country and its people from the category of a failed state into that of an emerging democracy. For Somalia's sake, and ours, we must persevere" (Albright, 1993).

In this regard, Clinton embraced a more assertive military stance, initially intending to disarm some of the local militias and then apprehend Mohamed Farah Aideed, a well-known warlord (Cameron, 2005, p. 21). In August 1993, following several assaults on US troops, Clinton gave the order for the specialized Delta Rangers to capture Aideed. On October 3, the attempt to do so disastrously failed, resulting in hundreds of Somalian casualties who were killed and wounded in a ferocious gun battle in the heart of Mogadishu (Cameron, 2005, p. 21).

Eighteen Americans lost their lives and 84 more were hurt in the ensuing 15-hour struggle. There may have been thousands of Somali deaths (Carroll, 2022, p. 705). The president and his national security staff faced heavy criticism due to the urban combat and the deaths of Americans. As the naked body of a US Ranger was seen on television being dragged through the streets of Mogadishu, public opinion was also abruptly altered (Cameron, 2005, p. 21). The incident shocked and outraged Americans, which significantly changed public perceptions of the mission. As the US troops started to leave Somalia, other nations soon followed. The mission's official conclusion occurred in March 1995, leaving Somalia in an ongoing state of anarchy and danger (Hyndman, 1999, p. 111).

Accordingly, a tragic chapter in the nation's history, the Somalia crisis of 1992 and 1993 served as a sobering reminder of the difficulties associated with humanitarian assistance. The crisis made evident how crucial it is for foreign actors to work together effectively, have enough resources, have clear goals, and have a thorough awareness of the local situation.

In this regard, the Clinton administration didn't seem well-prepared or confident to manage a complicated military situation in a region of the world they were unfamiliar with. They were aware of the mission's potential short-term outcomes, but they lacked certainty regarding its ultimate success (Chollet & Goldgeier, 2008, p. 55). Clinton argued that he "would have dealt differently with the conflict in Somalia seven years ago had he been more experienced" (as cited in Ellison, 2000).

The end of the Cold War was supposed to have opened new opportunities for the US abroad. The bitter politics that had animated the angry debates about American foreign policy since Vietnam were supposed to have ended (Chollet & Goldgeier, 2008, p. 79). Because of its embarrassing experience in Somalia, the Clinton administration initially resisted getting engaged in the Balkans and refrained from intervening in the genocide in Rwanda. Immediately after US forces left Somalia, President Clinton released an order that signaled a departure from his administration's earlier rhetoric of forceful multilateralism and projected a substantial reduction in American engagement in future armed humanitarian missions. Congress' attempts to reduce or limit American funding for UN peacekeeping were also a direct consequence of failings in Somalia (Cameron, 2005, p. 22).

The US' failure in Somalia has had a significant impact on both the nation and the surrounding area. The unsuccessful mission of the UN to establish peace and stability in the nation serves as a sobering reminder of the drawbacks of military intervention and the necessity of a more nuanced and locally based approach to conflict resolution. The ongoing conflict in Somalia serves as a stark reminder of the value of supporting local populations and collaborating with them to establish lasting peace and stability.

The catastrophe left fresh psychological scars on both the public and the political elite in Washington. They stressed that any military operation outside of self-defense has to be extremely risk-free and cost no American lives (Chollet & Goldgeier, 2008, p. 73). Diplomat Richard Holbrooke, who shortly helped the Clinton administration put an end to the Bosnian War, referred to this disorder as Vietmalia, the legacy of both Vietnam and Somalia (1998, p. 217).

1.6.3 BOSNIAN WAR

The Bosnian War was a pivotal event in modern European and global history that took place from 1992 to 1995. Between Bosniaks, Croats, and Serbs, the three major ethnic groups in the nation, the conflict in Bosnia and Herzegovina led to widespread violence, evictions, and fatalities. As a result of Yugoslavia's dissolution and the ensuing rise in nationalism and racial tensions in the area, war broke out.

The conflict arose soon after Bosnia and Herzegovina proclaimed their independence from Yugoslavia in April 1992. While Serbs, who made up about a third of the population, opposed independence, Bosniaks and

Croats supported it (Bowker, 1998, p. 1249). The Serbs intended to establish "Republika Srpska," a distinct Serb-dominated state within Bosnia, under the leadership of Bosnian Serb political and military leaders.

With massive atrocities perpetrated by all parties, the conflict swiftly grew more violent and prolonged. Mass rape, ethnic cleansing, and genocide were just a few of the war's many war crimes. The capital of Bosnia and Herzegovina, Sarajevo, was under siege for nearly four years, making it one of the longest sieges in modern times (Andreas, 2004, p. 36).

Up until 1995, when a NATO-led military intervention brought the warring parties to the bargaining table, the international community made attempts to mediate a peace agreement. However, their efforts were generally fruitless. The war was put to an end by the Dayton Accords, which were signed in December 1995 and gave Bosnia and Herzegovina a new governmental system (Caplan, 2000, p. 213).

One of the most catastrophic conflicts in Europe since the Second World War, the Bosnian War caused the relocation of around 2.2 million people and the killing of an estimated 100,000 individuals (Martin-Ortega, p. 139). The war also had important political and social ramifications since it brought to light the persistent ethnic tensions in the Balkans and the necessity of more concerted efforts at racial harmony and peacemaking.

Bosnia gained relevance as a symbol of the new era's challenge and an often used signifier for unwinnable "ethnic conflicts" in the context of institutional transformations in Europe and worldwide. As it is stated by Chollet and Goldgeier, the violence entailed a surprising degree of savagery in the former Yugoslav state with the greatest ethnic diversity. Numerous civilians—mostly Muslims—were harassed and expeled from their homes (Chollet & Goldgeier, 2008, p. 125).

In post-Cold War Europe, Bosnia eventually came to symbolize instability and Western failure. It gained strategic significance despite having no conventional strategic value or significance—the region's conflicts did not directly threaten NATO members, nor did they contain any important economic resources like petroleum—by virtue of its status as a symbol of Western failure and anarchy on the European continent (Tuathail, 1999, p. 517). However, as a result of its leadership position within NATO, the US military ended up being quite active in the area and launched the largest aerial bombing campaign in Europe since 1945 (Holbrooke, 1998, p. 319).

The US and European governments had diverging strategies in Bosnia. The European governments supported a multitrack strategy in Bosnia instead of direct intervention, including the deployment of UN peace-keepers under the United Nations Protection Force (UNPROFOR), the pursuit of negotiations, and the imposition of an embargo on all parties to the conflict through UN Resolution 713 (Onea, 2013, p. 53). However, the US did not approve of this approach and instead preferred the "lift and strike" strategy, which involved removing the arms embargo for Muslims and Croats while also launching limited airstrikes on Bosnian Serb strongholds close to Sarajevo. This suggestion was not accepted by the Europeans either (Onea, 2013, p. 53).

The Bosnian War was a test of the effectiveness of the foreign policy of the US. David Gompert, a former Bush administration official, said that US foreign policymakers were blind to the Yugoslav crisis and that the situation in Bosnia, in particular, "was setting the worst possible precedents for the new era. They did not appreciate the importance of defeating this case of malignant nationalism before it metastasized elsewhere in the former communist world" (Gompert, 1996, p. 141).

"Should American lives be sacrificed to put an end to ethnic conflict?" This was the question that America's strategy toward Bosnia under Presidents Bush and Clinton had captured (Chollet & Goldgeier, 2008, p. 126). Washington's Bosnian policy was not uniform. There was a division between national security officials. While Anthony Lake, Madeleine Albright, and Richard Holbrooke urged for more forceful action, another group involving Secretary of State Warren Christopher recommended the US manage or contain the issue rather than attempt to resolve it (Chollet & Goldgeier, 2008, p. 127).

On June 21, 1991, by stating, "We don't have a dog in this fight," Secretary of State James Baker implied that the US had no interests at stake in this conflict (Danner, 1997, p. 58). However, after four years, President Clinton and his team concluded that the US had a number of interests at stake in the course of the Yugoslavian War of Independence when Bosnian Serb forces attacked the eastern town of Srebrenica. The majority of the worldwide foreign community, which is made up of foreign policy experts, specialists, diplomats, defense analysts, and the international media, considered the Western powers', NATO's, and the UN's halfhearted engagement in the fight as a failure (Tuathail, 1999, p. 516).

The Washington Post journalist Bob Woodward mentioned President Clinton's statement, "This policy is doing enormous damage to the US and to our standing in the world. We look weak" (as cited in Woodward, 1996, p. 261). In addition, National Security Advisor Anthony Lake stated: "This is larger than Bosnia. Bosnia has become and is the symbol of US foreign policy" (as cited in Bob, 1996, p. 262). According to Secretary of State Madeleine Albright (1997b), "To suggest, as some have, that America has no stake in the future of Bosnia is to propose that America abdicate its leadership role in Europe."

On November 27, 1995, Clinton made a speech on Bosnia. His main point was the need for US leadership in an age of globalization:

> As the Cold War gives way to the global village, our leadership is needed more than ever because problems that start beyond our borders can quickly become problems within them ... nowhere has the argument for our leadership been more clearly justified than in the struggle to stop or prevent war and civil violence... There are times and places when our leadership can mean the difference between peace and war, and where we can defend our fundamental values as a people and serve our most basic, strategic interests. My fellow Americans, in this new era there are still times when America and America alone can and should make the difference for peace. The terrible war in Bosnia is such a case (Clinton, 1995).

According to the Clinton administration, major concerns about NATO's survival were generated due to the failure of the alliance to end the war in Bosnia (Chollet & Goldgeier, 2008, p. 125). In an interview, Deputy Secretary of State Strobe Talbott considered the Bosnian War as "a cause for deep skepticism and cynicism about whether NATO had any relevance to the post–Cold War world, other than as a standby defensive alliance against Russia in case it goes bad again" (as cited in Chollet & Goldgeier, 2008, p. 125).

In this regard, the end of the Cold War opened the door for a US foreign policy that was less ideological and imperialist on the one hand, and more cognizant of regional differences and the necessity of delegating authority to regional allies and international institutions on the other. The US' decision to defer to Europe in the handling of the Yugoslavia conflict was a crucial actualization of this, but it failed (Tuathail, 1999, p. 531).

The US originally resisted getting involved because it had concentrated on internal crises and the lack of public support for involvement, which also delayed the response of the international community. President Bill

Clinton authorized a limited air campaign against Bosnian Serb forces in 1995, which marked the beginning of American involvement in the conflict. The mission failed although the intervention did contribute to ending the conflict. The US took a long time to intervene in the crisis, and its initial emphasis on diplomacy and sanctions accomplished little to stop the killing. Ethnic cleansing had already started by the time the US entered militarily.

The Dayton Agreement ended the combat, but it didn't do much to resolve the underlying tensions and differences that led to it. Many war criminals were never brought to trial, and the Bosnian Serbs were allowed to create their own state within Bosnia. The credibility of the international community, and the US in particular, was damaged by the failure to stop ethnic cleansing and hold those responsible accountable (Altun, 2021, p. 33).

The intervention brought to light the constraints on the US military might as well as the challenges of interfering in conflicts with nuanced political and historical roots. The US and the international community's intervention in Bosnia were not successful to tackle the fundamental problems that had been causing the conflict, which had its roots in centuries-old ethnic and religious divisions. The inability to establish long-lasting peace in the area highlighted the difficulties in mediating conflicts with ingrained political and social divisions.

In this regard, the Bosnian War became a test of the US credibility. The US and its allies spent millions of dollars in a valiant effort to restore some kind of stability, order, and rebuilding to the area. However, the fact that the UN and Western nations failed to act decisively in the face of genocide for such a prolonged time shows that the American-led post-Cold War liberal order has significant flaws (Tuathail, 1999, p. 531).

1.6.4   KOSOVO WAR

The Kosovo War, commonly referred to as the Kosovo Conflict, was an armed conflict that erupted in the European Balkans in the late 1990s. The forces of the Federal Republic of Yugoslavia and the Kosovo Liberation Army (KLA), a separatist organization vying for independence for the then-Yugoslav region of Kosovo, engaged in combat. The battle, which lasted from early 1998 to mid-1999, was put to an end by NATO intervention, which led to the departure of Serbian forces and the installation of UN control over Kosovo.

The 1980s saw a rise in tensions between the Serbian minority and the Albanian majority in the Kosovo region, which served as the beginning of the Kosovo War. There was a rising sense of animosity among the Albanians, who felt repressed and sidelined because the Serbs, who made up just approximately 10 percent of the population, possessed the majority of the political and economic power (Stojanoavic, 2002). After Kosovo's autonomy was withdrawn and it came under the direct jurisdiction of the Serbian government in 1989, Milosevic, then-president of Serbia, made the situation worse.

In response, the KLA was established in the middle of the 1990s and started a guerrilla conflict in Kosovo against Serbian security forces (Krasniqi, 2019, p. 4). The KLA was committed to bringing about Kosovo's independence and was mostly composed of ethnic Albanians. As Serbian security forces started a huge crackdown on the KLA in 1998, there was an upsurge in bloodshed and violations of human rights.

As Milosevic increased his intimidation of the ethnically Albanian Muslim majority in the province of Kosovo, there were mounting calls to the US administration for yet another intervention in the former Yugoslavia in 1998 (Freedman, 2022, p. 341). Even though Milosevic appeared to have backed down in late 1998, after one final effort at a diplomatic resolution, the violence continued in early 1999.

The US and the EU, among other members of the international community, expressed growing concern about the situation in Kosovo and made efforts to mediate a compromise between the parties. The talks fell through, though, and NATO started a bombing campaign against Yugoslavia in March 1999, focusing on military and strategic targets.

After the Kosovo conflict was done, there was a divergence between the US and EU about the number of peacekeeping troops needed and who should pay for the province's restoration. Most US politicians typically forget or overlook the fact that the EU provided almost 70 percent of the soldiers and 80 percent of the cash for rebuilding (Cameron, 2005, p. 25).

By using approximately 1,000 aircraft flying out of bases in Germany and Italy, the war was fought mostly in the air (Freedman, 2022, p. 359). It took longer than initially expected, and the campaign's biggest loser overall was Milosevic. During two years of NATO's Operation Allied Force (OAF), the country was beaten in battle, isolated internationally, and under severe home pressure (Webber, 2009, p. 457). Even if the war's main goal of ending Milosevic's oppression of the Kosovan minority was achieved, as written in Ivo Daalder and Michael O'Hanlon's (2000) book, it was condemned as "winning ugly." Humanitarian costs were high, the bombing campaign took longer than intended, and there were severe conflicts between American military authorities in Europe and those in Washington.

In this respect, other nations and observers questioned the legitimacy and efficacy of the action, which made the bombing campaign contentious. The bombardment did, nonetheless, succeed in persuading Milosevic to evacuate Serbian soldiers from Kosovo, and the UN subsequently set up an interim government in the region.

In the years following the conflict, Kosovo became an independent nation, which many nations worldwide recognized but Serbia did not. With hundreds of thousands of people forced to flee their homes, along with numerous deaths and injuries, the conflict also had huge humanitarian effects.

Although there was little question that NATO succeeded in this battle more than the Serbs did, the Serbs did not lose all. It was plausible for Milosevic to think that his political approach was largely—though not entirely—working from the start of the war until mid-May. There was a lot of diplomatic assistance from Russia and the conflict appeared unsettling in Germany, Italy, and Greece (Posen, 2000, p. 66). The Serbs were able to produce many pulses of expulsions despite NATO airstrikes, indicating that they kept their tactical freedom of operation inside Kosovo. By the end of the war, the dominant political force in Kosovo was the UN, not NATO. As a result, Serbia had influence over Kosovo's political future thanks to two favorable big powers, Russia and China (Posen, 2000, p. 79).

Furthermore, with the Kosovo War, NATO's future position was called into doubt by Washington's and London's strategic mistake in urging take-it-or-leave-it discussions at Rambouillet and threatening an air war without the essential preparations for a ground campaign to protect Kosovans (Schwenninger, 1999, p. 54). In early 1999, Albright stated:

> [Kosovo] was emerging as a key test of American leadership and of the relevance and effectiveness of NATO. The alliance was due to celebrate its fiftieth anniversary in April. If my fears proved correct, that event would coincide with the spectacle of another humanitarian disaster in the Balkans. And we would look like fools for proclaiming the alliance's readiness for the twenty-first century

when we were unable to cope with a conflict that began in the fourteenth (1999, p. 391).

In this regard, similar to how it was in Bosnia, NATO's reputation over Kosovo was at stake, and its worth as a source of security was questioned. Even though it wasn't a direct participant in OAF, the EU was also significantly impacted by it. According to Alistair Shepherd (2009, pp. 513–530), the Kosovo crisis served as the crucial trigger for changing the EU's role in managing foreign conflicts. The crisis, which followed a weak performance in Bosnia, demonstrated that the EU was powerless to stop deadly conflicts occurring within Europe.

In addition, the Kosovo conflict has shown that NATO cannot serve as a stand-in for a more inclusive UN collective security system. With assistance from a small number of allies but against the will of the majority, the US had employed force against Iraq and Serbia in less than six months. Despite working with NATO, it has received criticism for being arrogant (Chollet & Goldgeier, 2008, p. 232). The US' treatment of Serbia had deteriorated into outright disdain (Posen, 2000, p. 49). As soon as NATO focused its strikes on Kosovo, it increased the claims of victory, although these assertions were false.

On the editorial page of *The New York Times* on May 23, 1999, President Bill Clinton claimed that NATO had already "destroyed or damaged one-third of Serbia's armored vehicles in Kosovo" and "half its artillery" (Clinton, 1999). Pentagon spokesman Kenneth Bacon also claimed that evidently, between 500 and 600 large weapons had already been damaged or destroyed (as cited in Posen, 2000, p. 64). However, these assertions were considered exaggerated, even inside NATO circles. Washington's calculations initially mentioned three or four times more than the reality on the ground. As of June 10, 1999, the Pentagon's estimate from mid-May had been reduced, implying the destruction of around 40 tanks, 50 armored personnel carriers, and 60 guns and mortars (Posen, 2000, p. 64).

In this regard, the US mishandled the Kosovo crisis. In the negotiations leading up to the 1999 Kosovo War, US officials largely ignored Belgrade's interests in the agreement that was crafted and assumed that Milosevic would surrender as soon as NATO demonstrated its willingness to use force. They also held Serbia responsible for the whole conflict (Walt, 2018a, p. 103). A protracted air campaign sped up Serbia's ethnic cleansing, which resulted in hundreds of civilian deaths and destroyed billions of dollars worth of property before the Serbs finally gave in, and

Belgrade did so only after negotiating a deal that was better than the initial US ultimatum. According to Mandelbaum, the entire conflict may have been averted if the US had been more sympathetic and adaptable from the beginning (1999, p. 103).

The Pentagon asserted that as the KLA launched its advance from Albania around the end of May, strikes on Serb ground units significantly increased in success and it is alleged that over 650 key Serb weapons were purportedly damaged or destroyed in less than two weeks. However, no one who had been to Kosovo since the war's end saw any proof of such widespread devastation, and a lot of Serb troops and equipment were spotted leaving Kosovo in fine condition (Posen, 2000, p. 64). The overwhelming body of evidence indicates that NATO troops launched the conflict over Kosovo without a well-thought-out strategy for using air power to directly impact Serb forces' capacity to operate in Kosovo. The first justification offered by President Clinton—that the conflict was intended to punish Serb soldiers targeting Kosovan Albanians and hinder their capacity to do so—had not been operationalized. In this regard, two simultaneous campaigns—one against Serbia as a whole and the other against the Serb troops on the ground—were initiated once it was obvious that the initially restricted air assaults would have little effect on the Serbs (Posen, 2000, p. 66).

In this regard, the Kosovo War was considered a peacekeeping failure. Washington's concept of the new NATO has been put to an early and perhaps decisive test in Kosovo, for which it is obvious that it was not well prepared. NATO had possibilities to reduce the likelihood of conflict but often did not take advantage of them. As it is stated by Daalder and O'Hanlon, in the simplest terms, it could have persuaded Milosevic to comply with its demands if it had combined more persuasive threats of heavy aircraft bombing with a demand that Yugoslavia permit armed NATO soldiers into Kosovo to provide security (Daalder & O'Hanlon, 2000, p. 185). It is not possible to absolve the Clinton administration and the alliance of responsibility for their general Kosovo policy. Although it was likely impossible to prevent the war, numerous steps could have been taken to reduce the likelihood of conflict.

Accordingly, notwithstanding the important role the US played in the conflict, the failure to stop ethnic cleansing and the inability to establish long-lasting peace in the area made the mission ultimately a failure. The Yugoslavian government launched a violent crackdown in response to the rising tensions, forcing thousands of ethnic Albanians to flee. The situation swiftly worsened, and the world community's alarm about the crimes being committed by the Yugoslav government grew.

The US played a leading role in the Kosovo War, but the mission was considered a failure due to the inability to impede ethnic cleansing and bring lasting peace to the region. The NATO bombing campaign did not stop ethnic cleansing. There were numerous allegations of war crimes and atrocities committed by both sides, as well as many displaced and slain Albanians. Although NATO was able to compel Yugoslavia to remove its soldiers from Kosovo, the intervention was unsuccessful in putting an end to the fighting and securing the area.

The lack of post-war reconstruction planning and strategy was condemned after the intervention. The territory was left in a condition of anarchy and instability when the Yugoslav army fled Kosovo, with competing militias seeking control. The UN-led government that was created in Kosovo was plagued by corruption and inefficiency, and the international community struggled to restore peace in the area.

In this respect, the Kosovo intervention served as a reminder of the American military's limitations and the challenges of intervening in conflicts with nuanced political and historical underpinnings. The US and NATO's intervention were unsuccessful in addressing the underlying problems that had long been the source of ethnic conflict and political oppression in Kosovo. The inability to establish long-lasting peace in the area highlighted the difficulties in mediating conflicts with ingrained political and social divisions.

To sum up, like the Gulf War, the operation in Somalia and the Bosnian War, the Kosovo War also had noteworthy ramifications for the liberal international order and prompted inquiries regarding the notion of hegemonic stability. The aforementioned conflicts have brought to light the inadequacies of the global system in addressing emergencies and upholding stability. They have underscored the difficulties associated with multilateralism and the constraints that international organizations face when attempting to respond to crises promptly and efficiently. Global terrorism became a significant obstacle to the liberal international order, endangering civil liberties, democratic governance, human rights, and the rule of law. Thus, the next chapter scrutinizes new challenges faced by the liberal international order within the framework of the war on terror.

CHAPTER 2

New Actors, New Challenges: War on Terror

2.1 UNEXPECTED CHALLENGES FOR THE LIBERAL WORLD ORDER

"Make America Great Again!"[1] This statement, which was Trump's election campaign motto in 2020, was utilized and mocked across many platforms, including newspapers, social media, academia, and TV channels. In addition to serving as a political campaign motto, Trump's statement can also be considered an exclamation and reflection of the US' perception of its image in foreign policy and how the US sees itself in the international community by being "great again."

Since the US was the leading force in the establishment of the liberal world order following the Second World War, it is difficult to imagine the liberal order without considering the creation of the so-called Pax Americana. As the Trump administration suggested with the aforementioned motto, does making America great again mean making the liberal order "great" as well? Arguments aside, this title seeks to address the current challenges of the liberal international order that was created after the Second World War and ascertain whether this order has come to an end.

In other words, American hegemony in the international system has recently entered a significant crisis, thus raising the question of whether it

---

[1] *It is a campaign slogan used by American politicians. Ronald Reagan first used it during his 1980 presidential campaign. Finally, it was used by Donald J. Trump in the 2020 presidential campaign. For details, please check the article on Trump's campaign: Karen Tumulty, "How Donald Trump came up with 'Make America Great Again'," Washington Post, (January 18, 2017). Available at https://www.washingtonpost.com/politics/how-donald-trump-came-up-with-make-america-great-again/2017/01/17/fb6acf5e-dbf7-11e6-ad42-f3375f271c9c_story.html.*

The Rise and Fall of the Eagle: An Assessment of the Liberal World Order.
Çağatay Özdemir (Author)
© 2024 Apple Academic Press, Inc. Co-published with CRC Press (Taylor & Francis)

will be replaced by a post-liberal order, granted the significance of the US' decline in hegemony in recent years, particularly in Western nations. This stands to be a heated topic of discussion in academic circles and the media.

Countries wanted to make sure that the world would never again descend into such heinous carnage after the Second World War, the bloodiest conflict in recorded human history. International organizations and agreements have been established by world leaders to advance international cooperation in areas of security, trade, health, and monetary policy (Kan, 2011, pp. 4–5). During the past 75 years, the US has promoted this structure, also referred to as the liberal world order. In this time, the world has experienced unheard-of peace and prosperity, yet, this system is showing signs that improvements may be necessary, as it currently faces challenges in addressing fresh sources of disorder such as a deadly pandemic and the looming threat of climate change. What's more, democracy is on a worldwide decline, authoritarianism is on the rise, and countries like China (Üncel & Güner, 2022, p. 50) are deliberately chipping away at the liberal world order, creating parallel institutions of their own like the Shanghai Cooperation Organization. Faced with these difficulties, will the liberal world order survive? If a new system emerges, what will that mean for freedom, peace and prosperity worldwide?

As was just indicated, the international order that emerged in the wake of the Second World War is in the process of gradually shifting. The end of the Cold War, the terrorist events that took place on September 11, the Arab Spring, the COVID-19 outbreak, and the war between Russia and Ukraine have all been significant turning moments pushing this change. Now, just as there were many conversations about the structure of the international system following the end of the Cold War, many talks are going on today regarding the structure of the international system in the current state of affairs. A non-US-centered world system as a post-American order (Schunz & Didier, 2019, p. 176), the establishment of a new world order led by China (Rolland, 2020), or a multipolar/multilayered power distribution system (Flockhart, 2016, p. 5) are the scenarios that come to the forefront in these discussions.

Which of the two scenarios will wind up being accurate is mostly dependent on a handful of important factors of the shift. These elements can be summed up as the decrease in the power of the US, the problem of global leadership, especially the problems at the UN, individualism, and the partial collaboration of states.

Pax Americana has not merely been threatened by a single event, but rather by a process that has taken many years to play out. The invasion of Iraq in 2003 served as a pivotal turning point in this process. Prior to that, NATO nations exhibited significant support for the US when the campaign in Afghanistan began in October 2001 following the 9/11 attacks, and Article 5 of the NATO Charter was put into effect.[2] The Afghanistan operation received no significant condemnation from the international community either, but when the invasion of Iraq started in 2003, almost the entire international community was opposed to it. The only exceptions were a few nations that supported the US.[3] As a direct consequence of this, an anti-American sentiment began to take root in a sizeable segment of the populace. The inadequacies of the occupation process led to an increase in criticism directed at the US, and its credibility came under close examination. So, this process of decline initiated and with it, the end of Pax Americana, but still, it may take years to complete. Since this title deals with the American liberal order's unexpectedly encountered challenges, it is essential to take the evaluation to its roots.

In addition to the pivotal turning points in world history, such as the great wars, theoretical arguments on international relations are particularly important in the establishment of international relations as a field of study. As is the majority opinion, the "Idealism-Realism Debate," also known as "The First Great Debate," served as the foundation for the development of the discipline (Akıllı, 2016, p. 13).

The "First Great Debate" was essential in the development of the academic field's distinct identity. At first, disciplinary practices were based on the chairs that had been established at universities, as well as lectures and research that had been conducted after the First World War. Idealism and realism were the most popular viewpoints at the time. After the end of the Second World War, in response to criticisms leveled against this tactic, the realism hypothesis was formed. In the wake of the fall of the Berlin Wall and in the years that followed, the Soviets voiced their disagreement with realism, which sparked the Second Great Debate. Traditionalism, behaviorism, structuralism; the Third Great Debate, critical theory, globalism, post-structuralism, feminism, and constructivist theory, which

---

[2]*For details, please see: "Collective defence and Article 5," the North Atlantic Treaty Organization, Available at https://www.nato.int/cps/en/natohq/topics_110496.htm.*
[3]*For details, please see: "2003–2011 The Iraq War," Council on Foreign Relations, Available at, https://www.cfr.org/timeline/iraq-war.*

rose to prominence in the 1990s, are some of the trends that have had a growing impact on the study of international relations.

Due to the breadth of the research being conducted, it is only natural that the content of the presentations and/or theoretical discussions that were essential in laying the groundwork for significant theoretical developments in the field of international relations will not be included here, but, to shed light on the liberal world order, it is necessary to provide a glimpse of liberalism in the theory of international relations.

Millions of lives were lost, those who followed the motive of "interest" bathed the world in fire, and the West was challenged by the West during the First World War. This is one of the few times in the history of the world where an event has produced a break. Idealism, which sprouted in such an environment based on the "Wilson Principles" (by US President Woodrow Wilson), envisioned the introduction of various innovations to prevent such a war from happening again (Kissinger, 2002, pp. 223–225). These reforms include the development of open diplomacy rather than secret diplomacy within the international system, the strengthening of international law, and the establishment of new international institutions. On the national level, these reforms included the establishment of democracies rather than authoritarian or absolutist governments.

In this particular setting, idealists regarded it as acceptable for the concept of national interest, as they believed that it would assure international peace and security if strengthening international organizations and creating means to avert conflict were pursued as this comprehension places the finishing touch on harmony and collaboration. Yet, according to Jeremy Bentham and John Stuart Mill, political decisions can be made in democratic governments that align with the interests of the community; to put it another way, the presence of national interests is only feasible with the assumption that liberal democracy exists. The politicization of the people, voting, separation of powers within the state, and freedom of the press are said to be the factors that have led to the development of this situation, according to the understanding that is in question. Idealism holds that a liberal understanding of democracy, in which the state does not interfere with the interests of the individual, is necessary for the possibility of national interest. In this context, national interest is defined as the interest of the society (Akıllı, 2016, pp. 14–15).

On the other hand, neoliberalism emphasizes the fact that "sovereign" states are not the only actors in the international system; rather, it recognizes that international organizations, multinational corporations, NGOs, and even individuals who try to be active in international politics are all actors in the system. In this context, neoliberalist discourse emphasizes that the concept of national interest is not dependent on a single actor but rather will be formed as a result of the interaction of various actors mentioned in the lines above. When evaluated in this context, the concept cannot be stable contrary to what realist theory claims. However, contrary to the realist theory's assumption that the international system is anarchic and that there is a constant power struggle between states, the neoliberal theory argues that cooperation is possible within this anarchic structure and that the concept of national interest will be kept at the highest level thanks to the development of this cooperation. In other words, according to the neoliberalist view, the essence of national interest is not the struggle for power, but cooperation for power. However, the neoliberalist view states that the topics to be cooperated with do not only consist of "high politics" (security, military, political, etc.), but also "low politics" (environment and economy, etc.). To recapitulate, the core of the neoliberalist theory is the principle of collaboration in any subject that can affect the interests within the anarchic international system. This principle is at the center of the neoliberalist definition of national interest.

In general, liberal theories place a strong emphasis on the idea that one of the most important factors to consider when evaluating the actions of states is how their internal affairs are conducted. Because of the nature of the regime, the dynamics of the connection between the state, society, and the person, as well as the presence of nongovernmental actors, need to be taken into consideration in the investigation of the behavior of the state. When we look at it in the context of identity, we see that liberal theories highlight the significance of the process of defining the interests of states and highlight the relationship between government and nongovernmental actors in this process. When we look at it in this context, we see that liberal theories emphasize the importance of the process of defining the interests of states. It is underlined that the participation of many other players operating within the state is an issue while discussing the development of the actor, which is believed to be a state, as well as questions related to foreign policy interests and behaviors. Participation in the formation of foreign policy decisions often includes nongovernmental actors, interest groups, and NGOs. On the other hand, both liberal theories and realist theories define the interests of states on a "material" plane. The entire state determines its political, security, and economic goals from the perspective of profit and loss, and thus shapes its behavior in foreign policy according to a more instrumental logic. To design the future relationships that will be formed with other states and institutions, one must first compute the potential profit and losses that will be revealed by these relationships. The "profit-loss perspective" is used to guide decisions on the nation's foreign policy. Liberal methods suggest that states are more likely to pick from a variety of decisions about their foreign policy, and rather than being driven by external imperatives, the behaviors of foreign policy reflect internal choices. As a consequence of this, the liberal theory postulates that the identities and interests of states are intimately connected to the internal characteristics of states, that these can change over time, and that the construction of identities and interests will be done through the "profit-loss perspective" (Akıllı, 2016, p. 15).

So, what is liberalism? In stark contrast to realism, liberalism is the belief in the possibility of peace and cooperation, the valuation of power through the economy of the state, as well as the notions of political liberties, rights, and other concepts of a similar nature. Fukuyama (1992) most famously evaluated the extent to which liberal democracies had overcome their violent tendencies and felt that progress in human history could be gaged by the abolition of world conflict and the acceptance of norms of legitimacy (Burchill et al., 1996).

2.1.1   BACKGROUND OF THE LIBERAL INTERNATIONAL ORDER

Since the late 1940s, the liberal international order has been the driving force behind the formation of relations between democratic, industrialized, and capitalist nations. In addition to this, it affects the state of international politics in general. As a result of the realization that the post-war era was characterized by ideas and institutions that prioritized the rule of law, democracy, human rights, the free flow of capital and goods, the provision of global public goods on a multilateral basis, and collective security, the liberal international order came into existence (Finnemore et al., 2021) from the end date of the Second World War, September 2, 1945, to 1991, the end of Cold War era, which spanned roughly 45 years. However, there are various perspectives on the incident or events that led to the Cold War. Fahir Armaoğlu asserts that Mikhail Gorbachev's resignation on August

24, 1991, as a result of the dramatic actions performed that day, marked the "official" end of the Cold War (Armaoğlu, 2010, p. 950). Raymond Garthoff, on the other hand, asserts that the sole events that led to the end of the Cold War were the unification of Federal and East Germany, the dissolution of the Warsaw Pact, and the removal of the Iron Curtain[4] that had divided Europe (Garthoff, 1994, p. 144).

On the other hand, Oral Sander (2010, pp. 584–585) emphasizes, in addition to the two developments mentioned by Garthoff, the disintegration of the Soviet Union ultimately brought the end of the Cold War. Similarly, John Morris Roberts (1999, p. 691) regards the dissolution of the Soviets as the finalizer of the Cold War. Eric Hobsbawm (1995, p. 759) also accepts the Soviet collapse as the only event that ended the Cold War. Former US National Security Advisor Zbigniew Brzezinski (Brzezinski, 1992, p. 33) also considers the collapse of the Soviet Union as the event that ended the Cold War. However, it is a fact that other events that occurred toward the end of the period affected this process. As can be seen, according to the general opinion, the main event that ended the Cold War was the collapse of the Soviet Union; however, it is a fact that the collapse of the Soviet Union was the main event that ended the Cold War.

The conclusion of the Cold War, which lasted for around forty-five years, marked the beginning of a transitional era during which a great deal of progress was made, as was noted in the lines that came before them. The failure of Mikhail Gorbachev's policies of "Glasnost" and "Perestroika," which were thought to be among the most significant of these occurrences, is the incident that can be considered the most important of these. In the superpower race,[5] as the polar leader in the bipolar world order, the Soviets gradually fell behind against the US, and the public marched in Moscow to end the monopoly of the Communist Party. Gorbachev, who took office

---

[4]*Iron Curtain/Iron Curtain: Winston Churchill first used the concept in his famous speech on March 5, 1946, in Fulton, Missouri (US). The concept, in essence, was used to describe the Western, Soviet Union, and Eastern European countries during and after the Second World War. Of course, the criticism of this characterization is directed toward the Soviet policy of Eastern Europe and its tendency not to establish open relations with the West. Source: International Relations Dictionary, (ed.) Faruk Sönmezoğlu, Prepared by: Deniz Ülke Arıboğan, Gülden Ayman, Beril Dedeoğlu, 4th Edition, Istanbul, Der Publications, 2010, p. 218.*

[5]*The Soviets did not have the economic and technological equipment to catch up with the "Star Wars," that is, the "Strategic Defense Initiative (Star Wars)" project, which would neutralize the long-range strategic missiles of the USSR with missiles to be launched from space. For details, please see Armaoğlu, ibid, p. 915.*

on March 11, 1985, then threw his support behind the "Glasnost" and "Perestroika" reform.

Because Gorbachev stated that with "Glasnost" (openness, transparency), the state and public institutions should be open to criticism from the public, and the Soviet economy should be restructured with "Perestroika" (restructuring) (Armaoğlu, 2010, pp. 913–915). On the other hand, it was around this time that it became clear ethnic tensions were beginning to emerge within the Soviet Union. In 1988, the Armenian community living in Nagorno-Karabakh aspired to join Armenia. With physical battles between Azerbaijanis and Armenians in the region, the region was split between two countries. On the other side, in the year 1989, the government of Yugoslavia attempted to put an end to these conflicts by deploying troops to the region of Kosovo, which was experiencing an increase in the number of ethnic clashes. In the same year, the Union Party, which would go on to become Uzbekistan's first non-communist political movement, was established. In Poland, free elections were held for the very first time. More than a hundred people were killed in Uzbekistan as a result of the battle that occurred between the Uzbeks and the Meskhetian Turks, East German leader Eric Honecker's stint as head of East Germany came to an end; the Berlin Wall came down; and thousands of East German civilians crossed into the Federal Republic by train. The end of the Cold War was officially declared by Ronald Reagan of the US and Mikhail Gorbachev of the Soviet Union on a warship off the coast of Malta.

In the year 1990, a battle between Georgians and Ossetians broke out, resulting in the military units of the Soviet Union intervening in the conflict. Baku was placed under a state of emergency after an uprising broke out there. A curfew was imposed as a result of the violence that broke out between Tajiks and Armenians in Uzbekistan. The Soviet Army pulled back from its position in Hungary. In Bulgaria, the former communist administration had been replaced by a coalition government. In Lithuania, elections were held for the first time with multiple parties participating. In Moscow, there was a big public march held to advocate democratic reform. A unilateral declaration of independence from the Soviet Union was made by Lithuania, followed by Estonia and Latvia, in that order. The two German states merged into one. The consequence of the referendum in Slovenia, which was one of the republics that comprised Yugoslavia, was an emergence of the demand for independence. In the year 1991, Soviet forces opened fire on residents in Lithuania. At the time, there was a sizable organization in Moscow that condemned these violent crimes in Lithuania. The desire for independence in Georgia evolved as a direct result of the referendum that was held in that country. First, the Council for Mutual Economic Assistance (Comecon) and then the Warsaw Pact dissolved. A coup attempt was made against Gorbachev. The coup attempt came to an end with the intervention of Russian Federation leader Boris Yeltsin. At the Almaty (Kazakhstan) meeting, where 11 (Soviet) republics came together, it was announced that the Union of Soviet Socialist Republics (USSR) had ended. Mikhail Gorbachev resigned. In 1992, the European Commission declared that it recognized Croatia and Slovenia. The Slovak Parliament declared independence. In 1993, Czechoslovakia was divided into two (Roberts, 1999, pp. 696).

Although the legal dissolution of the Soviet Union took place without any problems, the de facto dissolution of the said structure brought great difficulties for some countries. As a result of the bloody conflicts in Yugoslavia, which was perhaps most severely affected by the disintegration of the Soviet geography, the disintegration of Yugoslavia, as Akıllı emphasized, started with the declaration of independence of Bosnia and Herzegovina in 1992. The Bosnian Serbs, who were dissatisfied with the declaration of independence of Bosnia and Herzegovina, declared the Bosnian Serb Republic unilaterally and started ethnic cleansing in Bosnia and Herzegovina with the support of the Federal Republic of Yugoslavia and massacred hundreds of thousands of Bosnians. The massacre in question continued between 1992 and 1995, as a result of which around 300,000 people lost their lives, while around 2 million people had to leave their lands at the cost of their lives. In Bosnia and Herzegovina, where the human tragedy was experienced, this persecution could only be stopped in 1995 when NATO troops entered the country (Akıllı, 2016, p. 45).

While the events described in the previous lines were taking place in the former Soviet basin, in parallel with Saddam Hussein's actions in the region, the First Gulf War broke out in the Middle East as a result of Iraq's invasion of Kuwait on August 2, 1990. On the other hand, one of the most significant aspects of the First Gulf War was the fact that it provided a worldwide stage for the US to demonstrate its dominance as the lone leader of the emerging new world order. Another feature is that it demonstrates how the geography of the Middle East is truly rife with major crises; for example, during the First Gulf War, it was claimed that Iraq had nuclear weapons and the ballistic infrastructure to use them.

Just as world history witnessed a global breaking point after the end of the Cold War, it also witnessed a new breaking point as a result of the terrorist attacks on the World Trade Center's Twin Towers in the US on September 11, 2001. After the Cold War, the US was targeted by this massive attack on its own soil when a period of history was ending with the fall of the Soviet Union (Fukuyama, 1989), and it was believed that the liberal democracy of the West would dominate the world as the final stage of human socio-cultural development (Fukuyama, 1992). According to this view, reformation movements in the Soviet Union, the worst of the Cold War, and in Eastern Europe, the fact that consumer culture spread all over the world, declared the West's final victory. With the collapse of the Soviet Union, not only did the Cold War come to an end but it also marked the end of history. With the understanding that history continues through thesis and antithesis with a Hegelian reading of history, Fukuyama claimed that no system that could be an alternative to the West and thus cause conflict could not be found in the world. According to Fukuyama, Western liberal democracy was the final form of human government (Fukuyama, 1992). The terrorist attacks on 9/11 made it necessary to revisit the security maps that had been prepared. However, with the aftershocks of 9/11, a transition and change began in regional and global organizations, militaries, as well as socio-economic and political fields around the world.

2.1.2   THE DECLINE OF PAX AMERICANA

Before dwelling any further, it's important to ask, "What does Pax Americana mean?" Throughout history, several periods were named after Pax terms, such as Pax Romana and Pax Britannica, and for the liberal world order, it was also labeled as Pax Americana. In short, Pax Americana means, in Latin, "American Peace." In general, Pax Americana refers to the ceasefire between superpowers following the Second World War period. Other names for this period include the "post-war order" and "liberal world order." The Cold War saw the emergence of a bipolar system. As the USSR fell, the Western Bloc, led by the US, won the war. Human rights and democratic regimes were championed by the Western Bloc. As the Soviet Union fell apart, the US emerged as the sole great power.

As aforementioned above, this was viewed as a triumph of liberal democracies over communism. Furthermore, Fukuyama referred to it as "the end of mankind's ideological growth" (Fukuyama, 1989). Bill Clinton, the president of the US at the time, stated in a speech during his campaign that, "Freedom, not tyranny, is on the march and pure power politics is ill-suited to a new era" (Reuters, 1992).

According to liberals, the main concerns for the world order are trade, alliances, international law, multilateralism, environmental protection, and human rights (Ikenberry, 2017). Also, poorer nations have won the right to speak out through international organizations like the UN (Nye, 2017). This order was put in place by the US. For instance, the Truman administration gave post-Second World War economic assistance to European nations, and the Marshall Plan helped the US promote democratic rule in nations. The US also established NATO to safeguard world peace. Apart from that, the North American Free Trade Agreement (NAFTA), the Organization for Economic Co-operation and Development (OECD), and the World Bank, as well as international agreements such as the Nuclear Non-Proliferation Treaty (NPT), also known as the Warsaw Pact, were established as well. The liberal international order is characterized mostly by these traits.

Nonetheless, some people disagree with the statements made above. The character of the international system, which was defined as being liberal and international at the top, should be addressed first and foremost. According to Mearsheimer, if the international system is unipolar, the political ideology of the one pole matters; in other words, if we are going to talk about liberal democratic order that incarnates from the US, it has to be in a unipolar system so that a liberal democratic state as the dominant power can provide a solid ground for a liberal international order to emerge (Mearsheimer, 2019, p. 7).

At this juncture, it is necessary to shed light on the disparities between the popular concept of the liberal order and the definitions that are found in the literature. As was just indicated, various authors' definitions and understandings of the liberal order and their conceptualization of it can be found in the various conceptualizations of it. The majority of these started during the Second World War. For example, Lake et al. refer to the liberal international order as "a tremendously effective institution" and explain that it was established after the atrocities of the Second World War. The liberal international order is credited with encouraging the emergence of free trade and global capital mobility, promoting democracy, and protecting the West against the expansionist Soviet Union (Lake et al.,

2021, p. 226). Likewise, as mentioned above, Finnemore et al. also share the same perception of the liberal international order and consider the period after the Second World War (Finnemore et al., 2021). These kinds of descriptions comprise the mainstream definition regarding the liberal international order's lifespan.

Contrary to the mainstream definition, Mearsheimer challenges the definition and claims that the post-Second World War era was not liberal or international (Mearsheimer, 2019, p. 8). He also claims that the order that was constructed after the Second World War was a constrained system that was mostly restricted to the West and that it was a realist system in every significant way; it possessed some characteristics that were also in line with a liberal order, but those characteristics were grounded in realism logic. On the other hand, the post-Cold War system that the US has led is liberal and global, which is a considerable shift from the restricted order that the US dominated during the Cold War. This signals a significant departure from the system that the US created (Mearsheimer, 2019, pp. 8–9).

Apart from that, some studies focus on the dichotomy that Pax Americana and liberal international order are separate bodies. For instance, Ikenberry claims that the liberal order would endure despite US hegemony since it helps both emerging powers and Western nations (Ikenberry, 2018a, p. 8). Another claim implied that the US, the country that established and upheld this order, is currently experiencing a hegemonic crisis, not upholding the liberal order (Jahn, 2018, p. 43). In another view, Kurtbağ suggests that more liberalism will be the answer to the current liberal dilemma rather than less (Kurtbağ, 2020, p. 392).

Looking back to Mearsheimer's definition of the liberal international order, he explains the period as 1990 and beyond (Mearsheimer, 2019, p. 21). The dissolution of the USSR resembles the wake of the liberal international order championed by the US, which is evaluated as the "unipolar moment" (Krauthammer, 1991, p. 23). Mearsheimer (2019, p. 21) explains the situation as:

> The thick Western order that the US had created to deal with the Soviet Union remained firmly intact, while the Soviet order quickly fell apart. Comecon and the Warsaw Pact dissolved in the summer of 1991, and the Soviet Union collapsed in December 1991. Unsurprisingly, President George H.W. Bush decided to take the realist Western order and spread it across the globe, transforming it into a liberal international order.

Moreover, top officials sealed this by being the champions of the liberal order. Former US President George H. W. Bush said in a statement in 1990 that, "There is no substitute for American leadership" (Bush, 1990). Likewise, Secretary of State Madeleine Albright (Today Show, 1998) and President Barack Obama (2014) were confident in saying that the US is "the indispensable nation." All of these statements imply that the US is the core of the international system, and hence it's not possible to continue this international order without the leadership of the US. Nonetheless, some academic studies also implied the claim that the liberal world order is passing through systemic economic stress, growing nationalism, and general loss of confidence in established international and national insti-tutions; if the US chooses to abandon its key role as a guarantor of the system there will be consequences (Kagan, 2017, p. 1). To put it another way, the US and the liberal international order are interdependent in at least one respect. On the other hand, the question that needs to be asked is whether the deterioration of the liberal order in the international system coincides with the fall of the Pax Americana. The answer is going to be covered in the next heading.

2.1.3   CHALLENGES TO THE LIBERAL INTERNATIONAL ORDER

Under this title, challenges to the liberal international order will be discussed. But before explaining those challenges, it's critical to shed light on the definition of the liberal international order. In other words, what steps needed to be taken to constitute a liberal international order?

As Mearsheimer (2019, p. 22) suggests, there are three steps/tasks required to establish a liberal international system; first and foremost, it was crucial to increase the number of people who belonged to the Western order institutions and to create new ones when needed. In other words, it was crucial to create a web of universally recognized international organi-zations with significant influence over member states' behavior. Second, it was crucial to establish a free-trade-friendly, broadly inclusive global economy that promoted unrestricted capital markets. The economic order that predominated in the West during the Cold War was designed to be far more modest in scope, due to the presence of the Iron Curtain, than the hyper-globalized world economy, and finally, it was essential to force-fully promote liberal democracy throughout the world, a goal that was sometimes neglected when the US and the Soviet Union were vying for supremacy (Mearsheimer, 2019, p. 22). The US did not pursue this objective alone; most of its European allies supported it (Jawad, 2008, p. 625).

In the views of those who laid the groundwork for the liberal international order, the achievement of a robust and long-lasting liberal international order was conceptually identical to the achievement of world peace (Mearsheimer, 2019, p. 23). This long-standing mentality served as a powerful impetus for the US and its allies to work hard and persistently toward the establishment of that new order. As a result of this, Russia and China, as well as the interiors of their respective countries, have become targets for the expansion of liberal international order. The integration of China and Russia, in addition to the integration of each country's unique hinterland, was essential to the establishment of the liberal international order since China and Russia were the two most powerful powers in the international system after the US. The goal was to fully incorporate these countries into an open international economy, to incorporate these countries into as many institutions as possible, and to aid these countries in transforming themselves into liberal democracies. In addition, the enlargement of NATO into Eastern Europe is a classic example of how the US and its allies strive to turn the current Western-centric world order into a liberal one (Mearsheimer, 2014, p. 77).

Why is the liberal international order's continued extension and presence still being challenged despite the aforementioned steps and measures being attempted to maintain its safety and security? Evidence of increased protectionism, inaction on climate change, democratic backsliding, and escalating great power confrontation are some of the challenges that the Finnemore article points to as evidence of a deteriorating international order (Finnemore et al., 2021).

Furthermore, Finnemore et al. edited a special issue for the International Organization Journal to investigate and explain the challenges targeting the liberal international order (Finnemore et al., 2021). In their article titled "Challenges to the Liberal Order: Reflections on International Organization," David A. Lake, Lisa L. Martin, and Thomas Risse imply that the liberal international order has faced challenges from the start, including both internal and external factors as well as the interaction between interior and exterior dynamics of the system (Lake et al., 2021, p. 234).

Lake et al. stress that the nature of liberalism itself is the source of some of the liberal international order's current problems, which also fuel the rise of nationalist populism among the liberal international order's core members (Lake et al. 2021, p. 236). Furthermore, they explain that there are three main ways in which liberalism has faced problems: First, liberalism, especially neoliberalism, makes it worse for those who benefit and those who suffer from economic globalization. Although unappreciated, these impacts are generally predictable and also seem more nuanced than previously thought (Lake et al. 2021, pp. 236–237). According to Broz, Frieden, and Weymouth, the welfare and political ramifications of free trade and economic openness, which were exacerbated by the financial crisis of 2008–2010, are currently most apparent at the level of communities (Broz, et al., 2021, pp. 465–466). Apart from that, Rogowski and Flaherty (2021) claim that income inequality is a primary driver of populism and amplifies the effects of globalization disruptions (Flaherty and Rogowski, 2021, p. 498).

Secondly, liberalism has inconsistencies within its framework. Most crucially, liberalism had to be somewhat illiberal to establish itself, which made it less sensitive to the needs of the people (Lake, et al., 2021, p. 237). For instance, free trade policies required governments, particularly those in the US, to shield the decision-making process from pressure by protectionist groups (Goldstein & Gulotty, 2021, p. 525). Furthermore, opposing groups were left out of the process as free trade was institutionalized, and they eventually rebeled against it; similarly, Börzel and Zürn contend that to establish liberal internationalism, supranational institutions, particularly the EU, developed into more technocratic, invasive, and insulated from the general populace, which stoked discontent and a nationalist backlash (Börzel & Zürn, 2021, p. 303). The seeds of liberalism's very own problems are contained within in an almost dialectical manner; De Vries, Hobolt, and Walter claim that domestic opposition and new demands by mass publics for greater participation in politics have been spurred by international institutions, often rallied by the support for antiliberal policies (De Vries et al., 2021, p. 330).

Lake et al. explain that the third one is the fact that liberalism undermines ideas of national identity in both its economic and political manifestations (Lake, et al. 2021, p. 237). Simmons and Goemans extend the distinction between the Westphalian order and the liberal international order that they previously made and drew attention to an underappreciated conflict between territorial sovereignty norms, which are essential to the former, and universalist norms, crucial to the latter (Simmons & Goemans, 2021, p. 409). The contemporary era's nationalistic appeals and calls for the "repatriation" of sovereignty clash with these values. On the other hand, Goodman and Pepinsky stress the friction created by open-door immigration policies as well as the standards and laws limiting acceptable participation in a national polity, leading to fresh disputes asking "who are we?" today. This strikes the heart of nationalism and democratic political ideology (Goodman & Pepinsky, 2021, p. 435). Notwithstanding, Búzás characterizes the history of International Relations as an ongoing conflict between traditionalists who uphold racial hierarchies and transformationalists who support "multiculturalism" and are influenced by liberalism's belief in human equality (Búzás, 2021, p. 441). As Mearsheimer implies, nationalism is the strongest political ideology on this blue planet (Mearsheimer, 2019, p. 8) and adds that every time they clash, nationalism almost always triumphs over liberalism and weakens the liberal international order's very foundation of the established system. Moreover, Lake et al. mention that the liberal international order is facing significant nationalist-populist resistance from within core states as a result of these different issues; the West and other parts of the world are seeing an increase in parties and movements that exhibit some of the following three traits: nationalism, populism and authoritarianism (Lake et al., 2021, p. 238). As mentioned above, nationalism weakens the core of liberalism and when they clash, nationalism overcomes liberalism.

On the other hand, populism promotes society's interests rather than the opinions of elites. Generally speaking, populism involves rejecting the elite consensus and assuming a homogenous "will of the people" that opposes pluralism and is frequently characterized in exclusive nationalist terms. As mentioned above, nationalism is the nemesis of liberalism. Apart from those, authoritarianism is described as the denial of fundamental components of modern political systems, including free and fair elections, press freedom, and an independent judiciary (Lake et al., 2021, p. 238). These aforementioned three traits are on the rise, especially in the fortress of the liberal international order: Western states. A study conducted by Harvard Kennedy School shows that more than a quarter of European voters supported an authoritarian populist party in their national election, and many European administrations either include or depend on parliamentary support from those kinds of political parties (Norris, 2020, pp. 6–10).

An external challenge to the existing liberal order in the international system is posed by the growth of China as a key actor in the international system. One could ponder the reasons why the prosperity of a country in the Far East would threaten the free order of the international community. What about Japan or South Korea, given that this is the case? If this were the case, then the economic stability and prosperity of these two countries would make them competitors against the liberal international order as well. However, this is not the case, therefore they are not competitors. The significance of China lies in the nature of the state itself and the culture that it upholds within its borders.

Economic liberalism is accepted by the government of China, which is dependent on the liberal international order for growth. Some academics believe that China has successfully managed to strike this delicate balance up to this point in its history. Yet, at the same time, it contradicts some of the most essential tenets of the liberal international order, such as democracy, freedom of the press, and various other domestic human rights. The legal system is only partially acknowledged as legitimate (Weiss & Wallace, 2021, p. 663).

Nonetheless, China is hardly the only authoritarian nation that could oppose the liberal international order, or at least some of its provisions. Examples include Russia, Venezuela, and Iran; nevertheless, the list might be much longer. In other words, the emergence of non-Western major actors in the international system that hardly employ the main features of the liberal international order is considered a challenge to the order. This is because the main features of the liberal international order include things like free trade and democratic governments.

2.1.4 MULTILATERAL INSTITUTIONS BEING WEAKENED

The Nixon government abruptly ended the Bretton Woods monetary system in 1971 by severing the connection between the US currency and gold. The world was astonished by this decision, but it was made in response to several crises and what was an unsustainable relationship between the dollar and gold, creating the actual possibility of a run on US gold holdings. Similarly, when member nations refused to support the war in Iraq, the George W. Bush administration initially tried to win their approval before breaking off relations with the UN (Lake et al., 2021, p. 244). Furthermore, the EU could not act as a whole in the Bosnian and Kosovo wars even though these wars happened in the very heartland of the European continent. Furthermore, President Emmanuel Macron of France recently stated, "NATO is experiencing brain death because of Trump" (Erlanger, 2019). And this statement also demonstrates the lack of confidence in NATO. Those examples point to a loss of trust in multilateral institutions, but at this point, it is important to understand that this instance of distrust is dependent on the states that constitute those institutions. In other words, flag carriers of the liberal international order also indirectly undermine the order itself by weakening the core elements and successors of the liberal international order, such as multilateral institutions.

As mentioned above, the mindset of the liberal international order's founders, spreading liberal democracies all around the world, is the key element for establishing a strong, lasting liberal international order that was equivalent to bringing about world peace. Attempting such ambitious social engineering on a global scale is almost guaranteed to backfire and weaken the legitimacy of the venture itself. Intervening in the politics of nations to transform them into liberal democracies is extremely difficult and generally resisted by nationalist notions. For instance, after the 2003 US invasion of Iraq, Syria and Iran supported the insurgency in Iraq. Likewise, China and Russia have supported one another militarily, economically, and on international platforms like the UNSC (Mearsheimer, 2019, pp. 30–31). Furthermore, if attempts to alter the regime fail, there would be a considerable number of refugees flowing into liberal countries. Again, nationalism is the root of the issue and is still alive today, especially in cultures that pride themselves on being liberal. For a significant portion of the population living inside liberal democracies, especially the solitary pole, hyper-globalization has resulted in significant economic losses. The liberal international order is further threatened by these costs, which include lost jobs, stagnant or declining wages, and stark income disparity (Mearsheimer, 2019, pp. 31–32).

2.2   WAR ON TERROR AND US FOREIGN POLICY

On September 11, 2001, the US experienced a fresh breakthrough as a result of suicide attacks on the twin towers, much like the globe had a global breakthrough following the conclusion of the Cold War. The US was exposed to such a massive onslaught on its soil when the Soviet Union fell apart, signaling the end of history and the liberal democracy of the

West as the final stage of human socio-cultural progress in this era. It has become imperative to revisit the security maps that were drawn. Yet, as a result of the effects of 9/11, regional and international institutions, as well as the military, socioeconomic, and political spheres, began to endure a period of transition and transformation.

Fukuyama's *The End of History and the Last Man* (1992) was one of the two fundamental books regarding the future in the new order following the Cold War; the other was Samuel Huntington's *The Clash of Civilizations and the Remaking of World Order* (Huntington, 1996). According to Huntington's article *The Clash of the Civilizations?* (Huntington, 1993), the conflict in the post-Cold War world order would be between "civilizations" rather than ideologies and will pit the Western culture against its military might. It asserts that the enemy won't materialize until a strong axis between Islamic and Far Eastern civilizations develops. On the other hand, the "Alliance of Civilizations" (AoC) was established in the UN on September 2, 2005. The "Alliance of Civilizations" was an attempt to prevent the "possible" conflict situation, which Huntington hinted at in his book and article. The initiative was first emphasized by Spanish Prime Minister J. L. Rodriguez Zapatero on September 21, 2004, at the UN General Assembly; he stated that the conflict between the Western and Islamic civilizations should be prevented (Zapatero, 2004).

When considered cyclically, it is clear that two significant historical events—the end of the Cold War and the 9/11 attacks—had a significant impact on the radical shifts in the widely held notions of security. The concept of security in a bipolar system has altered since the end of the Cold War, which was brought about by the fall of the Berlin Wall, Gorbachev's departure, and the Soviet Union's admission that its material and economic infrastructure was unable to compete with the US and NATO.

The suicide attacks on the World Trade Center's Twin Towers in New York on September 11, 2001, however, marked the turning point in how people understood security. In essence, the issue of security should be discussed above all other issues to avoid being exposed to an event like the terrorist attacks of September 11. This idea of "sacrificing freedoms for greater security," which originated in the US after the relevant terrorist attacks and affected the entire world, refers to the condition of not having importance but still having.

However, in this context, "The Clash of the Civilizations" thesis has risen to the agenda as a result of the intervention process that began in the Middle East in the geography of Afghanistan after the 9/11 incidents, in the context of the "War on Terror" doctrine under the leadership of the US. Freedoms were given up to boost global security as a result of the new views that the 9/11 attacks caused in the concept of security, which was crowned by the "War on Terror" doctrine.

2.2.1   UNDERSTANDING THE "WAR ON TERROR"

George W. Bush stated the US' "War on Terror" doctrine as follows: "The attack (9/11) took place on American soil, but it was an attack on the heart and soul of the civilized world. And the world has come together to fight a new and different war, the first, and we hope the only one, of the 21st century. A war against all those who seek to export terror, and a war against those governments that support or shelter them" (Bush, 2001a).

Mearsheimer claims that the Bush Doctrine, which was created in 2002 and utilized to support the war in Iraq in March 2003, is an illustration of a significant US policy intended to create a liberal international order. After the terrorist attacks of September 11, 2001, the Bush administration concluded that to win the so-called global war on terror, Iran, Iraq, and Syria had to be confronted in addition to al-Qaeda (Mearsheimer, 2019, p. 24).

The term "War on Terror" is used to refer to the international counter-terrorism operation that the US has been leading after the 9/11 terrorist attacks. The war on terrorism was comparable to the Cold War in terms of its size, cost, and influence on international relations; it was meant to mark the beginning of a new era in world politics and has had significant ramifications for security, human rights, international law, cooperation, and governance (Jackson, 2020). Before the March 2003 invasion of Iraq, former President George W. Bush (2003) stated, "The greatest danger in the war on terror [is] outlaw regimes arming with weapons of mass destruction." These words sum up the mindset of the Bush administration. The Bush administration's fundamental core theory was that these alleged rogue states' regimes were closely connected to terrorist groups like al-Qaeda, determined to get nuclear weapons, and might even provide them to terrorists (Mearsheimer, 2019, p. 24). As Walt states, according to the Bush administration, the best method to deal with proliferation and terrorism was to transform all of the nations in the Greater Middle East into liberal democracies; this would convert the region into a sizable zone of peace and solve the twin issues of proliferation and terrorism (Walt, 2018a, p. 267).

Apart from that as the swift use of military force that followed the US' declaration of the "War on Terror" as an act of self-defense based on their determination, the UNSC adopted Resolution 1368 in 2001, which declared a "War on Terror" "to combat by all means threats to international peace and security caused by terrorist acts" (UNSC, 2001).

In his statement about the "War on Terror," Bush said: "It was an attack on the heart and soul of the civilized world" (Bush, 2001a), meaning an attack on the epicenter of the liberal international order. As Walt suggests, embracing the "War on Terror" doctrine of Bush is pursuing a liberalization spree for un-liberal governments (Walt, 2018a, p. 267); only by doing so, according to the Bush Doctrine (Bush, 2002), can peace finally be achieved. Nonetheless, the Bush Doctrine also aims to restore the liberal international order's challenged image; in this case, it can also be considered as Pax Americana's aim too, and surpass possible future challenges as well.

The Bush Doctrine opened the door for the US to employ force whenever and wherever it pleases, even though there is not yet a threat, by exploiting a notion like terrorism, which is difficult to define through possibilities. Unlike the Reagan Doctrine (supporting freedom fighters)[6] and the Clinton Doctrine (multilateralism),[7] the Bush Doctrine represents a blatant rejection of the law by the US, instead pursuing a more active, unilateral approach. In addition, through the Bush Doctrine, the US reserved this privilege alone and demanded everyone submit. In this situation, the US has stated that it will pursue an expansionist foreign policy in support of a unipolar world.

---

[6]"Reagan Doctrine," *US Department of the State Archive*, February 25, 2023, Available at, https://2001-2009.state.gov/r/pa/ho/time/rd/17741.htm .

[7]The Clinton Doctrine is an expert analysis of the key priorities in US foreign policy during the Bill Clinton administration (1993–2001), not an official government pronouncement. For an instance, please see: Patrick Clawson, "The Clinton Doctrine," December 28, 1997, *The Washington Institute*, February 25, 2023, Available at, https://www.washingtoninstitute.org/policy-analysis/clinton-doctrine.

2.2.2   US FOREIGN POLICY IN THE UNIPOLAR WORLD

As mentioned above, the 9/11 terrorist attack was a significant game changer not just for the US but also for the international system. Undoubtedly, the events of 9/11 in New York City marked a significant turning point in history; despite prior attacks against American forces and embassies, it was the first such attack on US soil. Thus, the Bush Doctrine, which is also known as the "War on Terror" doctrine, fueled foreign policy that dominated the early years of the 2000s in the US.

That dominant foreign policy was supported by the NSS in 2002 (Bush, 2002) and defined terrorism as planned acts of violence carried out with political motivation against innocent people. The NSS 2002 made it abundantly clear that no grievances could be used to justify terrorism, that the US would not give in to terrorist demands, and that it would use force against anybody who intentionally sheltered or helped terrorists; nonetheless, it is stated clearly that the US will pursue and persecute both terrorists and those who support them (Bush, 2002).

In the fight against terrorism, the Bush administration claimed to have adopted the stance that a strong offense was the best kind of defense (Bush, 2002). And this mindset orchestrated the invasion of Afghanistan and, months later, Iraq (Jacobson, 2010). Thanks to this mindset (Ramsbotham et al., 2011), the Washington-led coalition's invasion of Afghanistan was the US' initial response because the Taliban government in Afghanistan refused to turn over Osama bin Laden, the leader of the terrorist group al-Qaeda who was responsible for the 9/11 terrorist attacks. In preparation for an invasion, American and British armies began bombing runs in Afghanistan. A number of factors made Washington's choice to enter the Afghan conflict unavoidable. For instance, in the days after 9/11, the perceived threat of other terrorist attacks grew more urgent, making military intervention necessary to defend the (liberal) international order (Misra, 2004, p. 107). On the other hand, the Bush administration, "never really examined an alternative to war in Afghanistan," as Cortright (2011, p. 11) asserts. The US was propelled by ideological incentives to conduct the "War on Terror," as they supported regime change in Afghanistan and, as mentioned, saw little hope and possibility for cooperation with the incumbent government, instead of pursuing reconciliation in this manner. But as mentioned previously, changing the incumbent government to a liberal one is more appropriate for the sake of the liberal international order, according to the US. As Walt suggests, transforming non-liberal countries into liberal democracies is believed to provide a safer world order (Walt, 2018a).

The Bush administration's doctrine had long argued for a hegemonic approach based on the use of American military superiority (Jervis, 2003, p. 366). The Bush administration turned an entirely new page with the invasion of Iraq. On the one hand, it was crucial and imperative to react to a state that shielded the terrorists who carried out the 9/11 atrocities. On the other hand (as in the case of the invasion of Iraq) it was ill-advised, needless, and expensive to invade another state without solid evidence. The Bush administration's unfounded allegations that Saddam Hussain had aided al-Qaeda posed a very real threat to Washington. If Washington is lying to them, why (and how) can other nations risk the lives of their soldiers and populations for the US? As a result, since then, doubts have been raised about the US' credibility and validity (Connah, 2021, p. 71).

As Jacobson states, as the Iraq War came to an end, violence in Afghanistan grew worse and the number of victims escalated (Jacobson, 2010, p. 587). Indeed, the Bush administration's actions and choices, such as the Guantanamo Bay torture and war crimes, must be criticized for being undemocratic and/or illiberal (Soder, 2009). In other words, the US' reputation was tarnished by the invasion of Iraq. It demonstrated to the entire world that, despite its true intentions, the US was a nation seen as a legitimate entity capable of bringing democracy to other countries through the use of military force. Thus, the invasion of Iraq was a mistake from a foreign policy standpoint. Anti-American sentiment increased across the region as a result of Bush administration initiatives. It demonstrated the futility of states pursuing liberal ideals in a realist world (Mearsheimer, 2018).

Hinnebusch explains that three layers of analysis must be used to fully comprehend the invasion of Iraq: the US' grand plan internationally, the Middle East's strategic importance to the US, and the objectives of Bush's ruling coalition. Understanding the Iraq War reveals the fundamental tenets of US Middle East policy and the crucial position of the region in US global strategy (Hinnebusch, 2007, p. 9).

Moreover, in Quadrennial Defense Review (QDR) 2005, the "War on Terror" doctrine's parameters were widened (Spencer, 2005). As previously mentioned, it had broadened the definition of the fight to include all challenges to the Western-centered system and substituted the phrase "against terrorism" with the phrase "extremists who have chosen terror as a method." The "War on Terror" doctrine is favored because it has given the US measurable gains within the limitless room for movement, both in 2001 and beyond.

But, despite all the obvious advantages the "War on Terror" doctrine has given the US, it is impossible to declare that the doctrine's implementation and outcomes have been a success. The primary reason for this is that military tactics alone cannot address the systemic issues of American hegemony. As a result, on one hand, the US surrounded the EU, Russia, and China with its war on terrorism policy; on the other hand, it sped up the process of global competition and alliance formation. Also, it became clear during the process how incompatible the anti-terrorist policy was with the actual threat posed by terrorism, which gave rise to the imperialist nature of the US' purportedly "benevolent" hegemonic effort (Hinnebusch, 2007, p. 17).

The "War on Terror" doctrine's steady decline in credibility, due to inhumane acts toward prisoners and civilians during the Iraq War in 2003, caused its potential capacity to empower American hegemony to fall short. In other words, through that doctrine, the US foreign policy and the liberal international order in the international system stepped back. Aforementioned above, some authors heavily criticized the thought of considering the liberal international order, and the US employs that order to empower its influence in the international system. Notwithstanding the outcome of these discussions, the liberal international order will continue to exist until a non-Western world order takes shape.

2.3   9/11 AND GLOBAL TERRORISM

One of the most important problems facing the globe today is terrorism, which has an impact on political structures, the economy, and national security (Laqueur, 1999, p. 15). The phrase is generally understood to mean "the use of violence against civilians with the explicit purpose of spreading dread or panic among the public," despite the fact that there is no widespread consensus over its definition (US Institute of Peace, 2002, p. 3). The US Department of Defense (2011, p. 404) provides the most exhaustive definition of the term, which reads as follows: "the calculated use of violence or the threat of violence to inculcate fear; intended to coerce or to intimidate governments or societies in the pursuit of goals that are generally political, religious, or ideological." This is the definition that is considered to be the most accurate representation of what the term means.

Because "certain governments, particularly in Africa, Asia, and the Middle East were unwilling to classify groups as terrorists if they sympathized with their intentions, because of the derogatory features of the name," there is no universally accepted definition of terrorism. Nonetheless, this is not exclusive to Africa, Asia, or the Middle East; rather, "the West has also sympathized with groups that have perpetrated terrorist actions" (Bruce, 2013, p. 26). The government of the US, for instance, provided the Nicaraguan Contras with backing for a considerable amount of time. On the other hand, European countries sponsored the actions of the African National Congress, which were labeled as terrorist activities by the local governments in South Africa in the middle of the 1980s (Bruce, 2013, p. 26).

Because of this condition, it is now extremely challenging to identify and categorize terrorist activity across the globe. According to Richardson (2006, p. 28):

> The legitimacy or otherwise of the goals being sought (by a group) should be irrelevant to whether a group is (defined as) a terrorist group ... so a terrorist is not a freedom fighter and a terrorist is not a guerrilla ... A terrorist is a terrorist, regardless of whether or not you appreciate the goal that he or she is trying to achieve, and regardless of whether or not you like the government that he or she is trying to change.

Even though there is no consensus regarding the precise definition of terrorism, it is universally acknowledged that terrorist activities involve the infliction of harm and the instillation of fear in civilians. In light of this, Rapoport (2013, p. 50) asserts that the modern history of terrorism can be broken down into four waves: religious, anticolonial, anarchist, and new left. According to Rapoport (2013, p. 50), these waves are distinguished from one another based on the sources of the drive and energy that are behind the actions of groups and individuals. According to this, the first "anarchist wave" may be traced back to the beginning of the French Revolution. Assassinations of monarchs and presidents were the primary form of terrorist activity during this wave. The goal was to bring about social and political reform by targeting existing power structures. The anti-colonial movement was the second wave, which began during the First World War and reached its zenith during the Second World War. During this particular wave, the majority of terrorist acts were linked to groups that were striving to attain freedom and fight against mandates. The Vietnam War marked the beginning of the third wave, and during this wave, the primary focus of activity was on evading the invasions. The Iranian Revolution marked the beginning of the last wave. During this particular wave, religious convictions began to play a more prominent role as a motivating factor in terrorist acts (Rapoport, 2013, p. 61).

The events of September 11, 2001, were one of the most significant acts of religiously motivated terrorism (Rapoport, 2001, p. 420). On that date, the US was the target of an unprovoked attack that took place on its own soil and utilized a tactic that had never been seen before (Rapoport, 2002, p. 33). A passenger airliner that had been hijacked and flown toward New York City's World Trade Center collided with one of the twin tower buildings. Due to the fact that three further planes were hijacked that same day, it is believed that these collisions were not accidental. The second plane crashed into the other World Trade Center tower. The third plane crashed into the west wing of the Pentagon building in Washington, and the fourth plane, which was on its way to the US capital, crashed in Pennsylvania after passengers aboard attempted to regain control of the aircraft. The target of the fourth plane was either the Congress or the White House building (Jackson, 2021).

It was asserted that the Democratic Front for the Liberation of Palestine (DFLP) attempted to claim credit for the events that transpired shortly following the strikes on the twin towers. The authorities of the organization, who released a statement shortly after the news was announced, rejected the report by asserting that they had no connection with the occurrence. After some time had passed, an unidentified person called a newspaper in Jordan and claimed that the strikes had been carried out by the Japanese Red Army in retaliation for the bombings that were dropped on Hiroshima and Nagasaki. They asserted that the use of atomic bombs was an act of retribution. However, this piece of information had not been verified either. The initial claims brought forward by the Federal Bureau of Investigation (FBI) and the Central Intelligence Agency (CIA) painted a different picture.

According to the national security forces of the US, the planes were taken over by groups of Arab descent who, after receiving aviation training, seized control of the aircraft while it was in flight and then carried out suicide attacks on designated targets (The 9/11 Commission Report, 2002). Since the attacks, the US has adhered to this assertion as its official thesis. Just two hours after the attack, the southern building of the World Trade Center collapsed, and orders were given to evacuate government offices across the US. Every building, including the UN headquarters in New York City, was forced to evacuate, and the New York Stock Exchange, the financial center of the country, was also shut down (Scanlon, 2019).

After all the buildings in the northern part of Manhattan (symbols of the power and wealth of the US) were evacuated, the north tower of the World Trade Center also collapsed. While President George W. Bush was attending a meeting in Florida, he was whisked away to an undisclosed location. A special order forced all airplanes to make a detour via Canadian airspace, and vital facilities were placed under the protection of the military. Official statements indicate that the assaults that took place on September 11, 2001, claimed the lives of 3,225 people from 80 different nations (Klitzman & Freudenberg, 2003, p. 400). When it became apparent that what had occurred was not a series of accidents but rather a deliberate attack on carefully chosen targets, planned down to the finest detail, President Bush held a press conference and announced that those who were responsible would be found and severely punished. After the incident, flags were lowered to half-mast in numerous nations, spokespeople from all religions condemned the attack, and memorial services and meetings were held in honor of those who had passed away as a result of the attack.

2.3.1 THE TRANSFORMATION OF THE 9/11 ATTACK INTO A GLOBAL WAR

The FBI and the CIA both looked into the attacks. The FBI's probe, which was conducted with the help of 7,000 agents, was the most comprehensive inquiry in the agency's history (Federal Bureau of Investigation, 2006). On the other side, the CIA was involved in the investigation throughout its entirety and presented Osama bin Laden, the Saudi-born leader of the terrorist organization al-Qaeda, as the one who was responsible for the attacks. As a result of this study, it was determined that Islamist extremists were responsible for the actions that resulted in the deaths of thousands of people. The statement made by President Bush was that Osama bin Laden would be apprehended whether he was alive or dead, and that everything aiding his operations, even from the outside, would be destroyed. He then indicated that the Taliban administration in Afghanistan, which hosted bin Laden, would be the first target (Stout, 2001).

Following this, a declaration of partial mobilization was made, and the Senate gave the president the authority to decide whether or not the country would enter a state of armed conflict. Not long after, the decision was made by the US administration to launch an attack against bin Laden and Afghanistan (where he resided). In response to this, the UNSC issued resolution 1368 dated September 12, 1993 expressing its disapproval of the recent terrorist atrocity. They acknowledged and accepted that bin Laden's group as well as the Taliban regime, which provided him with assistance and protection, were responsible for the events, and they confirmed that the US had the legal right to defend itself (Ulfstein, 2003). The US brought the matter to the decision-making procedures of NATO, where it was acknowledged that the US was within its right to defend itself and wage war against the adversary (as determined in accordance with the criteria outlined in Article 5 of the NATO Treaty). Article 5 of NATO's founding declaration was put into effect for the very first time in the organization's 52-year history (NATO, 2022). According to Article 5 of the NATO Charter, the alliance counts the attack as one that was committed against all of its members. The US has never before been vested with the right to wage such an open war. On September 19, 2001 the US dispatched more than 100 combat and aid planes to sites located in the Middle East and the Indian Ocean. In addition, the marine force intended to take part in the event that Washington referred to as "Eternal Justice." The first air attacks of the war with Afghanistan were conducted on October 7 (Strong, 2017, p. 92).

On November 12, 2001 the Taliban withdrew from seven regions that they had held, bin Laden and his family departed Afghanistan, and the Northern Alliance took control of the country. A new constitution was approved by the people of Afghanistan, and Hamid Karzai was appointed as the leader of the interim administration. On the other hand, the US began holding secret hearings in the military court that was established at the Guantanamo naval facility in Cuba for the purpose of trying foreign nationals who were suspected of being terrorists (Chomsky, 2002).

The events of 9/11, marked a significant turning point in the history of humanity. The most important trade center in the US (the World Trade Center) was destroyed in a vicious and catastrophic attack, which resulted in the deaths of thousands of people (Jackson, 2021). The US, which was the only superpower in the world at the time, felt a direct military threat to its own country for the first time since the Cold War, and the Soviet Union's launch of Sputnik into space in 1957 (Khan Academy, 2023), which was an indication that the Soviet Union was capable of launching intercontinental missiles during the Cold War years (Licklider, 1970, p. 600).

The US had not been attacked on its own soil since the Japanese assault on Pearl Harbor on December 7, 1941, which took place during the Second World War. The attacks on September 11, 2001, represent the first attack on American soil since that time. On September 11, 2001, the possibility of an assault became a reality; however, this time it did not come from the Soviet Union but rather from a lesser enemy in the form of terrorism, which is very difficult to recognize and respond to tangibly (White, 2004, p. 293). Because of this, the US was rendered helpless following the strike. Due to Washington's confusion regarding the occurrence, the administration was unable to immediately provide a plausible explanation for the attack. Security measures based on the "state of war" were implemented by George W. Bush and other administrations (Katulis & Juul, 2021).

Following this tragedy, which caused a significant amount of shock in the US, important conversations took place regarding the country's intelligence organizations and security systems. Even more significant is the fact that the world's preeminent superpower, the US, which had not even been subjected to such an attack during the time of the Cold War, started a process that would activate its expansionist understanding and legitimize it in the eyes of public opinion around the world (Dunmire, 2009, p. 200).

This war was unique in comparison to others of its kind. The concepts of friend and adversary are as distinct as night and day within the scope of the conventional procedures that are practiced in the field of international relations. Subsequent assaults have demonstrated that this statement is no longer accurate. In an article that was published on September 12, 2001, in *The Washington Post* by David Von Drehle, he referred to this ongoing conflict as the "gray war." In the gray war, not only was it unclear who the opponent was, but it was also questionable whether or not the current scenario constituted a legitimate war. This so-called war did not have geographically confined fronts with military goals or armies fighting according to set laws, yet the carnage it caused resulted in the deaths of thousands of people. According to this interpretation, the incident in question signaled a significant shift in the way international affairs are conducted. Indeed, the US' rapid declaration of war against international terrorism following the events of 9/11 resulted in long-term behavioral shifts in international relations. These shifts have been brought about by the US (Drehle, 2001). As the recent terrorist attacks have proven, it is no longer possible to understand international relations in simple words such as "friend" and "enemy," nor is it acceptable to solely define international security in military terms. Both of these perceptions are no longer viable options (Özdemir, 2002, p. 155). The strikes that the US carried out in Afghanistan against the Taliban and Osama bin Laden, whom the US declared to be "terrorist organizations," as well as the war that it fought against Iraq in the spring of 2003, were projections of this tendency.

After overthrowing the existing governments in Afghanistan and Iraq and allowing artificial powers to take control, the US is patiently waiting for the opportunity to attack other Middle Eastern countries that Washington believes support "terrorism." Both of these "interventions" were undertaken to pave the way for the US to attack other Middle Eastern countries. In fact, many scholars argue that the US prioritized the elimination of terrorist groups less than the consolidation of its hegemonic position in the Middle East and the expansion of its control over the region's abundant supplies of oil and other forms of energy (Tellis, 2005, pp. 9–10).

2.4   AFGHANISTAN WAR

Once the US recovered from the shock of the attacks on 9/11, it immediately pointed the finger of blame at the terrorist Osama bin Laden, who had previously used similar tactics against the Russian occupation of Afghanistan (Karakoç-Dora, 2021, p. 176). The attacks that took place on September 11 on the World Trade Center, one of the largest financial hubs in the world, and the Pentagon, the headquarters of the US Department of Defense, are a testament to the potential impact that global terrorism can have. Following the assaults, President Bush declared that "the terrorists who carried out the attack on the US and the countries that backed this attack would not be separated" and would be subject to the same level of punishment. This statement unmistakably demonstrated the procedure that needed to be carried out (Akkurt, 2005, p. 97).

Osama bin Laden, who American intelligence agencies blamed for the attack, was the target of a request made by the US to the Taliban government to hand him over. However, the Taliban did not comply because they required proof that bin Laden was responsible (Hook & Spanier, 2013, pp. 294–295). Without receiving prior approval from the UNSC, the US and the UK initiated a military campaign against Afghanistan on October 7, 2001, which they dubbed "Operation Enduring Freedom." They justified their actions by citing the right to self-defense, which is outlined in the Article 51 of the UN Charter. As a result of this operation, the US established a more permanent presence in Central Asia, and not long after that, the Taliban government in Afghanistan was deposed (Halatçı, 2006, p. 81).

The most important factor in the decision to invade Afghanistan was a desire to exact revenge for the terrorist atrocities that took place on September 11, 2001 (Denek, 2016, p. 309). The US had the belief that Afghanistan was home to members of the al-Qaeda organization, which they held responsible for the attacks. The rise in the frequency of terrorist acts carried out by al-Qaeda, in addition to the events of September 11, 2001, prompted the US to eventually intervene in Afghanistan (Morgan, 2009, p. 222). Osama bin Laden, the leader of al-Qaeda, resided in Afghanistan during the time of the 9/11 attacks that targeted New York and Washington as well as the bombings that occurred in 1998 at the US embassies in Kenya and Tanzania. The US administration believes that bin Laden was the primary perpetrator of these attacks (Esposito, 2002, pp. 428–429).

In October of 2001, the US began a campaign of airstrikes on Afghanistan when the head of the Taliban, Mullah Omar, refused to hand over Osama bin Laden. As several people have mentioned, the US did not have any evidence of al-Qaeda's involvement. Despite this, Washington endeavored to convince the rest of the world that al-Qaeda is the most lethal and well-organized terrorist organization in the world. Al-Qaeda has its roots in the war that took place between Russia and Afghanistan in 1979. To put it another way, it is an organization, and its head, Osama bin Laden, was a fighter who was supported by the US against the Soviet Union, which occupied Afghanistan during the time of the Cold War. Multiple instances of research have made this observation (Uslubaş, 2005, pp. 210). According to the findings of numerous studies, Osama bin Laden was an Islamic warrior, al-Qaeda was an Islamic war organization in the context of the dynamics of the Cold War, and al-Qaeda was successful in Afghanistan with the assistance of the CIA. Several authors asserted that this group was successful in their battle against the Soviet Union, which had invaded Afghanistan, and freed Afghanistan from the shackles of "communism." As a direct consequence of this, the Islamic mujahideen, who had been trained to fight against the Soviet Union during the Cold War, were abandoned in the 1990s when they entered the battlefield. To some extent, the US was responsible for producing the group that committed the atrocities on September 11. Some believe that pride was a contributing factor in the decision to go to war. They believe that the US intended to demonstrate that, in the 21st century, they are still the only great global powerhouse (Arı, 2004, p. 176).

The invasion of Afghanistan by the US began on October 7, 2001, which was less than a month after the terrorist attacks (Congressional Research Service, 2001, p. 2). Earlier, on October 6, 2001, President George W. Bush delivered his weekly radio speech in Washington, where he announced that if the Taliban regime in Afghanistan did not hand over the Saudi-born terrorist Osama bin Laden, the Taliban would be forced to suffer the consequences (Öztürk, 2019, pp. 185–186). The US initiated its military involvement in Afghanistan with the bombing of Kabul, the capital city of Afghanistan. This was the first step in the process.

Shortly after, the US Department of Defense issued a statement confirming the news of the bombing. George W. Bush made a live broadcast in which he stated, "The uncooperative Taliban will pay the price," and "the US military has begun its offensive against al-Qaeda's terrorist camps and the military establishment of the Taliban regime in Afghanistan" (Sever & Kılıç, 2001, p. 287). Bush also stated, "The US will make no distinction between the terrorists who committed this act and the countries that protect and feed them," (Bush, 2001b) and stated that "Make no mistake, the United States will hunt down and punish those responsible for these cowardly attacks" (as cited in Campbell, 2001). Thus, the US declared war on the Middle East. In the attack against Afghanistan, in addition to the capital city of Kabul, the cities of Jalalabad and Kandahar, both of which were homes to the leader of the Taliban, Mullah Omar, were also destroyed. Airports and terrorist camps were subjected to intense bombardment as part of this operation, which also included the participation of British fighters and the employment of heavy bombers like the B-1 and the B-52. Cruise missiles were launched from submarines in the Arabian Sea. There was a great amount of support from all over the world. For instance, at the commencement of the strike, British Prime Minister Tony Blair announced that the goal was to break the military might of al-Qaeda and the Taliban rule. He said this in the context of the attack (Blair, 2001). Also, German Chancellor Schroeder made it clear that he agreed with the US' decision to launch an operation against terrorist targets in Afghanistan (German Leader Reiterates Solidarity, 2001). On behalf of the EU, EU Term President Guy Verhofstadt expressed the organization's unwavering support for the US and the other partners that were taking part in the operation (Drozdiak, 2001). Before beginning the campaign in Afghanistan, President George W. Bush shared his plans with Russian President Vladimir Putin. It was also mentioned that during the beginning of the air operations against targets in Afghanistan, US Secretary of State Colin Powell called the presidents of nine countries. On the other hand, the Taliban referred to the attacks that were carried out against Afghanistan as "acts of terrorism." The statement "We are ready for Jihad," which was made by Rahmetullah Kakazade, the Pakistani Consul of the Taliban government in Afghanistan, made the situation even more stagnant (Tek kişi kalsak da Ladin'i vermeyiz, 2001). Osama bin Laden, in his statement on a videotape broadcast on Qatar's Al-Jazeera television network, claimed that the war against Afghanistan and himself was a "war against Islam" (Bin Laden calls, 2001), and threatened the countries that support the US. Following two days of intensive bombing by the US and the UK, most of the Taliban's air force as well as its installations had been destroyed. As a result, the administration of the Taliban in Afghanistan took a significant and damaging hit. The US entered Kabul two days after the bombings, but after extensive searching, they were unable to locate bin Laden.

Following the attacks on September 11, 2001, the US, in accordance with the agreement reached in December 2001 and with the approval of the UN, launched "Operation Permanent Freedom." In January 2002, the UK took command of the International Security Assistance Force (ISAF), which consisted of approximately 5,000 soldiers from 21 different countries and immediately began their duties in Afghanistan (Khurami, 2023, p. 8). With the fall of the Taliban, the newly formed Afghan military and police forces required training. The ISAF, which first focused on providing security in and around Kabul in Afghanistan, was a participant in this process (ISAF's mission in Afghanistan, 2022).

The events of 9/11 have ushered in a fresh chapter in the annals of human rights history. The human rights conventions that rose to prominence during the height of the Cold War gradually began to lose their significance. Not only did the assaults of 9/11 result in the deaths of thousands of innocent people in the Twin Towers, but they also resulted in the deaths of a great number of individuals living in Afghanistan (The U.S. War in Afghanistan, n.d.). The current president of the US, Joe Biden, decided to entirely remove US forces from Afghanistan. After the former government fled the nation, the Taliban were able to regain control of the country and its governance. As a direct consequence of this, the conflict, which was responsible for the deaths of thousands of people and the destruction of a great deal of property, came full circle and concluded at the same location where it had begun (Baig & Muhammad, 2020, p. 51).

The so-called "Afghanistan Intervention," which took place between October 7 and December 7, 2001 (lasting for a total of two months), was successfully finished in favor of the US and its allies. As a direct consequence of its operation, the Northern Alliance was successful in accomplishing its aim, which was to remove the Taliban from their position as the governor of Afghanistan. Between November 27 and December 5, 2001, a conference was conducted in Bonn, Germany, to determine how the country would be administered following the intervention. The Northern Alliance, the Rome Group, the Peshawar Group, and finally the Cyprus Group, which consisted of Afghan refugees and different parts of Afghanistan, were all present at the meeting. The Rome Group was represented by the deposed King Zahir Shah. The Peshawar Group was ethnically Pashtun and supported by Pakistan (Akkurt, 2005, p. 289). In accordance with the agreement that was reached on December 5, 2001, it was decided that a provisional government would be established and that a member of the Rome Group named Hamid Karzai would serve as the chairman of the administration. In the interim administration established under Karzai, there were a total of 29 ministries, with 11 Pashtuns, eight Tajiks, five Hazara, and three Uzbek officials, with the remaining officials coming from a variety of different ethnic groups (Balcı, 2004, pp. 258–259). December 22 marked the beginning of the interim government's tenure.

During the negotiations in Bonn, important topics were discussed, and decisions were made that would impact the future of the country. These decisions included the economic, political, and social restructuring of Afghanistan, as well as the establishment of a national army and a peace-keeping force maintained by the UN (Akkurt, 2005, p. 287). The biggest challenge in the process of reconstructing Afghanistan was the unraveling of the social fabric that occurred as a direct result of the civil war, which lasted for a total of 23 years. It was said that restoring social order was the most essential objective of the Karzai government. The Kabul Agreement (also known as the Kabul Declaration) was signed on December 22, 2002, in the capital city of Afghanistan, Kabul, in the presence of representatives from the UN and diplomats from other nations (Dashti, 2022, p. 306). The proclamation was signed by the foreign ministers of the People's Republic of China, Tajikistan, Uzbekistan, Turkmenistan, Iran, and Pakistan. Pakistan's foreign minister was also present. The treaty's primary objective was to strengthen the ties that bind Afghanistan to its neighboring states and the government that was created on the same day (Akkurt, 2005, p. 310).

To facilitate communication between various government entities, the Department of Commerce of the US built an Afghanistan Information Center in the nation's capital. The "Preliminary Needs Report" (PNA) was prepared by the World Bank, the United Nations Development Program (UNDP), and the Asian Development Bank (ADB) for a meeting that was held in Tokyo on January 21–22, 2002, to discuss the recovery and restructuring of Afghanistan (Esmer, 2005, p. 34). At the Tokyo Conference, which was where the first report for the reconstruction of Afghanistan was created, participants addressed their provision of assistance to the country. The meeting was attended by representatives from over 60 countries and 21 international organizations (Akkurt, 2005, p. 309).

The US emerged as a world-dominating power for the first time during the First World War. The dwindling influence of Europe on the rest of the world following the First World War lent the impression that the US could no longer pursue an isolationist policy. Eventually, the Second World War proved this impression to be true. Though the US had hoped to return to its conventional policy following the war, the Cold War made it impossible. Unlike an isolationist, the US acted (at the time) as a gendarmerie force to protect the whole world from the threat of communism. In the end, the aftermath of the Second World War was a breaking point for US foreign policy. For particular interests, this transformation brought about a radical policy that spread violence everywhere rather than using force in limited territories. However, the years that followed did not bring about any other major breaking point. In fact, the US declared it would be influential all around the world under the motto of "New World Order" even after the end of the Cold War, pointing to a dominating force. While the form and content of the foreign policy outputs that followed the declaration have varied, the main motivating factor has remained intact.

What could have been a breaking point, the 9/11 attacks did not bring about a significant change in US foreign policy (Güdek, 2017, pp. 143–158). The assaults on 9/11 simply presented the US with a new ideological foe to replace those vanquished with the end of the Cold War. The US made efforts to legalize its operations across the world by creating reasons and mottos directed against this unseen enemy. If this were not the case, the dominance of the US over the rest of the world and the recognition of its own will by other nations would be met with negative reactions (Lyon, 2003, pp. 19–20). Because of this, the US has chosen to attribute the primary reason for the issue to acts of terrorism and unreliable states rather than engaging in major self-reflection to acquire insight into the factors that led up to the 9/11 attacks (Güdek, 2017, pp. 143–158).

The US restricted liberties following a series of reforms in domestic policy after the 9/11 attacks and began to reshape its foreign policy. Right after 9/11, the US administration launched a New NSS under the name of the "Bush Doctrine" starting on September 20, 2002. The New NSS highlighted how the US would stage a global war on terrorism and yet there was no single state, regime, or ideology targeted. This document declares that the US has the right to launch preemptive attacks against hidden and unpredictable threats and that the threats would be eliminated at the source. The US also emphasized that no distinction would be made between terrorists and countries that promote terrorism and that there is no need to wait for terrorists to strike the US to take action for the security of the American nation (Snauwaert, 2004).

After the invasion of Afghanistan, the discussions that had been sparked by the Bush Doctrine in the wake of the attacks of 9/11 took on a new and distinct form. The war in Afghanistan was the very first place where the Bush Doctrine was put into operation, and the US originally achieved military success thanks to strong international assistance. Moreover, Afghanistan was the very first place where the Bush Doctrine was tested. Professors of law and international relations in academia were mostly of the same mind over whether or not the war in Afghanistan was justified (Özlük, 2015, p. 36). The Obama administration believed that American power was being wasted in Afghanistan, and for reasons such as the impact of the global financial crisis in 2008 and the economic difficulties experienced in the US, it foresaw the withdrawal of American soldiers from Afghanistan to avoid further military adventures and establish its strategy on the development of the economy (Crowley, 2017, p. 285).

The capture of Osama bin Laden was a critical event that took place during the process of Obama's withdrawal from Afghanistan and affected Washington's strategy for the war-torn country. The capture and killing of bin Laden gave the American people closure. In addition to this, the capture of bin Laden created an image for the whole world, of the US overcoming the economic and political difficulties experienced in the country (Özdemir, 2018, pp. 78–79). In later years, American officials expressed concern about Afghanistan's progress in establishing itself as a nation. The American public also complained about Afghanistan-related issues, such as not being remunerated for the investments that had been made in the war-torn country. In this sense, the American people, who went through the most severe economic downturn in the past 80 years, did not want to support policies that veered away from domestic investments (Mandelbaum, 2016).

The process of pulling troops out of Afghanistan continued during the Obama administration, with the administration's focus being on preventing any operations with rising costs in Afghanistan. In addition to this procedure, further steps were made in Afghanistan, training their security forces, ensuring local authority, and handing authority to Afghan forces.

When it is taken into account that the turmoil in Afghanistan persisted and that peace was not reached during the Obama administration, it is possible to say that the conditions that gave Washington's interests priority triumphed over those of Kabul. Under the circumstances, it was more important for the US to prioritize its security concerns and interests than it was to ensure peace in Afghanistan.

It is possible that the terrorist attacks that took place on September 11, 2001, were the most significant acts in the history of humanity. This is due to the terrible character of the attacks, as well as the disruption that they generated within the framework of the international system. Following the terrorist attacks, human rights breaches were increasingly prevalent and were brought to public attention in a number of countries, including the US. Trust and stability trumped more traditional political ideals such as democracy, human rights, and freedom.

Wars were declared by many states against opponents both inside and beyond their borders to ensure power and security. But, in this path, the most fundamental rights and liberties were ignored. Thousands of innocent people were killed, many more were injured, and thousands more were labeled as "terrorists" and punished as such; they were deported, denied the opportunity to work, raped, humiliated, and insulted. The US and the rest of the Western world, which during the Cold War warned and put pressure on states in the Eastern Bloc and states that acted outside of their own policy on democracy and human rights, demonstrated to the rest of the world their hypocritical nature by applying different standards of treatment to different groups of people.

As a consequence of this, the operations that were carried out to undermine the idea of international security did not accomplish their intended goals, which were the promotion of peace and freedom; rather, they sowed the seeds of anarchy in the countries that were the focus of their attention. The terrorist attacks that took place on September 11 produced worldwide inequalities, power conflicts, and regular war and strife, particularly in the Middle East. After the US withdrew its forces from Afghanistan, the situation there was not significantly altered; the so-called "problem" continued to exist there.

2.5 IRAQI WAR

After invading Kuwait on August 2, 1990, Saddam Hussein was met with responses from the region and the rest of the globe that he had not anticipated. The UN, which during the time of the Cold War was unable to play an effective role due to ideological polarization, initiated a peace-driven operation in Iraq, which raised hopes about how a collective security system would function beyond the year 1990. During the operation, which was directed by the US, Iraq was kicked out of Kuwait, and important decisions concerning Iraq's disarmament were made. After the attacks of September 11, 2001, the US concluded that Iraq posed a threat to the peace and security of the world community. This resulted in the US declaring war on global terrorism based on the Bush Doctrine. The US referred to Iran, North Korea, and Iraq as "rogue states" and "an axis of evil" during this period because of their progress toward the acquisition of weapons of mass destruction. This was due to the fact that all three of these countries were located in the Middle East. Many individuals felt that the events of 9/11 marked a turning point in history, and as a direct consequence, the US profoundly altered the architecture of its foreign policy, which was subsequently confirmed by the Bush Doctrine (Özlük, 2015, p. 36).

Even though oil was a significant factor in the struggle between the US and Iraq, it should be noted that it was not the primary driver of the Iraq War. The primary justification for the intervention was the imminent risk to people's safety. This entails ensuring the safety of both Israel and the US (Crawford, 2003, p. 6).

At the end of the Cold War, the US emerged as the world's lone superpower, and as a result, it came to assume that it bore the burden of maintaining global and regional stability. Based on this belief, the US held the opinion that Saddam Hussein, a leader who fought with Iran, took up arms and conquered Kuwait, and adopted expansionist policies toward the area, had to be toppled and disarmed (Nazir, 2006, p. 52). Taking advantage of the climate generated by 9/11, the US attacked Iraq to disarm Saddam Hussein because weapon inspectors and the world community saw insufficient pressure being applied to Iraq (Malik, 2004, p. 86). The US attacked for a variety of reasons, one of the most important of which was the pretext that the country was stockpiling weapons of mass destruction. The US believes that Saddam Hussein would have been able to launch attacks against his neighbors and establish regional dominance had he been in possession of nuclear weapons. The US thought that even if the Iraqi leader did not possess nuclear weapons at the time, he would in the future, which meant that the situation necessitated intervention regardless of whether or not Saddam currently possessed nuclear weapons.

It wasn't a question of whether or not Saddam was too insane and aggressive; the issue was whether or not Saddam would attack the US with nuclear weapons for no apparent cause. The possession of nuclear weapons would have enabled Saddam to maintain his power for a far longer period of time and would have fueled his ambition to rule the Arab world. If nothing was done to stop him from finishing the development of nuclear weapons, then some of these weapons could have been transferred to Islamic terrorists or used by the regime in terrorist acts against the

US. Fear of what may be done if such states have nuclear capabilities was stoked by the attacks on Washington and other cities in the US on September 11, 2001. Also, in the past, al-Qaeda had made several attempts to acquire nuclear, biological, and chemical weapons (Gordon, 2002, p. 39). Even though Saddam Hussein was allowed to remain in power after the Gulf War, the possibility that he possessed nuclear weapons was the primary focus of US domestic and foreign policy. As a result, following the attacks on September 11, the US placed a significant emphasis on Iraq (Yüce, 2022, p. 254).

While preparations were being made to intervene against Saddam, a "psychological conditioning" was carried out that was difficult to reverse. If the US gave up, both its leadership and credibility on the global stage would have suffered as a result. This is one of the reasons why the US began its invasion of Iraq (McNeill, 2018, p. 4). The shared interests of the US and Israel were also factors contributing to the conflict. However, many other factors could have led to the war. For example, Saddam Hussein, who was anti-Israeli and launched 39 Scud missiles at Israel during the Gulf War, would have been deposed and Iraq would have had a democratic and secular framework, which would have allowed the US to settle in the region (Stradiotto, 2004, p. 3). Again, the willingness of the US to use its military and political power to restructure the balance of power and expand its own economic dominance throughout all of Central and West Asia, in addition to the regime change in Iraq, played a significant role in the events that took place (Arnove, 2003, p. 54). A regime in Iraq favorable to the US would have been installed if the war against Iraq had been successful, and the US government would have been in a position to restructure the surrounding area. Because of the intervention, Saudi Arabia's influence on oil prices would have been reduced, Syria and Hezbollah would have been intimidated, Iran's efforts to develop weapons would have been deterred, and the Arab-Israeli conflict would have been resolved in favor of Israel. All of these outcomes would have been the result of the intervention. Also, it would have been feasible to stop the spread of anti-American sentiment by reforming the Arab world. Another compelling reason for the US to wage war in the region is that it contains 65 percent of the world's oil reserves, has low costs associated with exploration and processing, and contains 36 percent of the natural gas reserves. The US would like to dominate the region and play a role in production and marketing. Despite the fact that the US claims it attacked

Iraq to rid the country of its stockpile of weapons of mass destruction, one of its main objectives was to get closer to the region's abundant oil resources (Gürseler, 2016, p. 80).

As Washington took control of the administration through the invasion of Iraq, it would also bring under its control the reserves in the Middle East and the Caspian Sea. It would also advance the political interests of China, which gets the majority of the oil it needs from the Middle East. James A. Paul stated the following as the reason for the war at the Global Policy Forum: Although the official statements of the US and the UK are built on "human rights" and "democracy," the real aim of the war (in Iraq) is to bring about regime change, which will bring in power the pro-US administration that will agree to reconsider the oil deals and to reshape Iraq policy. The options that are being debated in Washington focus entirely on the swift encirclement of oil fields, the reconstruction of the oil production infrastructure, and the protection of the oil production system from the influence of local politics (Paul, 2002).

It was to intimidate al-Qaeda and its sympathizers that they intervened in Iraq. It was also believed that terrorists would be dissuaded from planning any additional attacks against the US. In addition to this, the US could demonstrate that it is not weak, which would boost its prestige once more (Tunç, 2003, p. 34). This was stated by President Bush in his address to Congress in September of 2003 when he was requesting more funds to be allocated to the reconstruction of Iraq. Adding the answer "to demonstrate strength" to the question about Iraq, he added "they smelt the weakness of the USA" and referenced the withdrawal from Somalia and Beirut as an example. The question was about whether or not the US should display its strength in Iraq (Pfiffner, 2004, p. 30). Other reasons for going to war that were given by the US but were not accepted by the public opinion of the rest of the world include the following: the fact that Iraq did not comply with resolutions passed by the UN, that it possessed weapons of mass destruction, that it posed a threat to the countries of the region and the rest of the world, that the democratization of Iraq was necessary, and that it had connections to al-Qaeda. On the other side, Iraq was hoping to find a solution to the issue through the UN forum (Mazarr, 2007, pp. 12–13). As a consequence, it is possible to assert that the policies of the US and Israel are interwoven. Israel would be able to benefit from these resources and could breathe a sigh of relief when the pre-9/11 sympathy for Israel started to turn into anger because the US would take control of Iraq's oil and water. Israel's most dangerous adversary in the area would have been completely removed.

The mission of the UNSC is to maintain international peace and security among governments that respect each other's sovereignty and equality. Article 39 of the UN declaration states that the UNSC is responsible for determining whether or not there is a threat, an act that violates the peace, or an attack. In accordance with this judgment, a decision about whether or not there will be armed or unarmed sanctions is made. To summarize, under international law, it is illegal for a single state to make such a choice on its own (Binder & Heupel, 2015, p. 241). Due to the nature of tradition and international law, the Western world maintains its stance that every war must adhere to certain moral standards and be a fair war (Miller, 1964, p. 258). When assessing the possibility of war in Iraq, a number of researchers held the view that "there was no basis for war yet" (Langan, 2004, p. 1). There was no overt military conflict between Iraq and the US and its allies. In addition, there was little evidence to suggest a connection between Iraq and al-Qaeda. There was also no immediate threat that called for the implementation of a preemptive assault doctrine, thus this was not necessary. Several potential courses of action involving Saddam have to be taken into consideration. But the president formulated the strategy for war, and Congress gave its approval for the plan. There was discussion on whether or not international authority was required at this time, but the president and Congress concluded that approval from the UN was neither legally nor morally required (Abele, 2009, p. 34).

In reality, the Iraq War represents the expansion of the UN's non-interference in the domestic affairs of nations. This initial Iraq War lacked both worldwide community backing and international moral legitimacy. The exclusion of the UN played a crucial role in the asylum of the US, upsetting the UN, which was the most important factor in ensuring world peace following the Second World War and damaged international law. After Second World War, the US invasion of Iraq was a step toward a world system dominated by power politics and devoid of laws (İnat 2004, p. 23).

The Iraq War continued until May 1, 2003, when it finally came to a close. The single positive outcome of this conflict was the removal of Saddam Hussein from power in Iraq. After the conclusion of the conflict, neither the UN nor the forces of the US discovered any evidence of the presence of weapons of mass destruction (Rayburn & Sobchak, 2019,

p. 247). Now, the US officially states that there was no evidence that Saddam Hussein had contact with the terrorist organization al-Qaeda, which carried out the attacks on September 11 against the Pentagon and the World Trade Center. Because of this, the basis for intervening in Iraq is a topic of discussion in public opinion both in the US and around the world. As a result of these conversations, the US justified its presence in Iraq by stating that it was doing so to "deliver democracy to the Middle East, starting with Iraq" (Gözen, 2006, p. 59).

It is possible that resentment against the US, which Iraqis perceived as an invader, contributed to the high number of suicide attacks that occurred after the war rather than during it. The US lost more soldiers to suicide assaults than it did during the war. Not only has the anti-American feeling reached its zenith among the people of Iraq, but it has also reached its highest point among the populations of other Islamic nations. In addition, Islamic nations have shown an increase in their support for Osama bin Laden (Gunaratna & Jayasena, 2011, p. 7). According to research carried out by Pew Research Center, 65 percent of individuals in Pakistan, 55 percent of individuals in Jordan, and 45 percent of individuals in Morocco support Laden. The reason for this is that many people feel that the US invaded Iraq not to combat terrorism but rather to exert power over the Middle East and the rest of the world (Hinnebusch, 2007).

Following the conclusion of the war, Baghdad descended into complete lawlessness. Although all symbols of the government were set on fire, American forces did not stop the looting that was taking place. Store owners fought to keep their merchandise safe by brandishing firearms, and looting occurred even at medical facilities. In addition, tens of thousands of items housed within the Iraqi National Archaeological Museum were disassembled and looted, and the intervention that was begun by the US under the guise of liberation evolved into an occupation. In the immediate aftermath of the war, Baghdad lacked necessities such as electricity, water, and order. While Iraq lacked basic needs, President Bush believed that the adoption of democracy in other Arab nations would be encouraged by the liberation of Iraq. Yet, the anarchy that prevailed in the first month and a half after Saddam Hussein's administration collapsed contributed to an acceleration of certain developments, including a rise in anti-American sentiment and an increase in terrorist attacks across the Arab world (Önel, 2020, pp. 69–70).

The administration of the US believed that the triumph of the US military in Iraq and the fall of Saddam Hussein was a foreign policy event that occurred during the presidency of George W. Bush that will be remembered. The US established a more permanent presence in the Middle East as a result of its invasion of Iraq. The US believed that this would further democracy and regional balance in the region. The military might of the American armed forces were to be put to use in the construction of the Iraqi army, and if Saddam could be apprehended, the US will have contributed to the establishment of political stability, democratic institutions, and an economic agenda in Iraq. Baghdad, on the other hand, turned into a hostile environment following the conflict. They had high hopes that the people of Iraq would be overjoyed and that any resistance would vanish when American armed forces entered the country in March of 2003. These dreams were, sadly, shattered as the reaction of the Iraqi people was uncontrollable. For instance, at the beginning of Ramadan in the year 2003, a suicide vehicle bomb destroyed the headquarters of the Red Cross, and four police stations throughout the city were targeted. These attacks resulted in the deaths of more than 30 individuals and the injuries of more than 200 others. Rockets were fired at the Al-Rashid hotel in Baghdad, which was also the target of an assassination attempt on the mayor of Baghdad. Paul Wolfowitz, one of the most influential figures in the war's planning and execution, was also the target of a targeted attack but managed to escape injury (Shanker, 2003, p. 1). After the war in Iraq, there was no significant improvement in the condition. It was not simply attacks on US military personnel. The Jordanian Embassy in Baghdad was attacked on August 7 by a vehicle carrying explosives that were driven through the compound. Fifty-two people were hurt and 12 individuals were killed as a direct result of this attack (Tayal, 2003, p. 522).

On August 19, 2003, a truck loaded with bombs attacked the Kanal Hotel, which had been utilized as a building for the UN after this attack. There were 22 fatalities and 100 injuries reported. On August 29, 2003, a car bomb explosion resulted in the death of approximately 81 individuals, among them Ayatollah Mohammad Baqer al-Hakim, a prominent Shiite political figure in Iraq. Additionally, over 200 people sustained injuries in the incident, which occurred near one of the most sacred Shiite religious sites in Najaf. Ayatollah Hakim, the leader of the Iran-backed Supreme Council of the Islamic Revolution in Iraq (SCIRI), tragically lost his life shortly after delivering his weekly sermon at the Tomb of Ali in this revered city (Chronology of Events in Iraq, 2003). On October 26, 2003, a rocket attack on the el-Redid Hotel took place while Wolfowitz was present. As a result of the strike, 16 people were injured, and a US colonel was killed (Bonner & Shanker, 2003, p. 1). The attacks that took place on October 27, 2003 at seven different locations resulted in the deaths of 42 and injured 224 others. On October 28, 2003, six individuals lost their lives in the city of Fallujah. During November 2003, two American helicopters were brought down by enemy fire. Twenty-two soldiers were killed in the battle. In the attacks that took place on November 13 at the Italian headquarters and on November 12 at the Italian outpost in Nasiriya, a total of 28 people were killed: 18 Italian soldiers and eight Iraqis (Hooper & McCharty, 2003, p. 1). The difficulty of maintaining order in Iraq was made abundantly clear by all of these events.

Even though half a year had passed since the war was declared over, the resistance had not stopped. Despite this, the US administration claimed that the quality of life for Iraqi civilians was gradually getting better across the majority of the country. Yet, research conducted by organizations such as the Red Cross and other assistance organizations revealed that gang warfare was a threat to Iraq. In Iraq, the situation remained the same for a good number of years. It was impossible to bring order back to Iraq, and the Iraqi administration faced multiple problems at a variety of different times. As a direct consequence of this, the US decided to withdraw from Iraq. The memories of years of war and thousands of dead and wounded stayed in the minds of the populace that was left after an inconclusive conflict, just as they did in Afghanistan.

One may say that President Obama made an effort to bring an end to the conflict that had been initiated by President Bush. Terrorism, on the other hand, became a problem for Obama, and terrorist organizations in Iraq became a significant concern after realizing that the withdrawal of US forces presented them with a chance. Despite this danger, President Obama determined cutting the costs of the military as his most important objective, which necessitated the implementation of a new strategy. Within this framework, the president put into action an anti-terrorism strategy that was predicated on airstrikes and made an effort to eliminate terrorist targets in both Afghanistan and Iraq. When the ever-increasing danger posed by the situation in Iraq was taken into account, President Obama's approach, which anticipated a withdrawal, not only cut expenses but also played an important part in guaranteeing the safety of his troops.

The Iraq War provided the US with several crucial learning opportunities. The most notable of these is the fact that the US abandoned the concept of nation-building in Iraq due to the tremendous expenditures associated with doing so there, just as they did in Afghanistan. In fact, it had by this time become common knowledge that the US military should not attempt to participate in stability efforts. In this perspective, when we include Vietnam in square brackets, it is feasible to argue that the process of nation-building in Iraq was the most expensive mission in the history of the US (Tierney, 2012).

Once the US withdrew its forces from Iraq, a power vacuum was left behind, which provided a fertile ground for the rise of rival factions that vied for control of the country while vying for their own share of its resources (Hook & Spanier, 2016). Alongside these achievements, when the sectarian divisions that exist in the region are taken into account, it is possible to assert that there are significant obstacles standing in the way of the peace that exists within Iraq. It was also possible that Iraq's neighbors could be implicated in the tensions that were occurring in the country. On the other hand, the White House had the idea that it would prevent those countries from being involved in the conflict by applying pressure in the political, military, and economic spheres if they did get involved (Layne, 2009).

Although measures were taken to address the internal problems of Iraq, the administration of Barack Obama placed a higher priority on addressing the internal problems of the US. As a result, the withdrawal of troops from Iraq was carried out with this priority in mind, just as it had been in Afghanistan. At that time, the Obama administration was criticized for not being able to grasp the effects of Iraq's domestic politics while focusing on the withdrawal of troops from Iraq, and as a result, not being able to take a full role in Iraq's restructuring, and missing out on Iran's growing influence on Iraq (Dunne, 2011). It is possible to say that President Obama made a decision that put the US as the top priority and shifted his attention to the challenges that are being faced in his own country and that he only considered the situation in Iraq as an opportunity to withdraw his expensive soldiers.

The rise of terrorist activity in the country during this process also caused problems for the US, thus the impact of the events that took place in Iraq on the US was not limited to the withdrawal process alone. When confronting this challenge, President Obama opted to deploy less expensive airstrikes. When one considers the fact that terrorist acts continued to be committed in Iraq after Barack Obama was elected as president, one may conclude that this strategy did not yield satisfactory results in the battle against terrorism in Iraq. Nonetheless, despite the ongoing threat of terrorism in Iraq, President Obama was able to successfully implement the redeployment strategy, which resulted in the reduction of the cost to the US.

2.6   GREAT RECESSION

The Second Great Depression, also known as the Financial Crisis of 2008, began in the US but quickly extended throughout the rest of the world. It had a negative impact not only on the world economy as a whole but also on the economies of individual nations. Even though mortgage loans were the source of the financial crisis in 2008, real estate connected to housing loans on the futures market incurred large losses when the loans could not be repaid. This resulted in a precipitous drop in housing prices, which had earlier soared. Because of this, the financial crisis morphed into a crisis of liquidity and quickly spread from the US to both developed and developing countries in a short period. As a result, it caused increases in loan interest rates, a devaluation in currency, the decline of financial institutions, and the need for states to either provide financial support to financial institutions so that they could survive the crisis or expropriate them. The crisis significantly reduced the volume of global international trade, which contributed to a general slowdown in the economy around the world. The downturn experienced by the economy on a worldwide scale dampened the enthusiasm of multinational firms, particularly those based in developed nations, to engage in investment activity (IMF, 2009).

The global financial crisis evolved into one of the most pervasive and widespread crises the world has seen since 1929. The top two financial crises in the history of the globe, one in 1929 and another in 2008, both had such a catastrophic impact on the economy of the world that economists did not hesitate to use the term depression to describe the aftermath of both of these events. The Panic of 1857, the oil shock, the Japanese Crisis, and the Asian Crisis in 1997 were all unable to match the impact of the first two crises mentioned. As a result of the severity of the Great Depression in 1929, millions of people were forced out of their occupations, and severe employment issues were encountered as a direct result of the drastic reduction in the volume of world trade. This had a negative impact on the general standard of living. The government seriously contemplated taking measures to stimulate the economy, and certain steps were made as a result; however, the fact that Second World War immediately followed the financial crisis was an indicator that the recovery would not be simple.

Both the Great Depression of 1929 and the Financial Crisis of 2008 had their roots in the US. This is the only thing the two crises have in common. The fact that the US exerts a significant amount of influence over the economy of the world, despite the fact that the banking system is not resistant to crises, that the international financial system does not have sufficient wiggle room to tolerate crises, and that the public authorities have not effectively responded to the crises, caused the crises to spread to other countries. The analogy holds true for both crises.

As for the results of both crises, the stock market went bankrupt as a direct consequence of the 1929 crisis, and the rate of unemployment in the US grew to a quarter of a million people. After the financial crisis of 2008, the gross domestic product (GDP) of the US suffered a substantial hit, and the jobless rate more than doubled.

Indeed, the Financial Crisis of 2008 broke out with the subprime mortgage crisis in 2006 and the crisis became global once the Lehman Brothers filed for bankruptcy in 2008. Originally emerging as a financial crisis, it then morphed into an economic crisis upon spillover into the real sector (Eğilmez, 2013). The Lehman Brothers, the fourth largest bank in the US, filed for bankruptcy on September 15, 2008, with $619 billion in debt. This is billed as what sparked the 2008 financial crisis. "In two days following the bankruptcy, Americans withdrew nearly $150 billion from their money market accounts. In October 2008, the Federal Reserve and other central banks injected liquidity worth $2.5 trillion into the markets which had been the largest monetary intervention in world history" (Ataman, 2009, pp. 85–89). The failure of Lehman Brothers was merely a portent of things to come; the main reason for the subsequent economic recession and the financial crisis, which had a ripple effect all over the world, was the opportunity for people to gravitate toward real estate with low interest rates. This caused the recession that followed, which had a ripple effect all around the world.

The monetary policy that was implemented prior to the financial crisis of 2008, as well as the modeling of other regulatory transactions, was found to have a number of flaws. The fact that the system included some lacking modeling features as a component of the loaning system was the key factor that contributed to the failure of the modeling. Before the financial crisis, the monetary policy measures of the credit market did not lend themselves well to the development of accurate models. Thus, poor monetary and macroeconomic policies were the source of the crises that extended throughout the credit markets and relapsed. The authorities who had given the go-ahead for the interest rate decrease at the time neglected to take notice of the potential problems that could arise in relation to the parabolic rise in asset prices that the decision to slash the interest rates before 2008 led to (Stiglitz, 2011, p. 54). Among the main causes of the 2008 crisis are the supervisory and regulatory factors that can have an impact on the entire system causing financial crises, growth in the amount of asymmetric information brought about by the crises, changes in interest rates and accompanying uncertainties, balance sheet deterioration in the financial sector and deterioration of non-financial balance sheets caused by changes in asset prices (Mishkin, 2017). The causes of the Financial Crisis of 2008 didn't outbreak unexpectedly. The inflationist shocks in the 1970s and the shift in demand-supply economics radically transformed the post-war labor relations whereas the reverse labor relations caused inter-national differences, affecting the way the policy changes were introduced even though there are significant differences among the countries in terms of pace and form. Not only the US but also the EU and the Eurozone faced major problems in crisis management because of their different and conflicting market structures under their own umbrella (Brandl & Benchter, 2011).

The historical context of the financial developments in the country includes the factors that are responsible for the financial crisis that began in 2008 and revealed themselves first in the economy of the US. In fact, it was the US that pioneered the process that resulted in unrivaled capitalism and neoliberal economic policies rapidly expanding over the world beginning in the 1980s. This process began in the US. American capitalism plays a part in the shift in the commercial and financial centers of gravity across the globe. It had a role in this shift by acting as a global "transmitter" of the impact of the crisis that occurred in 2008 and of the crash in the system that occurred as a result of it. Within the limits of the US, the regulations of capitalist America governing money management and financial markets had global impacts with determining components.

The 2008 financial crisis was more profound than what many early projections indicated, and the recovery is reported to be gradual and diverse. While the growth has a slow pace in some countries, the global gross income has declined since the Second World War even though this experience was welcomed. The global economic crisis has brought about significant and diverse implications around the world. Since the inception of the crisis, many countries have reported adverse effects that vary by region, level of development, and challenges. According to Resolution No 63/303, the crisis has led to a global increase in unemployment, economic recession, deceleration in growth, adverse effects on the balance of payments and trade, contraction in direct foreign investments, contraction in global trade, decline in tourism revenues, and difficulty of access to loans and trade finance.

Nobel Prize-winning economist Paul Krugman (2009) referred to the 2008 financial crisis as follows: "This crisis is like no other." The 2008 global crisis poisoned all countries with financial links to the US through financial channels. A crisis is literally a case of cancerous cells spreading to other parts of the body. This crisis did not have the same effect on all countries in the world. While income distribution became unbalanced in the US, some populist problems cropped up in Europe. However, Asian countries including China, India, and Indonesia continued to sustain a trend of growth.

The IMF's World Outlook Report indicates that unemployment in the US, where the crisis originated, doubled during the recession. The unemployment rate, which was hovering around 4.6 percent for two consecutive years in 2006 and 2007, hit 5.8 percent in 2008 with a slight increase. However, the crisis made its presence felt particularly in the US labor markets when it reached 10 percent in 2009. The unemployment rate, which was 9.3 percent in 2009, rose to 9.6 percent in 2010 and declined to 9 percent in 2011" (World Economic Outlook Databases, n.d.).

Even Germany, the driving engine of the EU, experienced a decline in its workforce. The unemployment rate was 5.8 percent in 2006 and 2008, and 5.4 percent in 2007 and it rose to 8 percent in 2009 with a sharp increase as far as the performance of the G7, which was established by France, Germany, Italy, Japan, the UK, and the US back in 1975, and joined by Canada the following year, is concerned. The IMF reported that the unemployment rate, which peaked in the G7 countries at 8.3 percent in 2010, was around 7.9 percent in 2011. In Canada, the last country to join the G7, the unemployment rate, which was 6 percent in 2007, rose to 8.3 percent in 2009, but fell below 7.5 percent in 2011 (Marshall, 2012, p. 6).

The report published by the Financial Crisis Inquiry Commission (FCIC) founded in 2009 to specifically review the causes of the global crisis is one of the most comprehensive studies with conclusions drawn by the US government about the causes of the global crisis. The conclusion part of the report drawn up by the commission notes that the factors that led to the crisis unfolded as a part of a process and that it was a man-made crisis and the system was not a natural outcome of the process, meaning that the crisis was preventable. It was reported that the most influential factors behind the crisis were the low interest rates, the loan bubble created by the international investors who held US real estate, and the non-strict regulations, which made the crisis inevitable once the bubble burst as the risks grew. It was also noted that the failure to effectively make financial regulations and inform the market actors in a guiding light injured the economic stability of the US and that the government did not take action to avoid it and caused panic in the markets through errors of judgment made throughout the process. Additionally, companies that traded in the financial markets failed to manage the risk and this triggered the crisis to a significant extent. The report also pointed to the organizational structure that did not stop market actions that would hamper transparency and indicated that the conveniences provided at high rates for debts with no way to be paid off in a way to encourage high-risk investments expedited the devastating effects and spread of the crisis (FCIC, 2011).

The low interest rate on loans available in the US encouraged people with lower incomes to pursue the goal of home ownership. Significant financial repercussions were brought about as a result of an increase in the interest rate by the Federal Reserve and the inability of low-income people to pay their mortgages. The inability was reflected in international indexes as well. While the Case Shiller index, which measures real estate prices in the US, declined by 16 percent from mid-2007 to mid-2008, experts were suggesting that the index should decline by another 10 percent. Eğilmez explains:

> This was a great shock for the American people, who thought that their wealth increased with the price hike of their real estate, and they borrowed and spent money accordingly. Real estate owners in

the UK were in even more debt. So, the latest rise of capitalism was built on the inflation of real estate prices. The real estate prices were rising, and real estate owners thought they were getting wealthier and increased their spending by borrowing more, which boosted the economy and the real estate prices were rising even more. As the real estate prices increased, the demand for real estate also took an upward turn, and this time the financial transactions made with real estate documents grew more and more. Everyone was buying their second and third real estate for investment purposes. The underlying assumption of the purchases was that they could be sold at a higher price someday. The prices tended to decrease and the bubble began to deflate once it became clear that this assumption might not be true (2013, p. 67).

The desire to own a home is still prevalent, but it doesn't necessarily mean that there is demand for those who cannot afford it. Many Americans who take out loans to buy homes end up facing foreclosure if they can't make their loan payments when their financial situation changes. When there are too many foreclosed homes, they become unsellable due to oversupply, and their value decreases. This can lead to financial crises in many countries.

Since the 2008 global financial crisis, many people in economically developed countries have become disillusioned with globalization and laissez-faire economics. Liberal democracy and open borders have suffered as a result. The economic system that was supposed to be based on free markets and liberal ideals has become more focused on rent-seeking. The disregard of the elites toward the people who have been left behind has caused frustration and anger, leading to the rise of elected leaders who exploit this sense of unfairness.

CHAPTER 3

Quo Vadis: A New World

When the international order is examined in accordance with today's dynamics, theories of international relations are challenged with the questions such as: "How was the international order established? What are the necessities and the forms of international order?" along with philosophic approaches throughout history itself. Certain approaches to the international order have become more popular and coupled with certain factors such as the authority of the governments, acceptance of the economic system as well as societies with technical developments and cultural movements.

In simple terms, the international order refers to how countries and the other actors are ranked and how they exert their influence over each other. In light of this, the most important issues to answer are those about the ideas and goals of the players who are participating in the international arena as well as how they are operating for their own interests in the international domain. This leads to questions such as who the main actors are, how the first international order was established and evolved through the liberal order, how conditions have changed the root of the liberal international order, and why the applicability of the liberal international order is decreasing in today's new international system.

3.1 FALL OF THE LIBERAL ORDER

Following the termination of the Cold War and the dissolution of the Soviet Union, the US emerged as the most powerful nation on the face of the earth.

The Rise and Fall of the Eagle: An Assessment of the Liberal World Order.
Çağatay Özdemir (Author)
© 2024 Apple Academic Press, Inc. Co-published with CRC Press (Taylor & Francis)

Ikenberry referred to this as the "unipolar moment," and it had finally arrived (2018a). In addition, the deeply ingrained and comprehensive Western system that American politicians had established to deal with the Soviet menace remained safely intact, while the competitor's communist structure quickly fell apart in December 1991. This was the case although the system had been established to deal with the Soviet menace.

The US was the only nation to emerge victorious from the Cold War; nonetheless, the development of a liberal international order required the completion of three primary objectives. First and foremost, it was essential to broaden participation in the institutions that made up the Western order, as well as to construct new institutions wherever it was deemed necessary to do so. To put it another way, it was necessary to create a network of international organizations that welcomed everyone as members to facilitate and mobilize Western principles (Jang et al., 2016).

Secondly, it was of the utmost importance to include countries from all over the world in the open economic order that the US and its allies had fashioned during the time of the Cold War and to make that order even more open than it had been previously (Kagan, 2017). There is little question that after accomplishing this objective, the concept of globalization entered our lives in a way that has never seemed quite as powerful before. Since then, the world has turned into a borderless village in which people, products, and money are free to move about (Green & Ruhleder, 1995).

Finally, it was essential to vigorously promote liberal democracy and the ideals it upholds all over the world. This was a goal that the US regularly overlooked when it was engaged in a competition for pre-eminence with the Soviet Union (Barnett, 2021). As a result of the liberal philosophy's promotion of democratic ideas and standards, the so-called "free world" has grown to encompass countries that were previously excluded from its sphere of influence. Liberal internationalism is a collection of ideologies and goals that liberal democracies use to structure the world in accordance with their vision of "an open, loosely regulated, and progressively oriented international order," with the growth of the "free world" (Ikenberry, 2018b). These three goals find some support in liberal theory, which can be broken down into the following categories: liberal institutionalism, economic interdependence theory, and democratic peace theory.

Therefore, in the minds of those who conceived and designed the liberal international order, the construction of a strong and sustainable liberal international order was synonymous with the creation of a peaceful world, which was also determined by actors in the order. During the 1990s and the early 2000s, it seemed that the US and its closest allies were on their way to constructing a fully fledged liberal international order. Nevertheless, this did not turn out to be the case. There was no question that there were a few problems, but overall, the new order was operating very well. The fact that it began to break apart just a few years into the new millennium was something that very few people predicted would happen, but it did happen.

Throughout the years, while the US and its allies have successfully completed the three primary tasks of the liberal international order, the range of actors involved has become more diverse. This has been made possible by advancements in technology and communication, and it occurred at a time when the system was regarded as the hegemonic structure of the US (Alcaro, 2018). The structure of the liberal international system brings non-state actors, in addition to the US and its allies (Noortmann, 2009). In fact, the framework of the liberal international order is characterized by the presence of a diverse array of non-state players, which is an essential component that cannot be denied.

Some commentators believe that the current crisis in the liberal international order is evidence of a fundamental shift in the politics of international organizations. According to Duncombe and Dunne, we are currently residing in "a unique epoch in International Relations," in which "all major stream theories accept that the hegemony of the liberal international order is over" (Duncombe & Dunne, 2018). The breakdown of the international order maintained by the US appears to be providing emerging powers, particularly China, India, and other non-Western developing countries, with new opportunities to reorganize the world's political structure. To understand the deterioration of the liberal international order in three dimensions that are based on three aims that were highlighted in the previous chapter, this portion will be broken into three parts.

To begin, liberal institutionalism has, over the years, become increasingly problematic, particularly in terms of its role in tackling global challenges. In other words, the decline of multilateralism inside international organizations contributed to the deterioration of liberal order within the international system. Crises of multilateralism citing unilateral withdrawals from multilateral platforms, growing deadlock in major international institutions such as the UNSC or the WTO, and a general lack of adherence to existing international rule sets are the root causes of the problems (Ikenberry, 2018a).

Second, liberalism has also been credited with promoting the global expansion of free trade and capitalism. The concepts of free trade and market economies have been institutionalized through the development of several institutions like the IMF, the World Bank, and the WTO. It is predicated on the theory that global economic integration is beneficial to commerce and lowers the likelihood of war because war would be detrimental to the economic interests of the states involved (Rashid & Ghouri, 2021). The liberal international order facilitated economic interdependence, which had unforeseen consequences for various entities, particularly societies. A basic dependence on the forces of the market is imposed on human life by capitalism. This reliance on the system inhibits the ability to countervail elements, such as human rights, to effectively address the fundamental reasons that contribute to poverty and violence (Noonan, 2020). In this regard, economies that adhere to liberal principles in the West are still expanding, while those in the developing world continue to struggle. So, economic interconnectedness is now a force that undermines the liberal order of the international system.

Thirdly, the value-based liberal international order likewise suffers from deterioration over time. The US frequently inclines to view itself as an uncompromising "defender of human rights" and a proponent of liberal democracy. It gave the idea that it was on a mission to universalize Eurocentric principles to civilize "others" who had been the victims of human rights crimes in the Global South (Stokes, 2018). Under the pretext of "human rights and democracy," the US has actively pursued a policy of regime change and has become "especially adverse to alternative (and often non-Western) civilizational systems that reject its worldview," according to a recent report (Endaylalu, 2022). The subject of how emerging actors are striving to reform or rearrange the post-war rules and institutions is entrenched in the rise of China and Russia, which is something that will be highlighted in the following portion in relation to the Arab Spring and shifting dynamics in the international system. Alterations in US foreign policy, taken together with these established facts, will help illuminate theoretical debates concerning the formulation of US foreign policy.

3.2   TRANSFORMATION OF THE US FOREIGN POLICY

The disintegration of the Soviet Union has not only rearranged the power dynamics of international politics in the world of realpolitik, but it has also significantly altered the trajectory of research in the field of international relations. Particularly, the long continuing fight between two great ideologies of which the US and Soviet Union appeared to be their representatives became an end, and therefore, liberalism has appeared to gain an undisputable success. The sudden and dramatic shift in the structure of the international system was the impetus for the theoretical discussion on American foreign policy, which included constructivism, liberalism, and realism.

The reverberations of the dissolution of the Soviet Union were reflected in the theoretical discussions in international politics almost immediately after the conclusion of the Cold War. Fukuyama, the author of the "End of History" argument, has argued in a dialectical manner that democratic liberalism has become the final link in the ideological evolution of humanity, having ambivalently triumphed over its major alternative with the fall of the Berlin Wall. Fukuyama's argument is based on the fact that democratic liberalism has become the last chain in the ideological evolution of the human being. As a result, "the final form of human government" would be universalized as "the ultimate triumph of Western Liberal democracy" (Fukuyama, 1989). Although, for the time being, it would be a victory on the ideological level, he maintained that, in the long term, it would have an effect on the material domain (Fukuyama, 1989). As a result, he presents us with a universe that is split in two: i) The post-historical world, in which the economy serves as the primary motivating factor in interpersonal relationships and power politics play a much smaller role; ii) the historical world, in which religious, ethnic, and ideological conflicts, in addition to power politics, continue to be major concerns (Fukuyama, 1992).

In a similar vein, Doyle, using the democratic peace theory as his foundation and citing Immanuel Kant as his source, asserted that the possibility of an armed war breaking out between democratic nations is virtually nonexistent (Doyle, 1983). According to this idea, there is a direct association between the degree of democracy and the use of military means. This correlation is a positive direct one. As a result, Doyle contends that the proliferation of democratic and liberal ideals is a prerequisite for enduring peace in the context of international affairs. Fukuyama did not state it clearly, but he made it clear that he believed the US to be the sole dominant power in world politics due to the country's moral preeminence in the arena of international politics. The idea places the US in a post-historical reality in which the US is also one of the major representatives of democratic liberalism. This is due to the fact that the US has historically been one of the key representatives of democratic liberalism. This implied representation also came with a few duties and rights that were implied in the agreement. Since the end of the Cold War, the US has followed a course of foreign policy that reflects the implied rights and duties that are derived from the country itself. According to Mead's conceptualization, self-assignment, together with the idea that the US is unique, is one of the most consequential features of US foreign policy from a liberal point of view (Ateş, 2022). The US, in its role as the representation of the post-historical sphere, has charged itself with the responsibility of promoting democracy and democratic values and principles, as well as maintaining international peace and security.

Self-assignment, on the other hand, does not automatically entail a unilateralist approach to American foreign policy. When it comes to the conduct of its foreign policy, the US has consistently emphasized multilateralism. In the era that followed the end of the Cold War, the US has taken several steps through international organizations, increasing its engagement to address global problems. One obvious manifestation of such a perspective is the decision to channel foreign aid contributions through a multilateral organization, most frequently the World Bank, rather than acting on a lonesome initiative (Milner, Tingley & Dustin, 2012). The US has a propensity toward multilateralism and one extension of this policy is the cooperation between major world powers within NATO, such as the NATO-Russia Council. When it comes to solving global concerns like climate change and weapons, a perception quite similar to this one can be seen as well. Even if it is difficult to justify participation in armed conflicts according to liberal theory, the fact that the US has participated in military interventions does not completely violate democratic peace theory because of the asymmetric nature of the regimes. In this context, liberals emphasize the authoritarian governments that the US has participated in military interventions against. Claiming it is essential to uphold international peace and stability, liberal thinkers have provided an explanation for why the US has engaged in military action against non-democratic regimes as a last resort. In addition to this, they have emphasized the collaborative nature of the interventions, to which the US was one of the contributors (Rousseau, 2005).

As a result, self-assignment became more apparent during the Bosnian and Kosovo wars that took place throughout the 1990s because of interventions. Similarly, the self-assignment of US foreign policy was also manifest in the words of former US President Bill Clinton regarding the genocide in Rwanda, as he stated that the genocide in Rwanda was one of his greatest regrets during his time in office (Lynch, 2015). As pointed out by Shipoli, if President Bill Clinton were affiliated with a foreign policy doctrine, it would be interventionism (Shipoli, 2018). Another example of self-assignment can be drawn from President George W. Bush's following speech on the 2003 Iraqi invasion:

> As we enforce the just demands of the world, we will also honor the deepest commitments of our country. Unlike Saddam Hussein, we believe the Iraqi people are deserving and capable of human liberty. And when the dictator has departed, they can set an example to all the Middle East of a vital and peaceful and self-governing nation. The US, with other countries, will work to advance liberty and peace in that region. Our goal will not be achieved overnight, but it can come over time. The power and appeal of human liberty is felt in every life and every land. And the greatest power of freedom is to overcome hatred and violence, and turn the creative gifts of men and women to the pursuits of peace. That is the future we choose. Free nations have a duty to defend our people by uniting against the violent. And tonight, as we have done before, America and our allies accept that responsibility (Tucker, 2017).

The US, as one of the key representatives of the post-historical world, has been supporting liberal norms and values, democracy, and human rights through the multidimensional course of its foreign policy. This is taking into consideration everything that has been said above. Even though the methods used may vary, preserving international peace and stability on a worldwide scale should remain the overarching goal.

Realists are people who believe that states base their foreign policies on how powerful they are and what their interests are in international relations. This perspective places a strong emphasis on the relevance of power and interest in the dynamics that exist between states and posits the idea that governments will typically safeguard their own interests. Realists think that governments manage their foreign policies to further their interests, and they anticipate that conflicts will frequently arise in the context of international relations (Rose, 1998). In addition, realist theory downplays the significance of values in the implementation of foreign policy by focusing solely on objective metrics rather than those that are open to interpretation. Realists believe that objective metrics are more reliable than subjective ones. In accordance with this perception, the realist assumes that every state crafts its foreign policy in such a way as to maximize power by any and all methods, in addition to preserving its survival and security (Glaser, 2014). Neorealism and realism are two theories that evaluate states based on the assumption that the goal of a state's foreign policy is to maximize power and security regardless of universal principles, culture, or identity. Both theories view states as fixed and standard units (Viotti, Kauppi & Mark V, 2019).

This aspect of realism, which remains one of the most influential theories in the field of international relations, is rooted in a chain concept that includes statism, security, and self-help. This chain concept is what gives realism its distinctive quality. The term "statism" refers to the primary function and nature of states as individual units. Despite neorealism's significant emphasis on the international system itself, nations continue to be among the primary players in the ontology of the realist approach. Realist scholars, taking this into consideration, believed that international institutions carry less importance for politics on the world stage. The second link in the chain provides an explanation for the eventual failure of power maximization, which is that states are a component of an insecure domain. The third link in the chain gives an indication of the technique in such a way as to rule out multilateralism, as it signals that nations do not expect the help and assistance of other actors. This argues against the use of multilateralism (Dunne & Schimit, 2019).

Some academics believe that contemporary realist theories only take into account the US government's foreign policy because of the close and long-standing relationship between realism and foreign policy. This view is based on the fact that realism has been historically and closely tied to the foreign policy of the US (Jørgensen & Ergül Jørgensen, 2021). Realists have attempted to justify every action taken by the US government in its foreign policy by referring to the nation's interests. The fact that high-level US policymakers such as Brzezinski, Kennan, and Kissinger have conceptualized their policies in realist terminology and have also implemented this conceptualization has reinforced the belief that indicates an association between US foreign policy and the realist theory. This belief signifies that the US government adheres to a realist theory when formulating its foreign policy. For instance, Kennan devised the idea of containment to prevent communist expansionism, and the continued implementation of this strategy exemplifies how closely the realist theory and the US government's foreign policy are connected (Mirza, 2018). Although realist theory failed to provide satisfactory explanations for many aspects of US foreign policy in the early years following the end of the Cold War, the US' approach to foreign policy after the attacks of September 11, 2001, was evaluated based on security and survival. Realists frequently argue that a change in the structure of the international system cannot be accomplished without endangering the interests of other nations, which would cause those nations to reject such attempts, thereby increasing the likelihood of great power wars. Realists believe that achieving this change is impossible. These powers can refrain from adopting hegemonic goals because they ensure prudential debate. Even though those countries are allies of the US, the US has chosen policies that have put the interests of other great powers in jeopardy, which appears to be a violation of reality on the part of the US toward this issue in the post-Cold War era (Mirza, 2018).

To put it another way, when the Cold War came to an end, the US did not celebrate by dismantling its military organization or lowering its presence in the global military arena. Instead, Washington planned to maintain a position of dominance that would discourage potential competitors from ever considering a frontal challenge, and it also sought to construct as much as possible of a "liberal" international order (Walt, 2018c).

Around the same time that the Cold War was drawing to a close, the constructivism theory, which had its roots primarily in the domains of sociology and psychology, started to be applied to the field of international relations. While debates on positivism and post-positivism persist, constructivism has emerged as a third feasible option for describing the dynamics of international relations (Alvesson & Sköldberg, 2009, p. 16). This is because constructivism combines aspects of positivism and post-positivism. The theory of constructivism postulates that the behavior of actors can be understood as the product of how they interact with one another. In contrast to realism and liberalism, which attempt to explain the nature of international relations by appealing to the existence of human nature and rational actors, constructivism asserts that actors are constructed. Realists and liberals both try to explain the nature of international relations by appealing to the existence of human nature and rational actors (Wendt, 1987). Alexander Wendt, who was one of the most influential scholars in the field of international relations to introduce the social constructivism theory, built his theory on the interaction between actors and structure by combining positivist epistemology and post-positivist ontology. His theory was based on the idea that the social construction of reality is a product of both the interaction of actors and the structure that they operate within. Wendt's theory focuses on the dynamic relationship between actors and structure (Wendt, 1987). So, the beginning of a state's foreign policy is the time when it begins the process of building its own identity, according to the theory that Wendt presents. Because the identity of a state may be used to infer its interests, the construction of the identity of the state begins first, and then comes the formation of the interests in the state (Nau, 2002).

Alongside Wendt, Huntington argued that the end of the ideological rivalry with the fall of the Berlin Wall will eventually bring about a rivalry between different existing cultures and civilizations (1997). Considering civilizations to be identities is not a logical fallacy, and hence, it is not illogical to interpret this struggle as one in which identities are contending with one another. Huntington (1997) argues, based on this theory, that the identity of a state will impact both the foreign policies and the interests that it pursues when it is built.

The academics who adhere to the constructivist school of thought examine the terrorist attack that occurred on September 11 and the subsequent developments in the foreign policy of the US through the lens of identity. Theorists who adhere to the constructivist school of thought believe that in the aftermath of the terrorist attacks on September 11, 2001, the US interests have been molded as a result of the fact that this event has become an important factor in the reconstruction of its identity. The attacks provided the US with the opportunity to further solidify its identity and enabled the country to adopt a foreign strategy that was based on the "us versus them" dichotomy. As a result, the US has launched military operations in Afghanistan and Iraq to fulfill its duties related to maintaining international order and promoting democracy. Statements made by President George W. Bush in the early aftermath of the 9/11 attacks are a clear indication of the identity-based approach that the US takes to its foreign policy: "Every nation, in every region, now has a decision to make. Either you are with us, or you are with the terrorists. From this day forward, any nation that continues to harbor or support terrorism will be regarded by the US as a hostile regime" (Bush, 2001c).

The events of 9/11 shed light on the motivations for the US' decision to go to war in Iraq and the stress that was placed on the American identity in response to those events. Constructivists believe that the primary reason the US went to war in Iraq was due to the Bush administration's perception that the preexisting strategic cultural norm of pursuing geopolitical stability through multilateral deterrence had failed in its mission after the terrorist attacks that took place on September 11, 2001. As a direct result of this, the elites working within the administration interpreted the execution of democratic regime change in Iraq as an attempt to impose a worldwide norm of hegemonic global policing through unilateral preventative war (Lauterbach, 2011). The purpose of the Iraq War, according to this viewpoint, was to demonstrate that a new norm, known as unilateral preventative war, could be successful. Neoconservative norm entrepreneurs, conventional conservative converts, and Bush administration loyalists were the driving forces behind the establishment of this norm. This was an element of a bigger strategic cultural vision that called for the hegemonic propagation of democracy by the application of violent means.

In a nutshell, the US has made how it carries out its foreign policy the central focus of its identity, particularly in the wake of the attacks that took place on September 11, 2001. So, the US' interests have been affected by the identity that it has decided to embrace.

3.3   RISING POWERS: CHINA

As was covered in the first two sections, the liberal international order may be said to be dead or in the process of metamorphosis. This caused fundamental shifts in American foreign policy, which led to the rise of new actors that are prioritized by the US. There is no shadow of a doubt that China is one of the primary actors that we may refer to as a growing power. In this regard, the next section will concentrate on China's status as a rising power in relation to how it emerged as a key actor in the international system over several decades.

The re-emergence of China as an important political and economic actor following the liberalization that took place in the late 1970s is widely regarded as one of the most momentous events that have taken place in recent history. As can be observed by China's new position as the world's second-largest economy, China's economic influence is already being felt all over the world, and this can be shown by the fact that China surpassed Germany in 2009 and Japan in 2010 (China overtakes Germany, 2010;

Barboza, 2010). The discussion is actually triggered by Ikenberry on how China's growing economic and political might will affect the existing international system and establish institutional order (Ikenberry, 2008), which is based primarily on Western ideas and liberal values that China does not share. The viewpoint reflected in the aforementioned question is widely held in the West, which considers the growth of China to be a danger to the continued dominance of the US and a source of instability in the existing liberal international order. This perspective holds that crises are almost always unpleasant and that the existing liberal international order is unable to undergo any kind of fundamental shifts. The global drama that is currently taking place may, however, be understood in a variety of ways, and one of those ways allows for alternative interpretations of the crisis in the liberal world order and the rise of China. The question that needs to be asked is not whether China will overthrow the liberal global system or join it; rather, the one that needs to be asked is how China will adjust to the liberal world order, as well as how the liberal world order will change to accommodate China's membership in it (and potentially inevitable leadership). The answers to the questions are anchored in the history of China both economically and politically, and generated from ruptures in the liberal international world order.

Even as its military is being modernized and its expanding presence causes real concern about its influence on global stability and the international system, China is widely regarded as an engine of economic growth across the world. The US and the rest of the international community are recognizing that the most important challenge of the 21st century is going to be finding a way to deal with the rise of China. However, to develop a successful approach, one needs to know China's underlying social, political, and economic background, which is significantly more comprehensive and nuanced than that which is guiding the current public debate in the US and other countries.

When it comes to the economic expansion of China as a primary instrument of its rising power, some academics have referred to the country as a "dragon" (Ikenberry, 2016). China has developed into a leading economic powerhouse on a global scale. In less than half a century, China has transformed itself from a backward and impoverished developing nation into a global economic superpower. China's real GDP has expanded at an average annual pace of almost 10 percent from 1979, when the country's economic reforms first started, until 2017 (Morrison, 2013). Before 1979, China was run by Chairman Mao Zedong under the leadership of a centrally planned economy, sometimes known as a command economy. With the establishment of production goals, the regulation of pricing, and the distribution of resources throughout the majority of the economy, the state directed and controlled a significant percentage of the economic output of the country. During the 1950s, all of China's individual home farms were consolidated into large communal farming areas (Lippit, 1981). To hasten the process of industrialization, the central government incurred massive costs throughout the 1960s and 1970s in the form of expenditures on both material and human resources. As a direct consequence of this, by 1978, more than three-fourths of industrial production was being generated by state-owned enterprises (SOEs) that were managed centrally and had output objectives that were determined centrally. In most cases, private firms as well as corporations with foreign investments were forbidden (Lin, Xiaoyan Lu, & Ying, 2020).

According to the World Bank, China has "seen the fastest continuous expansion by a major economy in the history of the world—and has lifted more than 800 million people out of poverty" (World Bank, 2022). China's rise to prominence as a big economic force on the global stage is well documented. For instance, in terms of purchasing power parity (PPP), value-added manufacturing, products commerce, and holder of foreign exchange reserves, it is the largest economy in the world. According to the OECD (2022), it boasts the world's second-largest economy and holds the position of the top global exporter (Mc Kinsey, 2022).

In this regard, China's annual real GDP increased by an average of 9.5 percent between the years 1979 and 2018 (Zhao & Kao-Jen, 2022). As a result of these economic reforms, China has been able to double the size of its economy in real terms on average every eight years. The worldwide economic downturn that began in 2008 had a significant impact on the Chinese economy. At the beginning of 2009, the Chinese media reported that 20 million migrant workers had returned home after being laid off as a direct result of the global financial crisis. Moreover, the news outlets stated that real GDP growth had slowed to 6.8 percent year on year in the fourth quarter of 2008 (Buckley, 2009). The Chinese government's response was to enact a $586 billion economic stimulus program, the majority of which was directed toward supporting infrastructure and relaxing monetary policy to encourage bank lending (Barboza, 2008).

Large-scale capital investment, backed by huge domestic savings and foreign investment, as well as high productivity growth, are often cited by most economists as the primary contributors to China's rapid economic growth. It seems that these two factors worked together to bring about the desired effect. The economy became more efficient as a result of economic reforms, which led to an increase in production and the availability of resources for new economic investment. The rise of China's economy has not only contributed to the expansion of that nation's economy but has also had an impact on the economies of neighboring countries. Throughout the past four years, China has been South Korea and Taiwan's key source of economic development. This trend has also been observed in Taiwan. As a direct consequence of this, their reliance on the economy of China is increasing at a higher rate than their reliance on the economy of the US (Ross, 2006). In addition to this, South Korea and Taiwan are economically dependent on China at present, making them especially susceptible to disruptions in trade and preventing them from expanding their commercial linkages with other economic powers. These are the characteristics that Hirschman (1980) identifies as being crucial to the process of the development of economically substantial political dependence. Additionally, it is projected that these patterns will remain prevalent for at least the next few decades. In light of the fact that the economies of South Korea and Taiwan are relatively underdeveloped in comparison to that of China, full incorporation into the Chinese economy is very certainly going to take place (Hirschman, 1980).

China has altered global supply networks as well as international diplomacy, capitalizing on its success to become the key trade and development partner for rising economies in Asia, Africa, and South America. In this regard, having a solid understanding of the political and military facets of China as a growing force is absolutely necessary. To begin, it is important to point out that the rise of Beijing to global dominance has created challenges for the liberal international order. China's "silent growth" has since given way to more outspoken declarations of its desire to become a great power and to adopt a more assertive stance in the world, most notably regarding its territorial disputes in the South China Sea (Mahesar, Ghumro & Ali, 2021). The geopolitical repercussions of China's economic strength have been brought to the attention of Asia and the US as a result of this, in conjunction with Beijing's military modernization initiative.

The early forecasts that China's inclusion into the global economy would result in domestic liberalization and foreign moderation have been proven to be excessively optimistic. Unfair trade practices, such as forced technology transfers and other constraints on foreign enterprises operating in China, have resulted in a trade war with the US and growing opposition in Europe. This has caused crucial economic developments to be put on hold (Qin, 2019). Despite China's economic competition evolving into a challenge for the country's bilateral and multilateral ties, it can be seen that China has effectively used its economic might to develop new tools in its foreign policy, particularly in soft power. It is important to keep in mind that one of the most effective components of US foreign policy for developing connections with other players has been the utilization of soft power tools.

In a speech given to the Central Foreign Affairs Leadership Group in January 2006, Chinese President Hu Jintao emphasized that China's worldwide reputation and posture must be exhibited in both hard power—such as the economy, science and technology, and defense—and soft power—such as culture. This was the first time that China's soft power had been officially mentioned, and it was a significant moment (Xu & Wang, 2015). After 2011, the 17th Central Committee of the Chinese Communist Party (CCP) devoted an entire plenary session to the topic of culture, coinciding with President Xi Jinping's impending inauguration as head of state. According to the final communiqué, one of the nation's primary objectives is to "evolve our land into a socialist cultural superpower" (Qianming, 2021). In 2014, Xi also stated that, "We should boost China's soft power, present a positive Chinese narrative, and increase communication of China's signals to the outside world" (Albert, 2018). The world has been deluged with a multitude of new projects that have been launched by China under the leadership of Xi, such as "the Chinese Dream," "the Asia-Pacific Dream," and many more. Since then, the Chinese government has devoted significant time and resources to promoting Chinese culture in other countries to enhance its "soft power." This promotion of Chinese culture is based on three main pillars: educational exchanges, Confucius institutes, and international media.

In 2004, China opened up its very first Confucius Institute in Seoul, South Korea. Since then, more than 500 institutes have been established in different parts of the world. These charitable organizations, affiliated with China's Ministry of Education, offer workshops on calligraphy and

Chinese cuisine, as well as celebrations of China's national festivals. Similar to cultural institutions such as the British Councils in the UK, the Alliance Francaise in France, the Goethe Institute in Germany, and the Cervantes Institute in Spain, Confucius Institutes can be found in various countries.

China has quickly become one of the most popular destinations for educational exchange among students from other countries. The vast majority of students coming from other countries choose to pay for their own education; nevertheless, the China Scholarship Council provides financial assistance to students coming from other countries to study in China as well as Chinese students who are studying in other countries. In 2016, China was home to more than 440,000 international students hailing from 205 different countries (Ryan, 2019).

Furthermore, playing an important part in China's soft power is the media. Beijing has invested heavily in its news stations that broadcast in foreign languages to have more influence over the narratives about China. This not only allows Beijing to reach a broader audience for high-profile meetings between Chinese leaders and their foreign counterparts but also for China's less-publicized operations all over the world. The official news agency of the Chinese government, Xinhua, already has 170 worldwide offices and plans to open more in near future (Ables, 2018). Both *China Daily* and *Global Times* publish English-language versions of their newspapers, which are distributed internationally. *China Central Television (CCTV)*, which was formerly known as the *China Central Television Broadcasting News Service*, rebranded itself as the *China Global Television Network* in December 2016. It currently broadcasts six channels, two of which are in English, as well as channels in Arabic, French, Russian, and Spanish, and it has reporting teams in more than 70 countries (Gold, 2020). Even though there is much debate over whether or not China's soft power is effective, the country's budget for it is undoubtedly one of the largest in the world. It is important to highlight that Beijing hosts a large number of international events and organizations, which in turn brings a large number of foreign visitors to China.

While China expands its sphere of influence through the use of particular instruments of soft power, its military, which constitutes a component of hard power, has undergone transformations based on the country's strategic objectives. When the Soviet Union withdrew from Indochina, China emerged as the sole major force in the region. Since then, as China's economic and military reforms have developed, China's advantage over its close neighbors has risen, and China is now in a position to dominate these countries (Di, 2007). According to Favrel, the four most important strategic aims are maintaining territorial integrity, achieving national unity, ensuring maritime security, and maintaining regional peace (Fravel, 2008). In this regard, the Chinese mainland and the country's marine power have seen the most substantial increase in relative capacity growth over the past few decades. The People's Liberation Army (PLA) of the People's Republic of China has witnessed a considerable movement during its first drive for modernization in the 1980s and 1990s. This drive took place in the decades between 1980 and 1990 (Bommakanti, 2017). In a similar vein, throughout the past 15 years, Russian capabilities have decreased while China's capabilities have developed, which has resulted in an increase in China's power in comparison to the Soviet successor nations that are located on China's border in Central Asia. To better reflect the shifting requirements of warfare in the country, modernization efforts have included not just continual doctrinal changes but also modifications to both the equipment and the organizational structure. In addition, China has modernized its Special Operations Forces, which are primarily tasked with destroying the C4I (Command, Control, Communication, Computer and Intelligence) capabilities, airfields, and air defense capabilities of China's enemies (Flanagan & Michael, 2003). Third, elite personnel are the first to receive new equipment and priority funding for their training. This includes modern tanks, artillery, ground-transport vehicles, and heavy-lift helicopters, as well as Russian imports and other cutting-edge military hardware. In addition to this, they have benefited from the upgrading of China's C4ISR (Command, Control, Communications, Computers, Intelligence, Surveillance and Reconnaissance) infrastructure.

The way China conducts its foreign policy concerning Taiwan is also determined by its military modernization. China's relative military capability is also improving in the vicinity of the Taiwan Strait, which separates China and Taiwan. China is relying on air power in the Taiwan theater rather than ground forces to change the military balance and undercut the US' capacity to provide security for Taiwan (Wu, 2016). Although China has increased its relative military force on the Korean Peninsula and in the Taiwan Strait in the past five years, China has not yet increased its relative military presence in East Asian maritime regions that are outside the range of its land-based capabilities. The current Chinese drive for naval modernization may be traced back to the middle of the 1990s when looking at it from a historical viewpoint. Over the past 25 years, China has increased its fleet of nuclear and diesel-electric submarines while also deploying two aircraft carriers, scores of other cutting-edge surface combatants, and a multitude of other cutting-edge surface combatants. The number of "battle force ships," or vessels with a direct or supporting combat role, has increased by 119 in only the previous 15 years, and the People's Liberation Army Navy (PLAN), which currently has 360 battle force ships as opposed to the US Navy's 297, now outnumbers the US Navy in size (Sweeney, 2020). Due to the precision of the data and the figures, it is not simple to gain a comprehensive understanding of China's military modernization in a short amount of time. On the other hand, it ought to be made abundantly apparent that the modernization of China's armed forces tends to affect the power balance in the region, just as the military presence of the US in the region does.

If we look at the rise of China in the liberal international order through economic and political dimensions, we can say that it is quite a unique actor that the US needs to deal with. Pessimistic and cautiously optimistic schools of thought, which approximately but not exactly correlate to the realist/neorealist and liberal/neoliberal theoretical division in international relations, have dominated the discussion on the crises of the liberal international order through the rise of China and other developments. In the previous section, there was a theoretical discussion on American foreign policy and the liberal international order. In this regard, the population, size, and economic might of China, together with its distinct ideological stance, will constitute the primary challenge to the liberal order of the international system. It is important to keep in mind that not only maintaining global balance but also navigating shifts in global power is difficult and fraught with risk, particularly for East Asia. There will be fighting and conflict, and China and its allies will find themselves in incredibly difficult and competitive positions. Notwithstanding this, the shift in global supremacy has not yet sparked a fundamental dispute over the liberal international order. The first question that was asked is still relevant today: Can the liberal international order accommodate China? If not, how will the US structure its foreign policy in response to the challenges that are posed by China? Answers are not yet obvious, but Ikenberry's perspective should be considered as follows: The current order is in crisis as a result of the withdrawal of the UK and the US from their leadership roles; China is not to blame for this crisis (2020).

3.4   RISING POWERS: RUSSIA/ANNEXATION OF CRIMEA BY RUSSIA

Vladimir Putin came to power in Russia, ushering in a new era of political transformation in the country. Following the dissolution of the Soviet Union, the newly independent nation of the Russian Federation went through a period of profound political turmoil. Both the government and society in Russia were thrown into turmoil as a result of the numerous political and bureaucratic reforms that took place. As soon as Putin was declared the winner of the Russian presidential election in the year 2000, the country and its leadership immediately regained their great power thanks to Putin's vision and policies. After that, Putin was able to approach internal politics as well as a foreign policy with a newfound sense of clarity. The great power normalization model was embraced by Putin, and he adjusted it to meet his ethos regarding foreign affairs. At the beginning of his presidency, Putin made it abundantly clear that he was fearful of the actions and intentions of the US, and that he was acting in accordance with the statist ideology of multipolarity and great power balance that had been espoused by former Minister of Foreign Affairs of Russia Yevgeny Primakov. Yet, he was quite quick to point out what differentiated him from his predecessor (Tsyangkov, 2013). In fact, Putin's goal was to bring Russia back to life on all fronts—economically, socially, and politically—which are the primary foundations of the new Russia (Spechler & Spechler, 2019).

Because Russia aims to be a great state, Moscow's priority in terms of its foreign policy should be to restore Russia's reputation as an international superpower. Russia must exercise its strength in nearby regions since it is where the greatest challenges to Moscow and Russians are likely to originate and where Russia has traditionally had a sphere of influence. As a consequence of this, analysts have noticed the close relationship between Moscow's two primary foreign policy goals during Putin's administration: regaining its position as a great power and maintaining its dominance in the nations around it to ward off potential future security concerns (Spechler & Spechler, 2019). Putin has denied that he is aiming to reconstruct the Soviet

Union, but his actions make it plain that he has the desire to govern over the nations that Moscow formerly controlled as part of the USSR. This is despite the fact that Putin has denied that he is attempting to recreate the Soviet Union (Starr & Cornell, 2014). It wasn't long after he took office in 2000 that he made the statement that nearby states are strategically significant as part of the Russian sphere of influence.

Russian liberals, several economists, and other persons who can be referred to as "realists" have pushed in favor of the former option since they place a strong emphasis on Russia's limited resources (Tsangykov & Tsangykov, 2004). Realists believe that Russia should use its resources toward modernizing its economy and constructing new infrastructure rather than striving to grow its influence and provide security beyond its boundaries. Realists also believe that Russia should not try to expand its sphere of influence. On the other hand, Russian nationalists have insisted that Moscow has a divine obligation to bring the Commonwealth of Independent Republics (CIS) under Russian control and to defend their relatives living in those states from the persecution of non-Russian administrations.

It is true that an important official policy document known as the "Foreign Policy Concept of the Russian Federation," which was published in July 2008, advocated a vision of a Greater Europe in which Russia and its Western neighbors would simply be component sectors with equal status (Giusti & Penkova, 2008). As soon as it became clear that Western governments chose an "Atlanticist" policy in which their political institutions would prevail, Putin probably gave up on the idea of working together, though it is highly unlikely that he ever seriously entertained the thought, to begin with. According to Putin, democratic "color revolutions" supported by the West, such as those that took place in Georgia (2003) and Ukraine (2004), pose an existential threat not only to his authority but also to that of the powerful oligarchs.

Russia has officially expressed its commitment to defend these interests against Western and American invasions for as long as its strategic and historical (military and political) strengths are defined by its control over the area. This is the case so long as the territory is under Russia's control. This viewpoint is a reflection of the unease that exists in Russia as a result of the Color Revolution. In addition to this, the upheavals that are occurring run the possibility of leading to nearby nations becoming members of NATO, which would put Russia's safety in jeopardy (Frederick, 2018).

The most recent iteration of Russia's Foreign Policy Concept does the best job of describing the objectives of Putin's foreign policy. It demonstrates how important it is to bolster Russia's status as a vital center of power in the modern world (Stent, 2008). Putin believes that Russia's relationships with its surrounding countries will play a significant role in determining its success in accomplishing this objective (Stent, 2008). When seen from this angle, the most important development is the increasing multipolarity of the international system. Within the framework of this new international order, the US and the Atlantic Alliance will no longer have the preeminent role that they did in the decades following the Second World War. The military might, economic might and ideological influence of the West are being challenged by the emergence of competing power centers. This trend toward a multipolar world ought to be embraced by Russia, and the country ought to work to advance it (Turner, 2009).

The Russian government has in the past vehemently opposed the intention of the Baltic states to join NATO, and many Western politicians were apprehensive of upsetting the Russian government. However, since 2001, the prospect of the Baltic countries being accepted into NATO as part of the organization's second round of enlargement has become significantly more plausible, if not even likely (Kramer, 2002). In 2004, the Baltic states joined NATO, and later that same year, the West supported the Orange Revolution in Ukraine, which both alarmed and infuriated Putin (Kanet & Moulioukova, 2021). Russia's oil and gas income had started to climb considerably at that point after a prolonged period of extremely low prices. This is likely what strengthened Putin's resolve to hinder, resist, and combat both the development of NATO and the democratic movement in Russia's immediate vicinity. Improving Russia's position in the region was an essential component of Putin's new assertiveness, which was one of his primary goals. Putin profited from the growing support for Russia's hegemonic stance in the newly independent parts of the former Soviet Union among Kremlin leaders and a majority of the population. This support was particularly strong in the newly independent countries of the former Soviet Union. Moscow began to place a large amount of emphasis on its ability to generate revenue from energy exports to arm itself with a weapon to use against those of its neighbors who defied or enraged the Kremlin.

It is possible that in the future some small regions with sizeable Russian populations, like Abkhazia and South Ossetia in Georgia, may prefer to remain members of the Russian Federation rather than maintain their status as independent states recognized only by Russia and a small number of other nations worldwide. Until the annexation of Ossetia, no leader of the Russian Federation had expressed a desire to annex the nearby states. However, this may change in the future (Gerrits & Bader, 2016).

Significantly, Putin has denied having any ambitions for eastern Ukraine to be convincing in this regard. It is also possible that the primary motivation behind the retaking of Crimea, which is comprised mostly of Russian countrymen, was the desire to maintain control of vital naval resources in the port city of Sevastopol, which is located on the coast of the Black Sea. There is no need for Putin to pursue any further territorial expansion for Russia to achieve re-establishment as an important global force (Kotkin, 2016). In addition, his country does not possess the necessary raw resources for expansion. In the current iteration of the Russian Federation, in which Vladimir Putin's political standing is in jeopardy, Crimea is already costing the Kremlin a significant amount of money to pay pensions and improve health and education. To successfully absorb the areas of Luhansk and Donetsk in eastern Ukraine, much greater financial resources are required. Any kind of military action taken against the Baltic states will invariably result in a collective defense by NATO. It would appear that this effort is motivated both by ideology and by a desire to achieve a particular personal goal. Putin appears to hold the view that unrestricted democratic discussion, competitiveness, and decentralization of authority are terrible for Russia and possibly for any society as they promote volatility, disorder, and stagnation.

3.4.1 GRIDLOCK OF UKRAINE

In the preceding sections, we discussed the significance of the Baltic region and Ukraine for Russia. In other words, at no point in the history of Russia can Ukraine be left to its own devices to determine its own fate. Nashi is one of Putin's primary communication methods. It was created as a young movement that would be loyal to the state and its leader in particular while simultaneously fighting back against those who criticize them (Hemment, 2012). Nashi was formed as an "anti-Orange" force and comprises tens of thousands of young people who have been trained to be ready to enter the streets and intimidate protestors as well as violently disband any anti-government demonstrations that may take place in the Russian Federation. In addition, Putin began a series of measures in 2006 to suppress actual or potential dissent within the Russian Federation. These measures included the elimination of independent television stations, the expulsion of NGOs that received foreign funding, the sponsorship of legislation that severely penalized participation in demonstrations, the forcible dispersal of such demonstrations when they did occur, and the imprisonment of organizers (Hamlett, 2017). Putin has indicated that he places a high priority on ensuring that color revolutions do not take place on the frontiers of Russia, where they may potentially expand into Russia itself. Since 2004, when a protracted public movement in Ukraine toppled the pro-Russian administration, this has been his primary objective in the region (Allison, 2014).

Euromaidan, the protest movement in Ukraine, got its start on November 21, 2013, after President Viktor Yanukovych arbitrarily delayed the signing of the Partnership Agreement with the EU. The "Euromaidan Revolution" of 2013–2014 in Ukraine, an important buffer state between the Russian Federation and the recently expanded NATO alliance, put significantly more of Russia's interests in jeopardy than anything else (Shveda & Park, 2016). Kyiv is only 800 kilometers from Moscow, which means that the cultural, linguistic, demographic, and economic ties between Russia and Ukraine are stronger and more intimate than they are between the capitals of most post-Soviet countries, which are almost 2,000 kilometers away from Moscow. Ukraine was intended to play a significant role in Russia's plans to establish an economic union in Eurasia, which is a crucial part of President Putin's quest to reclaim Russia's reputation as a great power. The resounding vote in favor of independence in Ukraine in 1991 was a major contributing factor to the collapse of the Soviet Union. The decision by Ukraine's Yanukovich to forgo signing a painstakingly negotiated association and free trade agreement with the EU and instead forge deeper economic connections with Russia was what initially ignited the demonstrations that led to the start of the revolution in that nation. These demonstrations eventually led to the overthrow of Yanukovich and the establishment of a new government (Piper, 2013). Reportedly, they also put pressure on the Ukrainian administration to take any and all actions required to put an end to the rioting; nevertheless, the police assaults that followed on the protestors just helped to intensify the amount of violence that was taking place. In the view of Moscow, the crisis was caused by Western politicians and groups since they stoked the flames of unrest through their participation. The acts of the opposition amounted to an attempt to overthrow the lawful government of Ukraine via a coup (Mearsheimer, 2014).

Various academics approach this revolution from a variety of angles in their research. There have been assertions made that the Dignity Revolution was not a direct reaction to the abandonment of Ukrainian national ideas under the leadership of Yanukovych— though many people considered this an essential problem. The more fundamental causes were the citizens' outrage at the unprecedented rise in corruption, the failure to sign the Association Agreement with the EU for the possibility of rapprochement with Russia, and the brutal violence used by the police. Overall, the outrage of citizens was the most fundamental cause. On the other hand, Russian nationalists believe that this uprising was a Western plot to remove Ukraine from Russia's sphere of influence. They believe this because the West supported the rebels. Putin highlighted that Russia was now obligated to live up to its obligation to the agreement from 1994 that protected the sovereignty of Ukraine (Hale, 2004). After Yanukovich fled to Russia, Moscow issued a ruling declaring that it was illegal for the Ukrainian Parliament to remove him from office. Once the deposed president of Ukraine issued a public request for Russian troops to enter Crimea and establish themselves in the south and east of the nation, the Russian military invaded Crimea and installed themselves there. They provided assistance to pro-Russian counter-demonstrators in Donetsk and Luhansk who were attempting to form what would eventually become separatist states in those two cities (Hale, 2004). As a result, the Russian president was successful in elevating the standing of his country in the region while simultaneously strengthening his government's grip on power.

3.4.2   ANNEXATION OF CRIMEA

Ukraine is a substantial Slavic country that has been recognized as a separate state by the UN for a very long time. The city of Kyiv, which is now the capital of Ukraine, was the first major center of Russian nationhood. Before the start of the Second World War, a portion of what is now Ukraine was part of Poland. The East Slavic language (Ukrainian) is the official language, although Russian is also extensively spoken and understood. This also reflects Putin's speech, in which he used geopolitical justifications about Ukraine's inclination toward the West to defend these events. However, he also deftly drew attention to the fact that Russia is a divided nation and that it is Russia's moral obligation to care for Russian communities abroad and respect their purported desire to reunite with Russia (Laruelle, 2015). According to this point of view, the context for the annexation of Crimea was actually established during the protests, as was touched upon earlier. In addition to this, the Russian government has said that neo-Nazis and other organizations on the far right would engage in violent acts against Russian speakers and people of Russian ethnicity in Ukraine. The participation of these right-wing personalities lent credence to widespread portrayals in Russian media of Ukraine being dominated by a "fascist junta" that posed a threat to Russians (Biersack & O'Lear, 2014).

In addition to this context, historical facts seen from a Russian point of view played a major role in legitimizing annexation in the eyes of the Russian populace. This land had been donated to the Ukrainian SSR by the then-leader of the Soviet Union, N. S. Khrushchev. Despite the vehement objections raised by Western nations, the so-called "Republic of Crimea" was improperly returned to Russian control in a hastily held vote that was overseen by Russian armed personnel. This confusion in 2013 is likely what inspired the rebellion of pro-Russian separatists in Crimea, which is a peninsula on the Black Sea where a major section of the population is composed of Russians. More Russian troops arrived in Crimea to reinforce the ones that were already there, and they moved closer to the border with Ukraine. The Russian government, to impose Russian interests in Ukraine, utilized the creation of a Ukrainian threat as well as the chaos that was caused by the change in leadership. On the morning of February 27, 2014, troops in simple green uniforms with balaclavas covering their faces and advanced weaponry arrived around the Crimean Peninsula. It is presumed that the purpose of their arrival was to protect the public from impending violence instigated by the new acting government of Ukraine and its supporters in the right wing (Timeline: Political Crisis in Ukraine and Russia's Occupation of Crimea, 2014).

Instead, financial assistance in the form of loans from the IMF was made available to the Ukrainian economy. Because of the severe sanctions that the US and EU have put on Russian banks, long-term energy transactions within the Federation are currently impossible. During a similar takeover in April of that year, pro-Russian activists dispatched Russian soldiers to the southeast Ukrainian areas of Donetsk and Luhansk, outfitting them in unmarked clothing and providing them with huge pieces of weaponry (Kostyuchenko, 2015). Over the subsequent three years, 450,000 people managed to escape, the majority of them into Russian territory, while many others were killed in the fighting. The United Nations High Commissioner for Refugees (UNHCR) estimates that 1.6 million people were moving around within their own country (Over 1.3 Million Ukrainian Refugees, 2023).

To lend legitimacy to Russia's occupation of Crimea, Russian military personnel and their proxies on the peninsula organized a referendum on Crimea's independence from Ukraine. Both the breakaway of Crimea and its annexation by Russia violate international law. A referendum was scheduled to take place on March 16, 2014 by the "government" of Crimea and its armed supporters (Grant, 2015). By 2018, pro-Russian separatists had managed to take control of this region with the assistance of hybrid forces that were able to infiltrate enemy territory, cyberwarfare, propaganda, and economic extortion. Putin did not comply despite the separatists in the two provinces, who were ethnic Russians and Ukrainians, declaring their desire to become a part of the Russian Federation; this may have been because of the potential costs of energy, public sector salaries, and food aid, all of which were already a concern in Crimea. Alternatively, this may have been because Putin was concerned about the possibility of a military conflict between Russia and Ukraine. On the other hand, these individuals will have the opportunity to obtain Russian passports (Neil, 2019).

Putin was able to enforce the Minsk Protocol in 2014 because the Kyiv government was on the verge of economic collapse (national income dropped by approximately 16 percent between 2014 and 2015). The Minsk Protocol formalized an armistice that reduced but did not eliminate the fighting along the cease-fire line in 2014. The "Minsk II Agreement" from 2015, which was mediated by French President Francois Hollande and German Chancellor Angela Merkel, called for greater local self-government in the separatist eastern areas and did not condition peace in the Donbas on the restoration of Crimea to Ukraine (Zajac, 2016). The agreement was reached by Hollande and Merkel. The terms of this second agreement were not acceptable to any of the parties, and as a result, it, too, was unable to put an end to the violence and loss of life. In the four years that have passed since the deployment of Organization for Security and Co-operation in Europe (OSCE) forces, during which there have been both active combat and periods of cease-fire, the situation has not been altered in any way. In order to compete with a newly reconstructed Ukrainian army, the Kremlin has stationed an estimated 5,000 hybrid Russian soldiers there at a great financial expense to itself. Both of the Donbas's provinces are still administered and defended by their own independent armies and governments.

The current confrontation between East and West Ukraine has been significantly aggravated as a result of the Russian seizure of Crimea, which has transformed the dispute from an economic and diplomatic issue into a catastrophic geopolitical tragedy. In spite of having to pay a high international political and financial price for preventing a dismembered Ukraine from joining NATO—utility bills to the two regions remain unpaid and normal commerce is disrupted—Putin has successfully achieved his goals in this critical part of the "new abroad": no foreign forces (other than Russian), no economic integration with the EU, and a docile population and a regime anxious to avoid open conflict with Moscow (Yuri, 2016). Most importantly, Moscow is able to keep its access to the Sevastopol naval facility, which is home to Russia's Black Sea Fleet, because Crimea's sovereignty grants it such access. Because of its warm water port, its natural harbor, and its huge infrastructure, Sevastopol is considered to be one of the most important naval installations in the Black Sea. In addition, the Black Sea Fleet, in its current configuration, provides Russia with significant operational capacity in the immediate vicinity. Despite Russia's lack of a modern naval force, the fleet is able to deal with maritime threats to Russian interests in the Black Sea posed by other powers in the region.

It should not be surprising that many people on Ukraine's left bank prefer membership in the EU with Russia over membership in the Union. This preference is largely supported by people on Ukraine's right bank, primarily because Russian speakers are exposed to extensive propaganda through Russian media. Putin, however, cannot claim a complete win at this point. Putin most certainly anticipated that Crimea would serve as a symbol to persuade pro-Russian elements in Ukraine to embrace Moscow and resist Kyiv's efforts to further integrate with the West after the annexation of Crimea. While Ukraine is embroiled in a territorial dispute with Russia over Crimea, Putin may also be under the impression that Western nations will be reluctant to accept Ukraine into their ranks. The amount of business conducted between Ukraine and Russia fell by 30 percent in 2016 (Dragneva & Wolcznuk, 2016). Despite their pride in Russia's position in the international community, officials in Istanbul have recognized the Orthodox Church of Ukraine in a symbolic step that has been widely publicized and received approval from Kyiv.

Although Ukraine had to pay three to four times the price for natural gas than it did in the past, and that major new foreign investments were unlikely to arrive by 2017, Ukraine was able to obtain debt relief from the rest of the world, with the exception of its creditor Russia. This allowed Ukraine to slowly revive, and it was also able to pay off its debts. According to an article published in 2014 titled "Ukraine Wins IMF Deal; Faces $9 Billion in Debt Payments this Year," Ukraine was able to secure an agreement with the IMF, which means that the country would have to make $9 billion in debt payments this year. As a consequence of this, Russia does not have authority over the policies of Ukraine that it seeks. Senior European foreign ministers have met to explore the possibility of deploying a peacekeeping force and clearing mines from the area between the opposing sides of the conflict. In light of the circumstances, Ukraine made efforts to win over additional financial assistance and political support from Europe. To this end, it has proposed a number of different projects with fellow Organization for Democracy and Economic Development (GUAM) members Georgia, Azerbaijan, and Moldova, including free trade. Yet, there is typically a limited amount of financing available for endeavors of this nature. In an effort to reduce its dependency on fuels supplied by Russia, Ukraine has received more than $350 million in aid from the US, in addition to a shipment of anthracite coal valued at $80 million (Peterson, 2017; Wides-Munoz, 2022).

In conclusion, but certainly not least, the annexation of Crimea has had major repercussions for both the liberal international order and the politics of the surrounding region. To begin, despite the fact that Chancellor Merkel was the one who began the Minsk process, it is fair to say that the EU and the leaders of Europe did not react to the annexation as predicted. In comparison to the countries of Western Europe, Eastern European nations such as Bulgaria, Poland, and Romania responded more violently because of their historical anxieties (Gardner, 2016).

In the aftermath of Russia's annexation of Crimea, Germany, like other NATO partners, has been reticent to approve the stationing of rotating soldiers in the Baltic states and Poland. In addition, Berlin has not yet consented to the stationing of "permanent" military in Eastern Europe. The fact that Berlin was so dependent on energy sources during the later part of 2015 explains why it pushed so hard for the NATO-Russia Council negotiations to get back on track. In addition, shortly after the conflict in Georgia and Russia in 2008, France sold Russia the amphibious cruiser Mistral. Reportedly, this was done in an effort to bring Moscow closer to the NATO. Because of the likelihood that it will be utilized in impending Russian military operations, the US and NATO exerted pressure on France to renounce its intention to transfer the battleship. It appeared that Paris was using the battleship as a (failed) negotiating weapon to help "resolve" the Crimea crisis by delaying its transfer to Moscow despite Moscow having purchased it (Gardner, 2015). However, a deal was ultimately made to sell the Mistral to Egypt, which would be financed by Saudi Arabia.

Regarding the response of NATO, despite the fact that Ukraine is not a member of NATO and does not therefore require Article 5 security assurances, the US and its NATO partners have made it abundantly clear that they fully support the sovereignty and territorial integrity of Ukraine within its internationally recognized boundaries. As a means of addressing the issues that have been brought to light as a result of Russian actions, President Obama made it a requirement that a NATO rapid-reaction force be stationed in the three Baltic nations, as well as Poland and Romania. Elements of the navy, the air force, and special forces would be included in this force. There is a provision in the constitution that calls for full membership to both NATO and the EU. However, it is quite improbable that Putin's greatest nightmare will come true in the near future. There is not a single person in Ukraine who holds the opinion that Ukraine's membership bid to NATO will be successful in the foreseeable future. Jens Stoltenberg (2021), the secretary-general of NATO, has stated that "this depends on reforms." To put it another way, 2014 was a watershed year for both the regional politics and the international system, ushering in a number of unforeseen ramifications that are difficult to characterize. There is no question that Russia was successful in opening a route to influence Ukrainian politics in a more straightforward manner; yet, the responses of European countries and the US to the actual practice of annexation were rather different. In addition to this, it appeared as though NATO lacked the capability to discourage Russia. It is terrible for the liberal international order to realize that the economic and strategic dependency of European countries to Russia has generated undeniable restraint for these nations, which in turn has created a security conundrum for those countries. In opposition, Russia has once more militarily attacked the liberal international order that was established in the period after the Cold War. In conclusion, there is some room for judgment regarding the degree to which Russia has revised its appraisal of its policy toward Ukraine.

3.5   ARAB UPRISINGS AND US FOREIGN POLICY

After eight tumultuous years under the administration of George W. Bush, during which the US was placed in jeopardy of going bankrupt, President Barack Obama intended to alter the course of the future direction of the country's foreign policy. The new president made it a point, in both his words and his actions, to clearly contrast his vision of realism, pragmatism, and caution in foreign policy with those of his predecessor. He did this in an effort to show that his vision is more realistic, pragmatic, and prudent (O'Connor & Cooper, 2021). Obama thought that the US would come back to the world stage as a new, more progressive nation. Obama first capitalized the US' desire to abandon militant unilateralism and return to the traditional multilateralism in international affairs that had guided the country through the first decade following the end of the Cold War. Because the world is complicated, the new Obama doctrine, according to the presidential hopeful in 2007, would not be as dogmatic as the Bush doctrine. Then, in contrast to his predecessor who refused to "negotiate with evil," Obama vowed to cooperate politically with the country's adversaries as follows: "I will meet not just with our friends, but with our enemies, because I remember what Kennedy said, that we should never negotiate out of fear, but we should never fear to negotiate" (Ratnesar, 2011).

He claimed that engagement and diplomacy were more vital then than ever before for reestablishing "our alliances, repairing our relationships around the world, and actually making us more safe in the long term" (as cited in Gerges, 2013, p. 301). Obama argued that the Bush administration had significantly harmed both the critical national interests of the US and its moral position in the world by relying on hyper-militarism and avoiding direct interaction with opponents. Obama's argument was based on the fact that the Bush administration had avoided direct interaction with opponents. Obama has made an effort to transition away from depending on military strength and toward promoting and utilizing soft power in his administration (Lutter, 2015). As President Obama made clear in his inaugural address, his strategy for dealing with international issues was significantly distinct from that of the president who came before him. His new strategy for moving forward not only relied on immaterial moral principles or raw military power but rather on concrete relationships and long-lasting beliefs based on shared interests with other countries. After understanding how hungry the country was for a balance to be restored between domestic and foreign politics, Obama, as a final step, shifted his focus back to the issues facing the country at home. He achieved this by refocusing attention on core issues like the global financial crisis, unemployment, and the government debt here at home after the start of Bush's costly "war on terror."

One might make the argument that public opinion held the belief that the cost of the Bush doctrine was too large to bear and that it had weakened the nation's moral position in the world (Hartwig, 2008). The philosophy of "go it alone" and unilateralism was famously associated with former President George W. Bush. As early as 2006, Obama made it clear that, in contrast to his immediate predecessor, he was more of a realist than an idealist (Bejesky, 2011). His pragmatic and practical approach to foreign policy incorporated the ideals of collaboration, multilateralism, and shared security interests as guiding principles for international dealings. However, Obama's NSS from 2010 called for a rebalancing of American global commitments away from the wars in Iraq and Afghanistan, which had diverted the country's attention from its more urgent 21st-century challenges in the Asia-Pacific region. Although Obama has been reluctant to establish a doctrine in his name, he did call for a rebalancing of American global commitments in his NSS.

Obama recognized the perception the world harbored about the US and its mobilization of democracy. "We [Americans] promote our values above all by living them at home" (NSS, 2010). Obama made the veiled claim that all people share American values and that these shared ideals are what all of mankind desires, without explicitly specifying what those values are. In other words, Obama devoted a significant section of his NSS to strengthening the country at home compared to Bush's NSSs of 2002 and 2006. Obama believed that these principles would allow the US to extract itself from the "9/11 wars," moving its attention away from seemingly peripheral nation-building projects in the Muslim world and toward the challenge of a rising Asia.

On the other hand, during both his presidential campaign and his first six months in office, Obama repeated his priority of engaging Muslims and improving their unfavorable opinions of the US. This commitment was made during Obama's first six months as president. The incoming president reiterated on multiple occasions that, "The US is not at war with Islam, and it will never be at war with Islam" (Obama, 2009a). In an early effort to communicate with Arabs and Muslims, President Obama granted an interview to the Al Arabiya television network shortly after being sworn in as the nation's 44th president. Yet, in June of 2009, he addressed important issues and provided a wonderful approach for addressing relations between the US and Muslim countries in a talk that was widely recognized and delivered at Cairo University.

Not only did it contribute to momentum, but it also served as a long-term strategy. As Obama began his first year in office, he was immediately faced with the challenge of repairing the damage that had been done to the relationship between the US and the Muslim world by the previous administration, which had been led by Bush. To tell the truth, several former presidents of the US had traveled to countries in the Middle East, but they had merely come to deliver speeches rather than to listen. They all looked at the region through the same globalist glasses, which included the Cold War, geopolitics, Israel, and, more recently, the "war on terror" (Worthington, 2019). After understanding that this legacy, which had hurt the US' image in the region, was unsustainable, Obama attempted to use the authority of the presidential pulpit to start bringing American soldiers home. This legacy had tarnished the US' reputation in the region. Obama's predecessors had chosen a reductionist strategy of grouping all Islamists together, seeing mainstream and militant alike through the single lens of al-Qaeda, rather than taking a more constructive approach. This helped bin Laden's purpose by presenting all varieties of Islamic fundamentalism, from Hamas to the Muslim Brotherhood, as being comparable to jihadism, which is a violent, totalitarian fringe ideology committed to random devastation, worldwide enslavement, and the elimination of all non-believers (Gerges, 2005). Obama's speech in June 2009 sent a strong, fresh message in light of this context: "I've come here to Cairo to seek a new beginning between the US and Muslims around the world, one based on mutual interest and mutual respect, and one based upon the truth that America and Islam are not exclusive and need not be in conflict" (Obama, 2009a).

In his speech, he not only discussed Islam from a personal perspective, but he also pledged to clear up some of the misconceptions that Americans have about the religion in general. To further humanize the US in the eyes of Muslims and the 7 million Muslims who now call the US home, which he claimed have contributed to the prosperity of the nation, Obama suggested that Islam was a part of America's history. This was done to further humanize America (Obama, 2009a).

Obama, in contrast to his predecessor, did not include any references to the terms "terrorism" or "war on terror" in his message. In fact, the administration made a concerted effort to stop using the phrase "war on terror" to refer to the ongoing combat that is taking place all over the world. Given the turbulent and contentious climate in which Obama took office, his new lexicon of conversation, cooperation, and reconciliation between Christians in the West and Muslims in the East was a dramatic change from the rhetoric of the Bush administration (Singh, 2012). A fresh tone of humility and cooperation was established during Obama's talk in Cairo, which boosted hopes that he would change the direction of US foreign policy in the Middle East. Arab and Muslim opinion-makers of all shades praised Obama for his refined and courteous tone, even though they were skeptical. Nevertheless, they took a cautious approach and opted to wait and see what would happen. The difference between Obama's transformational words and his centrist deeds, which typically preserved the status quo, disturbed Obama's critics on the left and right in the US who demanded ideological purity and clarity. Disillusionment among liberals is widespread as a result of President Obama's reluctance to put a stop to the wars that were started by President Bush in response to the 9/11 attacks and to erase the aftermath of those attacks, particularly the American military prison at Guantánamo Bay. Even Zbigniew Brzezinski, who served as national security adviser to President Jimmy Carter and was sympathetic to the Obama administration, detected a disconnect between the rhetoric of the Obama administration and the reality of the situation: "I sincerely like his opinions and wisdom" (Brezinski, 2010).

When Barack Obama took office, he and his foreign policy team were unaware of the full extent of the painful legacy that the US had left in the Middle East, including the wars in Iraq and Afghanistan, participation in extrajudicial killings and torture, ties to repressive autocrats, unwavering support for Israel, and significant threats posed by Iran and Pakistan (Jervis, 2017). At the same time, President Obama was dealing with a slowdown in the domestic economy, and the development of China and India hinted at a shift away from a unipolar to a multipolar order in the world. In contrast to his conservative rivals, Obama and his advisors were acutely aware of American weakness in light of the new rising powers, and they desired to reorient foreign policy objectives away from the Middle East and toward the Pacific and Asia. Notwithstanding his lofty rhetoric about a fresh start in relations with Muslim nations, Obama did not make this region a particularly high priority throughout his presidency. The revitalization of the US economy over the long term and the consolidation of the country's debt were at the forefront of Obama's priorities. It was necessary to lessen the country's commitments to other countries, notably in the Middle East, where those obligations had exceeded the country's essential interests. In other words, the president began to shift the role of the US away from that of a guarantor of the liberal international order by placing a greater emphasis on domestic issues while simultaneously outlining a more assertive foreign policy toward the Middle East, which is a traditional area of conflict for the US.

Obama's priorities were domestic and primarily economic from the outset of his presidency. This is something that Obama's supporters have long disputed. The conflict in the Middle East as well as other global concerns were not high on his list of priorities. In light of this, it is easy to comprehend why President Obama opted, for the most part, to cut his losses and refrain from further growing the US role in the Middle East when confronted with challenges. Obama has consistently shown an inclination to avoid getting involved in the social and political instability and raging wars in the area, a decision that is in line with his worldview and the ideals he holds dear.

The unrest that broke out in Tahrir Square in Egypt in 2011 caught President Obama completely off guard. No one could fathom how one demonstration could set off a domino effect throughout a region and lead to civil war and chaos in some countries, such as Yemen and Syria (Açıkalın and Bölücek, 2014). The most influential people in US foreign policy dismissed warnings about public unrest as a domestic problem that the region's security services could control and did not give a post-autocratic Middle East any real thought (Dilanian, 2012). Although Obama was projecting a new rhetorical position toward the Middle East, he admitted that it is necessary to protect the vital national interests of the US, which include the security of energy supplies and the stability of longtime US allies. The Obama administration's covert embrace of pro-American authoritarian leaders like Hosni Mubarak in Egypt, whose assistance was required in combating terrorism, nuclear proliferation, energy security, and the Arab-Israeli conflict, is not surprising and was a result of incorrect ideas and presumptions about how Middle Eastern society and politics are structured—basically, a focus on high and elite politics rather than the importance of social movements and public opinion. Obama first adopted a tactful and non-interfering strategy for advancing democracy in the area (Banai, 2013). He argued in favor of open governments because they represent the choice of the populace—a subliminal jab at Mubarak and other Arab autocrats—but he omitted to mention the pervasive viola-tions of human rights in many Muslim nations. However, according to White House aides, in a five-page document titled "Political Reform in the Middle East and North Africa" that he sent to his closest advisors in August 2010, Obama urged them to question the conventional wisdom that the stability of the region always served the US' vital interests (Gerges, 2013). The hazards of both "continuing support for increasingly unpopular and oppressive regimes" and a "strong push by the US for reform" were apparently factors that Obama wanted to consider. Hillary Clinton, the secretary of state, and the Obama foreign policy team promoted human rights in a low-key, incremental manner (Forsythe, 2011). Yet, the Obama administration's foreign policy staff failed to foresee the storm that was brewing in Egypt or put pressure on Mubarak to abandon his dictatorial policies.

Both Mubarak and Obama were taken aback by the outbreak of popular upheaval on January 25, 2011, given the political climate in Egypt. The foreign policy team of the Obama administration initially responded to the emerging situation with hesitancy and reluctance. As the number of protesters increased and increased pressure was put on Mubarak to step down, President Obama shifted his strategy and eventually turned his back on one of the US' longest-standing allies in the Middle East. At home, the administration was criticized for sending contradictory messages to Mubarak and the protestors. At first, they chose to support Mubarak reluc-tantly, but later, they decided to fully support the demonstrators demanding his resignation. The government subsequently suffered criticism. As the storm grew stronger over several days, President Obama had to reconcile a divergence in policy within his administration. Diplomats from the State and Defense Departments analyzed the crisis through the lens of American strategic interests in the area, with a particular focus on the danger that it posed to the peace accord that had been signed between Egypt and Israel in 1979.

The management of crises and the smooth transition from one political administration to the next were Obama's key concerns. It was a concern that much as in previous uprisings, anti-democratic Islamic factions could take leadership of the Egyptian revolution. Organizations and groups that are rooted in Islam, such as the Muslim Brotherhood, Hamas, and Hezbollah, are often regarded as a threat to the national interests of the US and are viewed with mistrust in policy circles within the US. However, local autocrats who supported the West were seen as the better option due to their obedience, reliability, and predictability. Saudi Arabia opposed President Obama's sympathetic stance toward the demonstrators in Tunisia and Egypt. Saudi Arabia also rejected American efforts to persuade Gulf nations to carry out substantial changes and satisfy the justifiable aspirations of their citizens (Heydemann, 2014). The policies of the US were viewed differently in different countries. The Saudi Arabian government issued a statement in response to the Obama administration's initial feelings toward the Arab Spring. The conflict over Bahrain acted as a test of wills between two competing factions within the US government and Saudi Arabia, a steadfast neighbor in the region (Al-Matter, 2016). The authoritarian Al Khalifa royal family in Bahrain was first warned not to use excessive force against its citizens by the Obama administration's foreign policy team. King Hamad was also urged to implement significant reforms to prevent a prolonged political crisis and bloodshed.

Following this, the government of Bahrain permitted a Saudi military force to disperse the protesters while working under the auspices of the Gulf Cooperation Council (GCC). The Saudis and the Obama administration accused Iran of penetrating the Arab Shia community and utilizing its political aspirations for geostrategic benefit. They based their claim on the fact that Iran has a history of supporting terrorist organizations. This was done to provide a rationale for military engagement. When he met with King Abdullah of Saudi Arabia in April 2011, which was a meeting that signaled an easing of US-Saudi hostilities, Defense Secretary Robert Gates said that he did not even bring up the Saudi intervention in Bahrain. Gates also said that he did not bring up Saudi Arabia's support for the Bahraini opposition (Bumiller & MacFarquhar, 2011). The upgrade of the country's missile defense system was one of the most pressing issues that were brought up during Gates' meeting with the Saudi monarch. The events in Libya shed further light on what Obama refers to as his "anti-doctrinal philosophy." Because of the lessons learned from the Iraq War and the strain that is being placed on the domestic economy, the president demanded that his European and Arab partners take the lead in the effort in Libya. This was because he was unwilling to assume responsibility for it himself. "Leading from behind" was more his approach than "leading from the front," which was how George W. Bush operated. In the end, President Obama decided to back NATO's military operation in Libya because he was fearful that Muammar Gaddafi would massacre the rebels in Benghazi if he was not stopped.

3.5.1 EGYPTIAN REVOLUTION

Although some of the most important approaches and initiatives have been discussed in the preceding title, it is important to look at US foreign policy toward Egypt throughout the Arab Spring and afterward up until the Trump administration in a different context. Journalists, politicians, and intellectuals were taken utterly by surprise by the Egyptian uprising. Although it is too early to chronicle the history of that event, which is still evolving, we can certainly explain why so many Egyptians began taking to the streets on January 25, 2011. At first glance, it appeared as though Egypt was participating in a wave of unrest that had its origins in the spectacular overthrow of Zine El-Abadine Ben Ali in Tunisia.

Although the dramatic overthrow of Ben Ali in Tunisia was likely a major inspiration for Egyptian protesters—as evidenced by the heartfelt thanks to Tunisia offered on sites like Facebook and Twitter following Mubarak's resignation—the uprising itself could not have progressed without a series of significant developments in Egyptian politics in those years. The key explanation is that beginning in 2004, what Larry Diamond refers to as "liberation technologies" were being utilized by internet activists almost simultaneously. This was the primary explanation. It was anticipated that after the demonstration reached its peak, it would witness the democratic activities of the US. The most recent decade is typically the focal point of most evaluations about the promotion of democracy by the US in the Middle East. However, the origins of American funding for democracy in Egypt can be traced back to the early 1990s, when the US Agency for International Development (USAID) began to integrate aid for traditional development assistance programs. This was the beginning of a long and fruitful relationship between the US and Egypt (Ratrout & Köprülü, 2022). During that time, democracy aid was a new component of development assistance, and after the fall of the Soviet Union and the fall of communism in Eastern Europe, there was a growing enthusiasm for the encouragement of its spread. In order to combat terrorism during the time of the Cold War, the US facilitated systematic USAID assistance to Egypt. As a result of the attacks that took place on September 11, 2001, the overall structure of assistance was modified. It was the first time that the promotion of democracy was brought up as a national security priority, and assistance for democracy was defined as an essential instrument in the fight against extremism and, consequently, terrorism. The Bush administration expanded spending for democracy promotion from $500 million per year in 2000 to more than $2 billion by 2005 to accomplish this goal (Melia, 2005).

Questions still surround the efforts at democratization throughout the years and decades. Hosni Mubarak was a steadfast and trustworthy American friend while being a brutally dictatorial one. He abided by the terms of the peace accord that was signed with Israel in 1979, supported the peace process that was taking place between Israelis and Palestinians, provided intelligence on radical Islamist organizations as well as al-Qaeda, and contributed to the construction of the Arab bulwark against Iran. The realistic approach to Egypt was demonstrated by the US' willingness to disregard the repressive measures used by Mubarak's dictatorship while at the same time continuing to support the dictator (Jentleson, 2011).

From the beginning of the uprising until Mubarak's ouster, President Obama took a pragmatic approach to make the most of the limited influence that the US had to bring about change in Egypt (Morey et al., 2012). After Mubarak's confrontational address and refusal to step down on February 1, 2011, Obama eventually gave the green light to his advisors to push for genuine political reform to begin "soon." This came after Mubarak's announcement that he would not step down. As was to be expected, he did not want his administration to give the impression that it was supporting a tyrant against the wishes of the great majority of his people, particularly the young people, because doing so would run the risk of alienating the Egyptian population. Nevertheless, during the 18 days between the beginning of the "Egyptian Revolution" and Mubarak's resignation, as millions of ordinary Egyptians marched to the streets demanding democratic rights, the US shifted its priorities from interests to principles and promoted Mubarak's exit from office. The US employed both hard and soft force in its response to the unrest that occurred in Tahrir Square in 2011. The Egyptian military was warned by the Obama administration that US military assistance worth $1.3 billion would be cut off if the Egyptian government opened fire on its own people (Limited Benefits of US Ties to Egypt's Military, 2011). This step was essential in convincing the army that the people's demands were genuine, hence fueling the revolution against Mubarak.

In late June 2012, the Muslim Brotherhood's Mohamed Morsi was declared the winner of the runoff presidential election, defeating the military's candidate, Ahmed Shafik (a former Mubarak prime minister and, like Mubarak, a former Egyptian Air Force general), by only 840,000 votes out of the more than 25.5 million cast. The revolution that began in Tahrir Square was still in its early stages, and its course and eventual outcome were unknown at the time (Celebration in Egypt as Morsi declared, 2012). In the months that followed Mubarak's ouster, tensions between the US and Egypt increased. This trend continued with the detention in February 2012 of American citizens working in Egypt for pro-democracy NGOs such as the International Republican Institute, the National Democratic Institute, and Freedom House, among others. If the workers had been brought to trial, both Congress and the White House threatened to withhold $1.3 billion in annual funding for the military (Trial Is Adjourned, 2012).

A more serious crisis for Egypt and US-Egyptian relations erupted in the days leading up to the presidential elections in June 2012, when the Supreme Council of the Armed Forces (SCAF) reinstituted martial law and Egypt's Mubarak-appointed Supreme Constitutional Court ruled that the newly elected conservative parliament must be dissolved. After that, SCAF declared that it would be in charge of supervising the drafting of the new constitution and that a future civilian administration would continue to exercise authority over the military and the defense ministries (Sayigh, 2012). Nonetheless, protesters refused to accept the decision that was made by SCAF, and they returned to Tahrir Square once more. Now that they could not avoid it any longer, the US had to negotiate with the Muslim Brotherhood. There are some very good reasons to act in this manner: Egypt has the highest population out of nations in the Arab world and carries significant geopolitical and strategic weight for the region as well as for American foreign policy. The US wanted Egypt to maintain its membership in the anti-Iranian Arab camp while also guaranteeing that the future Egyptian administration would honor the peace treaty that had been reached with Israel in 1979.

On the other hand, having the Muslim Brotherhood in power could have put American ideals to the test. For example, what if Egypt's democratically elected leaders did not adhere to the democratic norms and principles with the Muslim Brotherhood in control? After the results were made public, President Obama extended his congratulations to President-elect Morsi on his victory in the election through Jay Carney, his press secretary. But while he was doing so, he underlined the necessity of democratic and pluralistic rights for women and Coptic Christians in Egypt (Obama Urges Egyptian Leader to Protect Democratic Principles, 2013).

At the beginning of Morsi's administration, Egypt's principal model of government did not revolve around emergency measures, for the first time in decades. As this was going on, the tough climate in which the president had to perform swiftly began to bring attention to situations that would eventually lead to the exception having to be reinstated. Major issues included the lack of a functional constitution in Egypt nearly 18 months after Mubarak's overthrow, the continued dominance of political conflicts between the army and the president, and widespread dissatisfaction with the composition of the constitutional committee. Morsi faced a significant challenge when it came to his legitimacy (Dunne & Hamzawy, 2017). On November 22, 2012, the president, who was concerned about the possibility of a constitutional impasse, issued a constitutional decree that granted him a wide range of new powers. In flagrant disregard for the rule of law, the decree granted the president increased legislative and judicial power, paving the way for the institution of emergency rule in the future (Ardovini & Mabon, 2019).

Unfortunately, throughout the 16 months that Morsi was in power, Egypt experienced a period of significant political instability, which culminated in Morsi's yearlong administration. Morsi took office on June 30, 2012, exactly one year and one day after he won Egypt's first presidential election that could be considered truly competitive. This marked the beginning of the end of a turbulent transition period that lasted for 16 months. Morsi's tenure pitted the Muslim Brotherhood and its Islamic backers against a broad swath of Egypt's public and business sectors, as well as the Coptic Church and the military, rather than solidifying democracy or civilian rule in the country. This put the Brotherhood and its backers in opposition to the Egyptian government. As a result of the climate of mutual mistrust, political deadlock, and popular discontent that permeated Morsi's administration, Egypt's military, which was headed at the time by Defense Minister Abdel-Fattah el-Sisi, had the opportunity to recover political authority. El-Sisi was in charge of the military. After several days of massive public protests against the administration of Morsi, on July 3, 2013, the military quickly ousted Morsi's government, suspended the constitution that was enacted during his tenure as president, and appointed an interim leader.

After Morsi, President el-Sisi initiated a massive assault on the Muslim Brotherhood and constructed a road map that effectively prevented the movement from participating in future constitutional and electoral procedures. This was done in response to Morsi. Tens of thousands of people, including supporters of the Muslim Brotherhood as well as other people, were arrested. The Muslim Brotherhood was not only declared illegal, but also a terrorist organization (even though Egyptian officials have yet to prove that the Brotherhood, as opposed to more extreme Islamist groups, is involved in terrorist operations), and the Brotherhood's supporters were declared illegal as well. Throughout the reign of Mubarak, the majority of US support and effort were directed toward the security partnership. Many reform programs (economic, judicial, and decentralization) that were agreed upon with the government received secondary attention. It was likely that the new Egyptian government, particularly el-Sisi's military, would be eager to return to that paradigm (Dunne, 2014).

3.5.2 MILITARY INTERVENTION IN LIBYA

Due to the fact that the Government of National Accord (GNA) in Libya does not have the power to maintain a monopoly on violence, there are still parts of the nation that are functionally lawless as a consequence of the country's current instability. Terrorists and other criminal elements now have an easier time traveling between Libya, Niger, Chad, and Algeria because these regions have made it simpler for them to do so. According to Thomas D. Waldhauser, the senior general for Africa at the Pentagon, the instability that has been plaguing Libya and the rest of North Africa may pose the most significant near-term threat to the interests of the US and its allies on the continent (Becker & Schmitt, 2018).

After the events of the Arab Spring, Libya was left in a state that was very near to complete chaos. Over the course of history, the country has evolved into three primary factions operating under the umbrella of the Libyan Unity Government, in addition to several other minor interests. These three primary factions eventually came together to form the Unity Government as a direct result of the Libyan Political Accord (LPA), which was brokered by the UN. The Presidential Council (PC), the first internal group of the Unity Government, was established to reign over Libya as the country's head of state. This was the primary motivation behind the formation of this body. Prime Minister Fayez al-Sarraj served as the presiding officer of the PC, which has a total of nine members. Abdessalam Kajan was an advocate for the Muslim Brotherhood in his capacity as a deputy in the PC.

Although the US officially backs the GNA, this affiliation with the Muslim Brotherhood created the possibility of problems with President Donald Trump. On his personal Twitter account, Trump regularly denounced the US ties with the Muslim Brotherhood. Since one of the two major militias is located in Misrata and backs the PC, the PC can claim a high degree of legitimacy. The operational headquarters of the council is in the city of Tripoli, which is located on the western coast.

The State Council is the second significant group. The Government of National Salvation, a competitor of the GNA, provides the State Council with its members. By creating a Libyan consultative committee that will help the House of Representatives (HOR) in making some appointments and decisions, the LPA aimed to include the opposing Government of National Salvation in the Unity Government. The temporary legislature known as the General National Congress (GNC), which was formed in 2012, served as the source of authority for the Government of National Salvation. The Government of National Salvation had no substantial assets following the movement of the bulk of GNC members into the State Council.

The third of the main groupings is known as the House of Representatives (HOR), and General Khalifa Haftar serves as its current head. General Haftar, who serves in a capacity analogous to that of a military dictator over the Tobruk and Bayda authority, did not hide his anti-Islamist viewpoint and worked to ensure that it is followed (Fitzgerald & Ugolini,

2015). In the current day and age, Haftar has the support of both Russia and Egypt, which is in line with the rhetoric that both countries have used against the Muslim Brotherhood (Becker & Schmitt, 2018). General Haftar is the leader of the Libyan National Army (LNA), a sizable military force in Libya that has enabled the HOR to thwart incorporation into the Unity Government. The House of Representatives will serve as the legislative branch of the GNA in accordance with the Libyan Political Agreement with the UN (Fitzgerald & Ugolini, 2015). Rather than fully complying with a protocol to become branches of the Unity Government, these parties' disagreement has been the source of the majority of the issues that Libya has been experiencing in maintaining its stability. Islamic State of Iraq and Syria (ISIS) and other terrorist organizations were able to flourish as a result of the division because it allowed for the spread of anarchy in areas that were contested by rival governments or in which those governments had abandoned to concentrate their forces in areas considered to be of greater strategic significance in their conflict with one another (Becker & Schmitt, 2018). General Haftar's reputation in Moscow has increased substantially as a direct result of the ferocity with which he has pursued the fight against ISIS. In recognition of all that he had accomplished, the Kremlin extended an invitation to him in January 2017 to tour one of their aircraft carriers. During this visit, the Kremlin sealed a $2 billion weaponry contract with Haftar's LNA. This occurred despite the continued sanctions imposed by the UN (Patil, 2017).

Russia has been allowed to expand its influence in the absence of US competition for international influence as a result of President Trump's erratic foreign policy, which alternates between a declared intention to completely withdraw from Libya and a declared determination to completely defeat ISIS. President Trump's predisposition to avoid engaging with the Muslim Brotherhood may be reflected in the fact that he won't participate in lengthy negotiations on the side of the GNA rather than the HOR. The desire of President Trump to work with Russia in the fight against ISIS has been made clear on multiple occasions by his administration. On November 11, 2017, Presidents Trump and Putin published a joint statement describing their shared efforts to battle ISIS in Syria. A civil conflict and areas of governmental vacuum allowed ISIS to flourish in Syria, just like they did in Libya. This issue was discussed in the joint statement (Joint Statement, 2017).

The fact that Russia openly backs Haftar and that Trump signaled his willingness to work with Russia to defeat ISIS raises questions for the GNA and those who provide funding for it at the UN. In addition, Egypt is transparently backing General Haftar in this conflict as reports indicate that Egypt sees General Haftar's dominance of the eastern half of Libya as being extremely beneficial to its own national security. Cairo is willing to support Haftar in his quest to strengthen his power since they view his sphere of influence as a barrier to the rise of ISIS. Egypt has substantially improved the LNA's access to arms, and a vast number of officials from the Tobruk government have traveled to Cairo on official errands (Fitzgerald & Ugolini, 2015). Because Egypt is prepared to provide Haftar with military support, the US has been placed in a precarious position. Given that Egypt is the second-largest beneficiary of foreign aid from the US, with $1.3 billion of that funding specifically intended for "Peace and Security," the commitment of the US to support the GNA is called into question. Despite the fact that the US formally supports the GNA, President Trump undermined efforts to bring the Libyan government together as a single unit by working with Russia on other similar programs in other nations and giving Russia room to act in Libya. These actions are taking place despite the fact that the US formally supports the GNA.

3.5.3   SYRIAN CIVIL WAR

Since the beginning of his administration, President Obama had shown reluctance to use force, except for instances in which the national security of the US was directly threatened. Even in these challenging circumstances, he consistently placed a greater emphasis on a drawn-down plan rather than an escalation (Gerstein & Epstein, 2011). Syria is a good illustration of this. Despite pressure from Republican legislators and a slaughter in Syria, President Obama chose to ignore calls for urgent participation in the conflict. Despite having pledged not to put US forces in harm's way unless it was absolutely necessary to protect American primary interests, the Obama administration did not believe that Syria, a small and impoverished country, posed a threat to the primary interests of the US. Instead, President Obama limited the US involvement in Syria to providing the opposition with political and financial support while simultaneously engaging in economic warfare against the Assad government.

In his testimony before the Senate Armed Services Committee in February, the chairman of the Joint Chiefs of Staff, General Martin E. Dempsey, stated that the Pentagon, including Secretary of Defense Leon E. Panetta, supported a proposal to supply Syrian rebels (Stewart & Zengerle, 2013). According to *The New York Times*, the plan was developed in 2012 by David H. Petraeus, who was the director of the CIA at the time, and was supported at the time by Hillary Clinton, who was the secretary of state at the time. The plan called for screening rebels and training fighters who would be given weapons (Gordon & Lander, 2013).

Despite the fact that the Obama administration was adamant that Bashar al-Assad must vacate his position as president, it did not express a desire to take military action because of the risk of regional and global escalation. A repetition of the circumstances in Iraq and Libya, as well as the growing prominence of hardline jihadist organizations like the Al-Nusra Front, are additional causes for concern for the administration. In a press conference that took place in November of 2012, President Obama stated:

> We have witnessed the infiltration of radical forces into the opposition. You know, one of the things that we need to make sure of—particularly when we start talking about arming opposition figures—is that we are not inadvertently putting weapons into the hands of people who would otherwise engage in activities that are detrimental to the safety and well-being of the American people. This is one of the things that we need to be on the lookout for (Dreyfuss, 2012).

Concerns were raised by terrorist organizations like the Al-Nusra Front and al-Qaeda in Iraq's involvement with rebels, and the US was "deeply concerned" about Assad's stockpiles of chemical weapons, as John Kerry reaffirmed after being confirmed as Secretary of State by the Senate. Close aides to President Obama had the belief that big military successes by the opposition would force Assad to quit without the need for direct military action by the West. In addition, they believed that Moscow would shift its attitude in Syria and increase the amount of pressure that was being applied on Assad to accept the inevitability of the situation. Neither tactic turned out to be successful. As a direct consequence of this, there was a stalemate on all fronts (political, diplomatic, and military). According to reports, the Obama administration was in the process of reevaluating its policy regarding Syria. As part of this process, the administration was reportedly considering direct engagement with the armed opposition, sending humanitarian aid directly to the political coalition of the opposition, and providing equipment such as body armor and armored vehicles in addition to possibly providing military training. This assessment indicates a new direction for the administration of President Obama in terms of the policy.

The lessons that President Obama gained from his experience in Iraq are the most cogent justifications presented for his reluctance to have a direct role in the situation in Syria (Schulenburg, 2019). It is not in the best interest of the US to become militarily involved in distant regions, particularly the Middle East, unless it can be demonstrated that its long-term strategic interests are in jeopardy and that there is a general consensus in the international community that can be formulated into a resolution by the UNSC. Obama made it a point to repeatedly stress the significance of the social and economic problems facing the US, as well as the fact that, in contrast to his predecessor, he put more of an emphasis on nation-building at home rather than on military operations and nation-building abroad.

In light of the Arab Spring of 2011, President Obama needed to reevaluate his participation in the region. In a speech given in May 2011, in which he outlined his strategy for responding to the Arab uprisings, Obama tried to refocus American foreign policy in this region. In that speech, he stated that the US had an interest not just in the stability of states but also in "the self-determination of individuals" (Obama, 2011). Obama announced what amounted to a new American strategy for the Arab world, promising to support democratic transitions, while also promoting significant political and economic transformation across the region. He emphasized the following; "Today I am making clear that it is a major priority and must be converted into tangible measures, supported by all of the diplomatic, economic, and strategic means at our disposal. Our support for these ideals is not a secondary interest" (Obama, 2011).

The inconsistent American support for change in various Arab countries, in particular its inability to assist the Palestinians or the ambitions of the people of Bahrain, is one of the primary reasons why Arabs do not trust the US. Whatever governments emerge from the rubble of political authoritarianism in the Arab world, those governments will have powerful foreign policies that support Palestinian rights and challenge Israel's hegemony. Recent uprisings in Arab countries are an example of how events in the Middle East can take on a life of their own and alter the direction that American administrations want to take their foreign policy. In this respect, Obama was not an anomaly but rather the norm. The upheavals in Arab countries convinced him to redirect his focus once again toward the Middle East, even though this was not his original aim. Obama was taking huge risks because he did not have a clear strategy for dealing with the disruption caused by the revolution and because he had limited capacity to affect the events that were going place there.

One of the questions that arose after the Arab Spring was whether or not it altered the regional and global order. The answer is "yes," but how? It is not yet entirely obvious. There is little question that the power dynamics in the Middle East region have undergone significant shifts. It is impossible to deny that the Arab Spring countries have undergone not only regime transitions but also a social and political revolution. From a theoretical standpoint, liberals highlight the positive effects of the Arab world's liberalization processes on rising prospects for cooperation both within the Middle East and between the democratizing region and demo-cratic powers. This is based on the pacifying and cooperative effects of liberal mechanisms such as "democratic peace," international institutions, and rising economic interdependence with the West and within the region. Liberals also emphasize the positive effects of the liberalization processes on rising prospects for cooperation between the democratizing region and democratic powers. The influence of domestic events on international policy and the results of those policies is, in the view of realists, overrated.

Also, its position in the global liberal peace project was dependent on international agreement, which was rapidly dissipating—just as it had done during the invasion of Iraq by the US in 2003—as regional actors sought to fill the void and steer this regional transition. Moreover, the US had a position in the global liberal peace project. The countries of Libya, Yemen, and Syria, in particular, have been hit hard by humanitarian crises, large-scale challenges with population relocation, and high-profile diplo-matic blunders. In each of these places, the UN came under increasing suspicion of being involved in some kind of conspiracy. In the case of Libya, for instance, Jeff Bachman (2017) represented a large number of anti-NATO interventionists when he held the UN accountable for legiti-mizing NATO's possible "crime of aggression" and violations of interna-tional humanitarian law through its regime change agenda. According to him, this agenda resulted in more harm than good for the Libyan civilian population (Bachman, 2017).

As a final point, it has been mentioned that the terrorist attacks on the US on September 11 sparked an unprecedented globalization of the discussion on democracy and political change in the Arab world. The Bush administration asserted that the attacks started in the Arab world and saw them as the product of a widespread authoritarian culture that promoted terrorism and extremism. At the time, it was abundantly evident that the US did not really pursue a democracy promotion agenda in the Arab countries. In addition, one could argue that the US' support for authoritarian Arab governments, along with those governments' apparent submission to the demands of the US and Israel's regional hegemony, was one of the primary factors that contributed to the dissatisfaction of the Arab masses with their governing elites. Nonetheless, despite the fact that Obama was awarded the Nobel Peace Prize, the position of the US in the liberal international order has been eroded to a greater extent than it was before the Arab Spring. In a peculiar turn of events, officials of defunct pro-American governments in Egypt and Yemen have volunteered to take on these responsibilities. Those who played significant roles in previous autocratic regimes are now spearheading the development and administration of democratic policies for the first time. In the case of Libya, a comprehensive reorganization took place, during which revolutionary forces were marginalized and a new pro-American administration was established. This administration succeeded the insubordinate and very unpredictable dictatorship of Gaddafi. With covert military intervention, the US was able to put an end to the revolutionary developments that were taking place in Bahrain. In light of this, it is of the utmost importance to keep in mind that these strategies did not address the major concerns that were the root causes of the revolutionary turmoil that occurred throughout the Arab world. Instead, they made them longer and opened new doors, which could lead to other revolutions across the Arab world. The US' unwavering support for Israeli activities in the region is one of these issues, and it is perhaps the most obvious one. The continuation of neoliberal economic policies, which have increased the gap between the wealthy and the poor to an unprecedented degree in recent Arab history, is another one of these issues. These steps will unquestionably result in an increase in anti-American sentiment throughout the area.

CHAPTER 4

Death of the Liberal World Order

4.1 POST-SECOND WORLD WAR ORDER IN CRISIS

The US was crucial in establishing the post-Second World War liberal international order. According to Henry Kissinger, no country other than the US would have had the idealistic spirit, resources, or ability to successfully tackle a wide variety of difficulties. The development of a new international order was fueled by the idealism and exceptionalism of the US (Kissinger, 2014, p. 371). This American liberal hegemonic system expanded after the Cold War and appeared to provide the entire world with a unifying rationale for international politics. Particularly over the past three decades, the liberal part of the international order has frequently meant promoting a particular type of global economy, including free markets, unregulated forms of capitalism, and the reduction of governmental intervention in the domestic economy. However, in recent years arguments have arisen that the liberal international order, which cannot be separated from the formation of American hegemony (Pax Americana), has entered a severe crisis leading to the belief that the unipolar moment has come to an end. Some analysts contend that the current crisis in the liberal international order is a reflection of a major shift in world politics.

In addition, critics point out that the mythology of American hegemonic power has always had a significant amount of fiction mixed in with reality. According to Nye (2017, p. 17), the liberal order should be viewed as a restricted international order rather than an all-inclusive global system as it was far from benign for many developing countries. From the view of some analysts, it was never truly a global order, more of a coalition of like-minded nations concentrated mostly in the Americas and Western Europe,

The Rise and Fall of the Eagle: An Assessment of the Liberal World Order.
Çağatay Özdemir (Author)
© 2024 Apple Academic Press, Inc. Co-published with CRC Press (Taylor & Francis)

which wasn't always beneficial to those who weren't members (Nye, 2015, p. 398). Kissinger (2014, p. 2) claims that there has never been a universal world order. The American international order only encompassed less than half of the world's population since the major nations—China, India, Indonesia, and the Soviet Union—were not participants. The US was not a hegemon in terms of the balance of world military power (Nye, 2015, p. 398). The liberal institutions, laws, and practices that were developed by American leadership in economics, but for just half of the world, ruled the global economy. Hence, Nye (2015) suggests the concept of a "half-hegemon" as a more appropriate term to use.

In this regard, recently more than ever, it has been questioned whether the order is desirable and sustainable. There are various arguments regarding the interrogation of the liberal international order. For years, academics who believed that international cooperation was bound to fail have now come back with different arguments. According to some scholars, the liberal order's propensity to put international institutions ahead of national interests and its strong belief in porous, if not open borders have had negative political repercussions among the prominent liberal states themselves, especially the US unipolarity (Mearsheimer, 2019, p. 8). When one considers how the Cold War ended 30 years ago, the current liberal crisis is all the more unexpected. There was a consensus at the time that liberalism was the dominant ideology in the US. It was on the march, and nationalism was seen as a defeated force. This invention was predicted to have a profound impact on all nations in the world. However, that prediction clearly failed, not only in the US but in other liberal democracies as well (Mearsheimer, 2020).

Accordingly, in recent years, different explanations in the literature arose regarding the crisis of the liberal international order. Mearsheimer claims that those liberal policies "clash with nationalism over key issues such as sovereignty and national identity. Because nationalism is the most powerful political ideology on the planet, it invariably trumps liberalism whenever the two clash, thus undermining the order at its core" (2019, p. 8). Furthermore, the liberal world experienced employment losses, wage declines, and a rise in income inequality as a result of hyper-globalization, which aimed to reduce obstacles to international commerce and investment. In this regard, it damaged the stability of the global financial system, resulting in ongoing financial crises. Then, as a result of these issues evolving into political issues, support for the liberal system continued to decline (Mearsheimer, 2019, p. 8). Another manner that a hyper-globalized economy threatens the system is by fostering the rise of nations other than the hegemon, which has the potential to erode unipolarity and collapse the liberal order. As it is stated by Mearsheimer (2019, p. 8), this is what the growth of China is bringing about, together with the resurgence of Russian dominance, which has marked the end of the unipolar period. In this regard, liberal hegemony is considered as being in serious jeopardy today that cannot be fixed. Ultimately, it bears the seeds of its own demise. That decree is doomed for yet another reason: It seems conceivable that the rising of China and the resurgence of Russian strength will result in a realist international order (Mearsheimer, 2019, p. 7). Similarly, Christopher Layne (1993) also argues that unipolarity was solely an illusion. Power balance, or the propensity for states to unite in opposition to a hegemon, is both normal and unavoidable; it may even be considered a rule of international politics.

According to Ikenberry (2009), who has significantly contributed to the dissemination of the concept of the liberal international order as a more comprehensive notion, the crisis of the current liberal system is related to the authority problem. New standards for national security and human rights are placed in the international community, but who has the authority to act on its behalf has become important (Ikenberry, 2009, p. 80). In the Cold War period, American leadership of the liberal international order was rendered tolerable for other nations because it offered safeguards when there were communist dangers on the horizon. American authority is now less firmly entrenched, and the post-war international order's hierarchical, American-centered nature is a bigger concern. In this regard, as stated by Ikenberry, the greatest issue facing the liberal international order is how to create legitimate authority for concerted international action on behalf of the global community while doing it at a time when the established norms of the order are crumbling (2009, p. 80).

Ikenberry (2020, p. 269) considers the crisis of liberal international order as a slow-motion response to the post-war Western order's globalization. As the liberal system became more globalized, the qualities that made it steadfast and robust throughout the Cold War—and hence appealing to governments in transition after the Cold War—were weakened. For Stokes (2018, p. 135), these aspects of the global system have produced new winners and losers as well as the growing economic gap in the West eroding support for the US' hegemonic position. The largest challenge to the liberal international order is this simultaneous crisis of weakness in Western strategic agency and in the social contract, not least because the US still benefits greatly from the arrangement it helped construct. Elites in the US may prefer to return to the status quo ante but given that globalization frequently harms American living standards, the West, which is closely related to American leadership, will continue to experience systemic shocks (Stokes, 2018, p. 135).

Something has obviously gone wrong with the liberal order, not just in the US, but in other liberal democracies. The crisis experienced by the liberal international order also exists in Europe. The lengthy post-war goal of creating a stronger union simultaneously seems to be coming to an end in light of Britain's choice to exit the EU and a plethora of other issues plaguing Europe. The uncertainties in Europe, which serves as the lone bastion of the larger liberal international system, are significant on a global scale. Moreover, populist, nationalist, and xenophobic strands of backlash politics have spread throughout the liberal democratic globe while liberal democracy itself looks to be in decline (Ikenberry, 2018a, p.7).

In this respect, as stated by Mearsheimer (2017, p. 352), liberal hegemony is ineffective. It was attempted for a long time, but the result was a legacy of pointless conflicts, bad diplomacy, and decreased reputation. In addition, liberal hegemony comes at a high cost to the American people, both financially and in terms of life. Mearsheimer claims that the harm it does to the American political and social fabric may be the biggest cost of liberal hegemony. In a nation devoted to waging wars, individual liberties and the rule of law will not survive (Mearsheimer, 2017, p. 352).

In addition, Ikenberry states that what we are seeing may be a "crisis of transition," in which the old US-led political basis of the liberal order will give way to a new arrangement of global power, new alliances of nations, and new institutions of governance (2018a, p. 8). This change may be bringing about a post-American and post-Western system that is still mostly open and governed by norms. Some other scholars perceive a more serious issue. According to this perspective, the global system is moving away from free commerce, multilateralism, and cooperative security in the long run. Several combinations of nationalism, protectionism, areas of influence, and regional Great Power projects are replacing the global system. In essence, liberal internationalism cannot exist without American and Western hegemony, and that era is coming to an end (Ikenberry, 2018a, p. 8). By going even further than this, some scholars like Mishra (2017) argue that the lengthy period of "liberal modernity" is coming to an end. The growth of the West and the Industrial Revolution looked to follow a fundamental developmental logic as the world's history changed from the Enlightenment onward. Reason, science, discovery, innovation, technology, education, constitutionalism, and institutional flexibility propelled this progressive movement. This widespread modernization has driven the entire planet in its grip. Perhaps the current crisis signals the end of liberal modernity's global course. It was a relic from a certain era and location, but times have changed since then (Ikenberry, 2018a, p. 8).

In this regard, this post-Second World War liberal hegemonic order's underpinnings are eroding. In a basic sense, this is the tale of significant changes in the balance of power and their effects. When the US and its allies created the post-war system, they were stronger than today. The era of unipolarity, during which the US dominated global economic and military rankings, is coming to an end. Japan and Europe have also suffered. Hence, this traditional trio that supported the post-war liberal system as a whole is gradually losing influence in the larger global power structure (Ikenberry, 2018a, p. 17). The effects of these shifts in global dominance are amplified by the political issues facing Western liberal democracies. As mentioned above, internal problems and discontent are present in all democracies. The more established Western democracies are dealing with growing political division and stalemate, economic stagnation, rising inequality, and budgetary crises. The massive third wave of democratization appears to have peaked and is already subsiding. Democracies' domestic credibility is eroded when they fail to solve issues and is further threatened by rising nationalist, populist, and xenophobic forces. Combined, these events put a bleak pall over the future of democracy (Ikenberry, 2018a, p. 17).

Accordingly, liberal internationalism's underlying principles have changed. The system is no longer based on parity or balance between the major nations. The traditional agreements and institutions are no longer tenable due to the unipolar distribution of power and the emergence of new players in the global system. More successfully than anybody in the 1940s actually imagined possible, and virtually overlooked during the Cold War, a liberal international order was established. Yet, challenges regarding the functioning of that liberal international order have been caused by different variables including the deterioration of the previous standards of sovereignty, the growth of international human rights norms, and the emergence of new types of threats of collective aggression (Ikenberry, 2009, p. 80).

Leading liberal governments have supported the idea of a liberal international order at different points throughout the past 200 years. It is a conception of order that has been more properly implemented in some periods than in others, and its logic has been more strongly represented in some parts of the world than others. The liberal order's building agenda has likewise developed and altered. The goals of today are still different from those of Woodrow Wilson and Harry Truman (Ikenberry, 2011, pp. 493–494). The development of law and structured collaboration in the modern age has been supported by a Westphalian system of balanced power and sovereign nations.

As it is stated by Ikenberry (2011, p. 495), liberal internationalism faces challenges as a result of the system's deteriorating balance-of-power foundations in recent years. The underpinnings of liberal order are brought into question. The post-war liberal international order produced laws and institutions that boosted nations' capabilities, which helped international law and institutions grow in the West and beyond. This statist desire for capacity-enhancing laws and institutions, however, is lost in situations where state sovereignty is being undermined and where states are deeply ingrained in larger international networks. This underpinning political support for rule-based order is not considered when the liberal internationalist agenda turns to the administration of post-Westphalian international relations. These destabilizing risks have come to light as a result of the 2008 global financial crisis and economic depression, which has also highlighted the ongoing conflicts between international openness and national stability. The neoliberal international market system has replaced the social contract that served as the cornerstone of liberal hegemonic arrangements with one that is more free-wheeling. Given these more contemporary circumstances, the liberal order—or at least its market-based components—seems to undermine rather than strengthen the capacity of the state to fulfill its domestic social and political obligations (Ikenberry, 2011, pp. 497-498).

The margin of advantage of the liberal coalition of nations, which continues to support the liberal system, has significantly shrunk. According to Lind and Wohlforth (2019, p. 74), in 1995, the US and its main allies generated around 60 percent of the world's production (measured in terms of purchasing power parity); in recent years, that percentage is now 40 percent. At the time, they oversaw 80 percent of the world's defense spending; yet recently, they only make up 52 percent. Maintaining the order, let alone extending it, is getting harder. As everything is going on, the order is experiencing an internal crisis of legitimacy that is already posing a problem as war-weary Americans, Euroskeptic British, and other Westerners have turned out to vote to denounce so-called globalist elites (Lind & Wohlforth, 2019, p. 74).

In the liberal hegemonic system, major powers maintain order through a balance of power and the restraints of state sovereignty. However, this Westphalian structure has been changed in the decades after the end of the bipolar world under conditions of unipolarity and crumbling standards of state sovereignty. The rationale and rules of the American-led international order have changed as a result of these new conditions. These changes have made it more challenging for the US to lead a liberal hegemonic order, as well as for other states to comply with and support it (Ikenberry, 2011, p. 394).

The problem of American liberal hegemony has been strengthened by other changes in the global system. The fear of great-power war in the post-Cold War order has given way to increasingly dispersed and decentralized threats from unstable parts of the world. In addition, the 2008 financial crisis and global economic recession have exposed the changing nature of global economic interdependence and America's role as the world's economic leader. Emerging powers from the developing world are now increasingly engaged in the global economy and want a bigger say in how it is governed. Hence, this unipolar liberal international order proved unworkable and met with controversy and resistance both domestically and overseas (Ikenberry, 2011, pp. 394–395).

Similar to Ikenberry, Lind and Wohlforth (2019) also state that the liberal order of things is in jeopardy. This international network of alliances, institutions, and standards is now under more threat than ever, years after the US contributing to its founding. Due to the awry foundational principles that the post-Cold War liberal international order was built upon, it was destined to fail. According to Mearsheimer, (2019, p. 7) promoting liberal democracy, which is crucial for creating such an order, is not only incredibly difficult but also destabilizes ties with other nations and occasionally sparks devastating conflicts. The major impediment to the advancement of democracy in the target state is nationalism, although the balance of power politics also plays a significant role as a deterrent. Hence, the order is battling nationalism and populism from within. The liberal international order has faltered in the past 10 years as a result of financial crises and populist uprisings (Altun, 2021, p. 17). On the outside, it is under increasing pressure from a brazen Russia and a developing China. Not just the order itself, but also the unheard-of economic success and tranquility it has fostered are in jeopardy (Lind & Wohlforth, 2019, p. 70).

Niblett (2017) also makes an inward-looking analysis regarding the crisis of the liberal international order. He states that the biggest threat is coming from within the liberal international system and the dominant nations of the system are dealing with persistent domestic political and economic unrest (Niblett, 2017, p. 18). The attraction of globalization has been diminished by more than 25 years of stagnating median salaries in the US and several regions of Europe. Although countries have been more open to foreign commerce, investment, and immigration, this has not resulted in significant local advantages for most of society. People's trust in governments has been broken by inadequate financial regulation that led to the 2008 financial crisis and the bank bailouts that followed it. The Great Recession also made them less supportive of free capital markets, which appeared to benefit mainly a small global elite (Niblett, 2017, p. 18).

The liberal international order has thrived for more than seven decades because of the protection that the US has supplied. Yet as compared to any time since the Second World War, the US has become more parochial (Niblett, 2017, p. 20). For a long time to come, the US is expected to maintain its position as the top military force. However, as seen by the US invasion of Iraq in 2003, a greater military might not always convert into geopolitical dominance, which is a crucial condition for unipolar stability (Acharya, 2018, p. 64). Although some of the anti-Americanism brought on by the unilateralism of the George W. Bush administration was reversed by the election of Barack Obama in 2009 and his foreign policy, Obama did not substantially extend US influence abroad (Weber & Jentleson, 2010, pp. 377–378). In the period of the 2008 presidential campaign, Barack Obama stressed ending the US engagement in the Afghanistan and Iraq wars, avoiding getting the country involved in new conflicts, and focusing on nation-building domestically rather than overseas. However, he was unable to significantly alter the course of American foreign policy (Mearsheimer, 2018, p. 347). At the time he departed office, American forces were still engaged in combat in Afghanistan, and he supervised

American involvement in the overthrow of governments in Egypt, Libya, and Syria. He evacuated American troops from Iraq in 2011, but in 2014 he brought them back to fight ISIS, which had taken over huge portions of both Iraq and Syria (Mearsheimer, 2018, p. 348). While the Obama administration renewed aspirations for the American-led liberal order to maintain its supremacy, some analysts indicated in 2013 that China will surpass the US as the world's biggest economy.

In this respect, the main pillars of the US-led liberal order were weakened in the post-Cold War era. With new goals and ambitions, more and more states of varying backgrounds joined the order. Together with these hitherto unrecognized and intricate global problems, the post-Cold War era also saw the rise of populism, the fall of transatlantic relations, the inefficiency of international organizations, the COVID-19 outbreak, the Russia-Ukraine conflict, and an increase in cyber terrorism. These are particularly challenging topics for the foundations of the liberal international order and governments from widely different areas, with correspondingly diverse political philosophies and degrees of development, to come to a consensus on. As a result, multilateral collaboration has faced more difficulties. The issue of governance and authority has been at the heart of these difficulties. How to rearrange the governance of this order is a challenge that is contributing to the current crisis of liberal order. In this regard, the fall of the liberal order is a significant threat to the stability and prosperity of the world. Old foundations have been undermined, but negotiations for new agreements and governance structures have not yet been completed (Ikenberry, 2018a, p. 19). The US has been the driving force behind the creation and maintenance of this order since the end of the Second World War. However, the foreign policy choices of the US to deal with what the world experienced in recent years have shown the erosion of American supremacy and exposed the weaknesses of the US-led liberal order. Hence, the decline of US hegemony is closely tied to the decline of the liberal order and the crisis in the liberal order has led to a quest for a new world order.

4.2   QUEST FOR A NEW WORLD ORDER

Unprecedented challenges from a variety of sources have resulted in the erosion of the liberal order and the quest for a new world order as countries and institutions seek to find a new system that can address the challenges of the 21st century. The pursuit of a new world order is manifesting itself in diverse ways, ranging from the creation of new organizations and accords to the forging of novel coalitions and associations. Certain nations are advocating their distinct perspectives on worldwide governance, whereas others are endeavoring to reform established organizations such as the UN and the WTO.

When the subjects of the American decline and the quest for new world order are considered, even analysts with different ideological points of view agree that the decline of the US power may not be beneficial for the future of international order in general or in particular domains like development, governance, and international justice. According to the general agreement, the decline of American supremacy will lead to increased international instability (Acharya, 2018, p. 98). Liberals argue that international cooperation and conflict management will decrease due to the decline of the US power. Realists argue that conflict may occur when failing states frequently become the objects of opportunistic attack by other powers and coalitions or turn hostile themselves. Hence, both realists and liberals believe the decline of the US power will bring danger, confusion, and collapse (Acharya, 2018, p. 98). According to Kraut-hammer (1990/1991, p. 27), the effects of losing US leadership would include "insecure sea lanes, impoverished trading partners, exorbitant oil prices, explosive regional instability." Although Layne (1993, p. 51), a realist scholar, is suspicious of unipolarity, he also worries that the eventual demise of the US would lead to "the resurgence of traditional patterns of great power competition."

In this regard, the liberal hegemonic system, led by the US, is at a standstill. There is a legitimacy problem inside the liberal international order. Within the liberal international system at large, there is disagreement on the nature of hierarchy and rule. The US position in the world system is under attack. The hegemonic character of the liberal international order is up for debate. On the other side of this crisis, it is expected that some form of liberal international order will manifest (Ikenberry, 2011, pp. 487–488). As a result, a more decentralized and shared structure of power and control will likely replace American hegemony within the order.

The complexity of contemporary international politics necessitates a deeper examination of the US-led liberal international order. Today, liberalism is perceived as demanding and expecting "the rest" to adhere to values it asserts that were exclusively formed in the West—although the most advanced liberal Western states flagrantly disregard them. Hence, it will be even more difficult to promote liberalism to the rest of the world with it now under opposition at home (Acharya, 2017, p. 283).

As it is stated by Nye (2017, p. 12), some critics suggest that Washington would be better off handling its relations with other countries that it "wins" rather than "loses" on each transaction or commitment since the costs of upholding the order exceed its advantages. Others contend that the underpinnings of the order are crumbling as a result of a long-term shift in global power brought on by the sharp ascent of Asian countries like China and India. Others believe it is challenged by a wider transfer of power from states to nonstate actors as a result of continuous developments in politics, society, and technology. In a nutshell, the order is dealing with its most difficult issues in decades (Nye, 2017, p. 12).

On the other hand, some analysts are more optimistic about the liberal order's future. For instance, the editors of International Organization argued in their anniversary issue that "rumors about the loss of the liberal international order have been grossly exaggerated" (Lake et al., 2021, p. 225). In addition, Ikenberry (2018a, p. 8) claims that liberal internationalism still has a future despite its problems. Although the American hegemonic liberal order is waning, liberal internationalism's more overarching structuring principles and impulses continue to have a significant influence on global politics.

In this respect, "What follows the liberal hegemonic order?" has become a significant question in recent years. Accordingly, Ikenberry claims that the old liberal order is unlikely to disintegrate or vanish in the absence of war or economic catastrophe (2011, p. 563). The liberal international order will change, as in the past. With changes in how governments distribute and use their power and authority, the nature of governance will alter. Leading and emerging nations in the system are not attempting to undermine the fundamental rationale of liberal internationalism as a system of open and rule-based order, precisely because the crisis of liberal order is a crisis of success. Instead, the system's allocation of tasks and duties is where the pressures and incentives for change are felt (Ikenberry, 2011, p. 563).

Ikenberry (2018a, p. 23) states that when alternative orders are considered, the sources of continuity in the liberal post-war international system become apparent. Several types of closed systems—a world of blocs, spheres, and protectionist zones—are the alternatives to the liberal order.

The fact that more people will suffer than benefit from the collapse of some kind of liberal international order on a global scale is arguably the best news for liberal internationalism. This does not imply that it will last, but it implies that there are supporters, even in the traditional industrial civilizations of the West. Despite this, a liberal international system has simply no significant ideological rival. The rest of the world does not find China's or Russia's model attractive. These nations are capitalist autocracies. Yet, this kind of condition does not convert into a substantial array of different concepts for the structure of the global order (Ikenberry 2018a, p. 23).

The question of whether the liberal international order will be replaced by a post-liberal order and the role that the decline in US hegemony will play in this regard has been intensely debated in recent years, especially in the academic circles and media of Western countries. There are increasing pressures and incentives for reform and restructuring since liberal internationalism is in crisis. The liberal global project is continuing to develop, as in the past. A new order is taking the place of the previous American-led liberal hegemonic system. Yet, what the new liberal internationalism will be like has become a significant question (Ikenberry, 2009, p. 80).

Accordingly, Ikenberry suggests that three possibilities exist for departing from liberal internationalism. Each route entails a unique arrangement of sovereignty, laws, institutions, and authority (Ikenberry, 2009, p. 81). In the first possibility, the US would have less authority over the laws and institutions. The US would continue to perform distinctive system roles for the wider order while simultaneously transitioning to work within more comprehensive and concerted great power institutions. The authority would shift in this post-American liberal order toward universal institutions, or at the very least, toward international organizations with a more diverse global membership. Post-hegemonic liberal internationalism would have a different hierarchical structure. Though typically flatter, a hierarchy would still exist; it just wouldn't be an American-dominated hierarchy (Ikenberry, 2011, pp. 521–522). America's unique privileges and rights would diminish as other nations grew in importance and power at the top table of international politics. The US and Europe would see their voting shares decline while nations like China and India would see their voting shares increase in the governance of these international institutions. In addition, liberal internationalism's hierarchical structure would evolve. In general, it would be flatter, but hierarchy will still exist;

it would just not be an American-dominated system. The increased group of powerful nations that would hold leadership roles in the UNSC and other less formal international organizations would make up the hierarchy of a post-hegemonic liberal order. These states would together offer the numerous functional services that the US historically supplied (Ikenberry, 2009, pp. 80–81). These nations would jointly assume responsibility for ensuring security, preserving free markets, and other functional services that were formerly supplied by the US. It would be a global system that has fewer ties to the West or the US (Ikenberry, 2011, pp. 526–527). Liberal internationalism may also follow a different route that is less drastic. In this adaption, the US would renegotiate the agreements and institutions from earlier times while continuing to be the world's dominant power. For Ikenberry (2009, pp. 80–81), the US would continue to offer useful services for the larger system under this reformatted liberal hegemonic order, and in exchange, other nations would accept the hierarchical norms and institutions ruled over by Washington.

There is a second route that liberal internationalism may go that is less radical. It will be based on a shared authority and rule. Under this adaptation, the US would rewrite the agreements and institutions from earlier decades while still maintaining its hegemonic leadership role. In this modified liberal hegemonic order, the US would continue to contribute useful services to the larger system, and in exchange, other nations would accept the hierarchical norms and institutions that Washington ruled over (Ikenberry, 2009, pp. 80–81). The core of this advanced liberal society consists of collective institutions and universal laws. Ikenberry (2011, pp. 527–528) calls this order a "reformed American-led liberal hegemonic order." In this regard, the US would renounce some of its hegemonic advantages and entitlements under this reformatted American-led order, but it would preserve others. The US would concede power and allow for growing nations in the political and economic spheres. Ikenberry likens the Obama administration to a reformed American-led liberal hegemonic order in terms of aiming to renegotiate hegemonic agreements and rebuilding the US influence throughout the international system. The Obama administration recognized the need for reforming international organizations to better meet contemporary issues and give emerging states more influence. Accordingly, in his speech at West Point, President Obama (2010) stated that, "As influence extends to more countries and capitals, we also have to build new partnerships, and shape stronger international standards and institutions." Hence, these statements by the Obama administration imply a willingness to repair and modify the American hegemonic structure. In addition, under all circumstances, the US would consent to further authority and decision-making sharing inside international organizations for security and economics (Ikenberry, 2011, p. 531).

A disintegration of the liberal international order is the third potential outcome that leads to a system with more competing spheres or blocs. This does not only include the transfer of authority and influence away from the US but also the dissolution of international norms and institutions. In this regard, Ikenberry calls this scenario "a breakdown of liberal international order" (2011, p. 532). If the order were to become much less open and rule-based, this would take place. The open, international trading system would disintegrate, ushering in a world of mercantilism, regional blocs, and bilateral pacts similar to that of the 1930s. Liberal internationalism institutions, laws, and framework for security and politics of liberal internationalism might split up into rival geopolitical blocs institutions (Ikenberry, 2009, p. 83). Such a breakdown just indicates that its open, rule-based, multilateral nature has come to an end; it need not result in the total collapse of order. The American hegemonic order might easily give way to an international system in which many powerful nations or centers—such as China, the US, and the EU—create separate economic and security sectors. Regional regimes would develop as relatively distinct, divided, and competing geopolitical domains, while the global order would become a less cohesive and united within its set of laws and institutions. That breakdown need not result in the total collapse of the system (Ikenberry, 2011, p. 533).

On the other hand, Patrick (2020a) makes some predictions regarding the possibilities for the future of the liberal international order, and he provides more optimistic sentiments. For him, the feasibility and desirability of revitalized American internationalism and multilateralism can be possible. The trajectory of history is contingent upon the extent to which the US adopts a policy of constructive internationalism. The sustainability of this approach hinges on a concomitant shift in the national mindset, whereby US citizens are convinced that their country's sovereignty can coexist with internationalism (Patrick, 2020a).

When Acharya's (2018) analysis of the future of the liberal international order is concerned, the maintenance of international order does not necessitate a renewed American hegemony. In this regard, the future of international order doesn't depend on any one or all of the new powers working alone or in unison with the incumbent powers. Hence Acharya expects a different kind of world order that is "complex, decentered, but interdependent" and he calls this new order "a multiplex world" (Acharya, 2018, p. 37). He defines multiplex world order as "a world without a hegemon, culturally and politically diverse yet economically interconnected, where security challenges are increasingly transnational but the power to break and make order is dispersed and fragmented" (Acharya, 2018, p. 37). Multiplication of significant actors including non-state actors (such as terrorist networks), movements, and the public, is another feature of the multiplex world. Hence, a multi-level governance architecture featuring official and informal institutions, networks, and hybrid structures at the global, regional, national, and sub-national (such as city) levels became prominent (Acharya, 2018, p. 37). In this regard, a multiplex world would be a diverse and complex society, with a decentralized type of order management, showcasing ancient and new powers, and with a larger role for regional administration.

In this respect, the quest for a new world order is taking many forms, and it is distinguished by a transition toward multipolar power distribution as emerging powers contest the predominance of established powers such as the US. According to Mahbubani (2020), the world is moving back toward a state that resembles a historic balance between various human cultures in the field of civilizational dynamism. The US-China rivalry will take place in a very different global setting than the Cold War because the world has grown more complex. For the ensuing 10 or 20 years, America and China will continue to engage in global competition (Mahbubani, 2020, pp. 24–25). Hence, the emergence of multipolarity poses a range of prospects and obstacles for the global system. From one perspective, the establishment of a multipolar system has the potential to foster both collaboration and rivalry, thereby facilitating advancements in economic prosperity and governmental steadiness. Conversely, a multipolar system has the potential to result in escalated conflict and instability, as various dominant entities compete for control and access to resources.

In this regard, the American hegemonic order may easily be replaced by an international system in which several major powers—such as China, the US, and the EU—create separate economic and security sectors. As a result, the global order would lose some of its coherence and unity, and regional systems would instead develop into geopolitical domains that are more separate, divided, and competing. According to some experts, when the American-centered unipolar system breaks up, there will be a "return to multipolarity." In this scenario, the existing world order, which was centered on a single dominant power, disintegrates and is replaced by a multifaceted, competitive structure. The system's foundation disappears. The US no longer serves as the center of gravity for the functioning of the larger international order (Ikenberry, 2011, pp. 533–535). According to the National Intelligence Council's survey of global change, "By 2025 the international system will be a global multipolar one … Power will be more dispersed with the newer players bringing new rules of the game while risks will increase that the traditional Western alliances will weaken" (2008, pp. iv-vi). In this regard, a spread of power away from the unipolar state is one step toward multipolarity. Therefore, a system where power is more broadly shared might simply and gradually emerge from the current distribution of power.

Accordingly, for some scholars, rising states, particularly China, India, and other non-Western emerging nations, would appear to have new chances to restructure the international order as a result of the crisis of the American-led system. For the past 10 years, the main question in discussions about the future of the international system has been how emerging powers want to modify or restructure the post-war institutions and regulations (Ikenberry, 2018b, p. 17). In fact, as it is reflected in the US' NSS in 2010, the Obama administration centered its foreign policy on the difficulty of integrating emerging powers: "From Latin America to Africa to the Pacific, new and emerging powers hold out opportunities for partnership, even as a handful of states endanger regional and global security by flouting international norms … New and emerging powers who seek greater voice and representation will need to accept greater responsibility for meeting global challenges" (NSS, 2010, pp. 8–13). In addition, Secretary of State Hillary Clinton in her 2009 speech at the Council on Foreign Relations stated, "In short, we will lead by inducing greater cooperation among a greater number of actors and reducing competition, tilting the balance away from a multi-polar world and toward a multi-partner world" (Clinton, 2009).

In this respect, there is a general consensus in the existing literature that a long-term global power transfer will take place due to the crisis of the liberal international order. Power and wealth are dispersing, moving away from Europe and the US. Although China's swift economic ascent has slowed, and the fast expansion that characterized the non-Western emerging states over the past 10 years may have come to an end, the general trend of development is still in place. Ikenberry (2018b) separates American hegemony from the liberal international order and claims that similar to the US, emerging powers also support many of the same international laws and organizations while opposing the ratification of others. The hegemonic order that rising states must contend with is not a single, cohesive one (Ikenberry, 2018b). An array of alternatives and selections are available under the international order. They may adhere to some laws and institutions but not others. These nations desire Western standards and organizational concepts but may not prefer Western domination of international organizations. Hence, an international system based on laws is something that the developing non-Western nations are likewise interested in preserving and, maybe, expanding (Ikenberry, 2018b).

Defenders of the status quo present the problems of the liberal international order as a conflict between liberal nations attempting to uphold the status quo and disgruntled authoritarians aiming to change it. However, the international order created by and for liberal nations has been radically revisionist, fiercely promoting democracy abroad, and growing in both depth and breadth (Lind & Wohlforth, 2019, p. 70). Accordingly, regarding the future of the international system, Lind and Wohlforth (2019, p. 70–71) suggest making the liberal order more conservative by stating that the US and its allies should consolidate the benefits the order has obtained rather than extending it to new locations and new areas.

In this respect, it's difficult to refute that the US bears a disproportionate portion of the responsibility for global problems. However, American leaders' attempts to transform the globe for the good of all countries fell terribly short in recent years despite their greatest efforts and highest ambitions. As it is argued by Mearsheimer (2018), the US dedication to a grand strategy of "liberal hegemony," an ambitious attempt to utilize American power to transform the globe in accordance with US political beliefs, was the primary cause of these shortcomings. The liberal international order was confirmed as an ambiguous ideal. The plan was unsuccessful on the most fundamental level because it was based on false assumptions about how international politics actually function. It overestimated America's capacity to alter foreign societies and undervalued the capacity of lesser players to oppose American objectives (Mearsheimer, 2018, pp. 71–72).

The global system is currently experiencing a period of unpredictability and insecurity. It is not unexpected that problems and conflicts exist within the liberal ideal and its actual political structures. There are political as well as intellectual issues here. These conundrums and conflicts have always been present. However, the validity and durability of the liberal international order have started to be questioned since they have recently surfaced in new and particularly obvious ways (Ikenberry, 2011, p. 480). The liberal international order has faced significant challenges in recent years, including the rise of populism and nationalism as well as the emergence of new geopolitical realities. The crisis and the problems of the liberal international order have highlighted the need to question the existing order and contemplate the future of the world order. Hence, the liberal international order's ability to respond to these new threats may determine its destiny.

4.3   TRUMPIAN FOREIGN POLICY

The 2016 US presidential election was characterized by significant controversy, making it one of the most contentious in the nation's history. Many millions of people have been highly dissatisfied with the current international order, and they have made their dissatisfaction known by casting a huge number of anti-establishment votes. Different political parties have used this to represent themselves. In many nations, it has assumed various shapes. Every country has unique characteristics. Populism is increasing in the rich and democratic West and it certainly poses a serious danger to the existing order (Cox, 2017, p. 12).

The emergence of populism as a prevalent phenomenon in the US and globally has been a progressively increasing trend in recent times, with the election of Trump being regarded as a significant milestone in this trajectory. The populist rhetoric of President Trump garnered support from a significant portion of the electorate who expressed discontent with the nation's trajectory and perceived a lack of representation from the political establishment. The ascent of populism in the US and the subsequent election of Donald Trump were influenced by multiple factors. The country experienced a notable trend of economic insecurity and inequality. The profound impact of the Great Recession of 2008 and its aftermath was experienced by numerous Americans, especially those residing in rural and industrial regions who witnessed the disappearance of their employment opportunities and the decline of their communities. Trump pledged to revitalize the economy and create employment opportunities in these regions, garnering support from individuals who believed that they had been excluded from the recuperation of the economy.

An additional contributing factor to the rise of populism was the shifting demographics of the nation. The emergence of multiculturalism and the growing heterogeneity of the populace has generated a feeling of unease and ambiguity among a significant number of white Americans. The appeal of Trump's message of nationalism and cultural conservatism was rooted in the perception among some that their values and way of life were being jeopardized. There was a growing sense of distrust and disillusionment among Americans regarding the political establishment. A significant portion of the electorate held the perception that the governing body was tainted by corruption and that elected officials were disconnected from the issues that mattered to them. Trump presented himself as a political outsider and this stance appealed to individuals who were dissatisfied with the prevailing state of affairs.

However, with Trump's election, the liberal international order experienced an erosion that originated internally and threatens to overturn long-standing norms of authority and power. Due to the Trump administration's resignation from the US position as the head of the order, the crisis has been labeled as "the absence of strong American presidential leadership" (Lute & Burns, 2019) or the "crisis of the empty throne" (Daalder & Lindsay, 2018).

The US chose a president who openly opposes liberal internationalism for the first time since the 1930s. On several topics, including trade, alliances, international law, multilateralism, the environment, torture, and human rights, Trump made remarks that, if followed through with, would essentially eliminate the US' position as the driving force behind the liberal world order (Ikenberry, 2018a, p. 7).

An outpouring of worry about the sustainability of the liberal international order arose as the US set a new course in its foreign policy under Trump. His foreign policy demonstrated a dramatic departure from the conventional American strategy, particularly concerning the liberal international order. Trump adopted a foreign policy approach that was characterized by unilateralism, authoritarianism, and hierarchy. Additionally, his economic policy was based on mercantilism. He advocated an "America First" foreign policy throughout his administration, highlighting a unilateralist and protectionist approach that questioned the core underpinnings of the global liberal order. During his inauguration speech on January 27, 2017, Trump cautioned the world that "from this day forward, it's going to be only America first, America first." According to Kupchan, the president's speech to the UN General Assembly on September 25, 2018, represented a shift from Washington's grand strategy, which has been in place since the Second World War. In his speech, Trump indicated, "We will never surrender America's sovereignty to an unelected, unaccountable global bureaucracy" (as cited in Kupchan, 2018).

The post-Second World War liberal international order is built on a set of values that place a high value on international collaboration, free commerce, and the rule of law. The foundation of this order is the idea that shared responsibility and collaborative effort are the keys to achieving both global stability and economic progress. The US was instrumental in forging this system by advancing a liberal democratic worldview via the use of its economic and military power. Though the US had contributed to the establishment of this arrangement, it started to doubt its worth under the Trump administration. Trump believed that the liberal international order placed limits on American dominance and that the US was unfairly required to pay for upholding international stability. Trump thought that by taking advantage of the US' generosity and openness, other nations were taking advantage of it. As a result, he adopted a foreign policy that stressed economic nationalism and put a premium on defending US interests.

There are different theoretical explanations regarding Trump's foreign policy decisions. According to Barnett (2018, p. 41), it is possible to understand Trump's foreign policy as being within the parameters of realism, but perhaps because realism is so flexible, it is suitable in every situation. One of Trump's most well-known slogans was "Make America Great Again," which might be taken as restoring American supremacy and enhancing American strength, security, and economic standing from a realist perspective. Although Trump's foreign policy choices seem to depend on mainly realism, many times his foreign policy decisions were considered ambiguous. Trump changed US policy on Syria and believed that allying with the ISIS is the best course of action since it poses a larger threat to the country than Syrian President Bashar al-Assad (Barnett, 2018, p. 42).

Trump was a pragmatist. Although he threatened a trade war with China, he took considerably more cautious measures. Trump painted US alliances as liabilities rather than strengths, and he vowed to decrease or downgrade the US' security commitments, both to NATO and in East Asia. In doing so, he disregarded the hard-learned lesson that the greatest approach to safeguard American security and economic interests is to support the security of the country's friends (Niblett, 2017, p. 20). NATO was seen by Trump as a useless deadbeat. He is hardly the first US official to criticize the partners for taking advantage of NATO or to doubt its value. According to realists, Trump should disregard values in favor of the national interest and the allocation of material power (Barnett, 2018, p. 42). Hence, governments should act in accordance with their interests and not allow moral principles to impede them. He disrespected morality, ethics, rights, and laws. He rejected all higher authorities, including positive law, common morality, and ordinary ethics. He criticized the American heritage of moralizing, waging war, and attempting to shine a light on America for the rest of the world. He enjoyed bargains more than ideas and he was an individual without ideology (Barnett, 2018, p. 42).

Trump also eluded institutionalist theory. Institutionalists view governments as logical agents who prioritize money and security, similar to realists. Yet, unlike realists, they believe that states often do not need to worry about extinction, acknowledge that they have convergent interests that may progress their shared goals, and believe that the future has a long shadow. States work together far more frequently than most realists think. Institutions play an important part. States also aim to have a solid reputation for being dependable. States' adherence to their pledges can be explained in part by institutions and reputational consequences (Keohane, 1989, pp. 1–20). Trump did not specifically oppose globalization; rather, he claimed that since US negotiators are corrupt and dishonest, they consistently strike the worst bargains for the US. He contended that because he closed the best deals, he could perform better. The US should have the most flexibility possible to renegotiate or withdraw from these agreements, as well. Deals were made and broken by Trump. Moreover, it appeared that he was unconcerned with reputational consequences (Barnett, 2018, pp. 44–45). Trump, therefore, believed that institutions are at best superfluous and at worst detrimental. With the Trump administration, the lengthy Trans-Pacific Partnership (TPP) lasted just a few days. He pulled the US out of the Paris climate pact. He considered the UN as worse than useless and the WTO as detrimental to the US economy. Hence, Trump was outside the bounds of institutionalism due to his abnormally high discount rate, make-or-break perspective on business dealings, and attention to both absolute and relative benefits (Barnett, 2018, p. 45).

In this regard, Trump demonstrated impulses for unilateralism, protection, and isolationism. He also showed a disregard for advancing democracy and had a negative attitude toward immigration. Trump was inaugurated as the 45th president of the US when it seems like liberalism is the greatest loser. Before Trump came along, liberal internationalism was already beginning to falter. He doesn't appear to care about liberalism or its principles. The Wilsonian tradition in American foreign policy was buried by him. He characterized immigrants as criminals, rapists, economic drags, and diluting the imagined pure US.

Constructivism likewise failed the Trump test since it is based on structure and rationality. Constructivism introduces the social into the social structure by identifying how discourses, ideas, and values shape society. Because it also contributes to the creation of the material and impacts the interpretations that actors make of the world, the social is more than just another component that places restrictions on actors. Constructivists, similar to realists, institutionalists, and liberal internationalists, do not believe that structure is all-powerful enough to reduce actors to nothing more than cultural pawns (Barnett, 2018, p. 47). Furthermore, constructivists (Wendt, 1999) also attribute rationality to actors, much like the previously mentioned theories, but they go a step further and distinguish between instrumental and value rationality. Strategic planning and means-ends analysis are analogous to the instrumental. The value takes into account how society shapes actors' subjectivity, identity, interests, and methods of giving the world purpose (Barnett, 2018, p. 47).

Constructivism is a social theory. First and foremost, constructivism aims to challenge the identities and objectives of states and demonstrate how they have been socially produced. Social constructivists, in contrast, contend and have demonstrated that even identities, both the general identities of nations as states and their unique identities, such as the US' feeling of distinction from the Old World, are formed in part by international contact. The idea of structure in social constructivism is permeated with ideational elements at the level of global polity. Constructivists contend that the conduct of international relations cannot be jointly understood in the absence of mutually accepted constitutive principles based on collective intentionality (Ruggie, 1998, p. 879).

In this regard, constructivists find it difficult to predict the near future of the US hegemony since their core ideas about identity, interests, and structure are always changing. International and local society both influence how people define themselves. Constructivists who can deal with fixed identities are best equipped to predict what actors would do. Yet during the past several years, it appears like the American identity has turned into a battleground divided by race, which has gotten worse with Trump's victory (Barnett, 2018, p. 48–49).

There was a widespread belief before Trump that the emerging nations, led by China, would pose the greatest threat to liberal hegemony. The liberal order is crumbling just as many of these powers are experiencing declines in their own fortunes. The election of Donald Trump and the vote for Brexit both indicate that the liberal order is facing both internal and external threats (Acharya, 2018, p. 287).

Hence, the victory of President Trump shook the underpinnings of the liberal international order. Trump administration questioned long-standing American international security alliances like NATO and observed the promotion of economic nationalism that poses a danger to the advancement of globalization.

In this respect, the election of Donald Trump marks a reaffirmation of the nation-state as the primary political unit, a break in the post-war liberal international system, and a sharpening of geopolitical revisionism (Stokes, 2018, p. 133). He claimed in his 2017 inauguration speech that the US had benefited nothing from these partnerships:

> For many decades, we've enriched foreign industry at the expense of American industry; subsidized the armies of other countries, while allowing for the very sad depletion of our military. We've defended other nations' borders while refusing to defend our own. And spent trillions and trillions of dollars overseas while America's infrastructure has fallen into disrepair and decay. We've made other countries rich, while the wealth, strength and confidence of our country has dissipated over the horizon (Trump, 2017).

For many years, Republican and Democratic administrations expanded US security commitments in Europe, Asia, and the Middle East, confronted or overthrew dictatorships, and used military force and economic clout to force others to conform to US values and preferences, all in the name of the grand strategy of liberal hegemony (Walt, 2018b, p. 102). The disastrous outcomes in Iraq, Afghanistan, Libya, and Yemen are proof that this approach has failed. When the US citizens voted for Donald Trump, the majority of Americans sent a message that they didn't want the US to be the one to maintain international order. Hence, the voters were receptive to Trump's "America First" message because it implicitly rejected liberal hegemony and reflected the views of a populace that is growing warier of America's hyperactive global role. Hence, he desired an international agenda that would be more self-centered, nationalistic, and purely transactional. He had little interest in forming new connections (Daalder & Lindsay, 2018, p.65).

In the NSS of the US issued by the White House in December 2017, Trump states: "[The] American people elected me to make America great again. I promised that my Administration would put the safety, interests, and well-being of our citizens first" (NSS, 2017, p. I). The America First concept is stated in its most comprehensive manner ever in the NSS. The slogan "America First" requires taking a myopic perspective of US interests. It implies abandoning efforts to maintain norms in the international system, renouncing the pursuit of denying great powers their spheres of influence and regional hegemony and abandoning the sacrifice of short-term interests (in trade, for example) in favor of the longer-term goal of maintaining an open economic order (Kagan, 2017). According to this policy, the US' priority should be protecting and advancing its national interests. It must be able to operate independently, without having to adhere to the demands of other nations (Walt, 2018b, p. 102).

According to historian Jeremy Suri (2017), the Trump administration "launched a direct attack on the liberal international order that really made America great after the depths of the Great Depression." In addition, Thomas Wright (2017) states that Trump "wants to undo the liberal international order the US built and replace it with a nineteenth-century model of nationalism and mercantilism." Hence, the 2016 US election demonstrated the fragility of liberal hegemony. Several of the fundamental convictions and principles of liberal hegemony were called into question by Donald Trump's win. The American public has been dissatisfied with the liberal hegemony that both Trump and his predecessor Obama were elected by campaigning against it. In contrast, Hillary Clinton vigorously maintained liberal hegemony in 2008 and again in 2016, losing both elections to Obama and subsequently to Trump (Mearsheimer, 2018, pp. 349–351).

In this regard, the Trump administration has posed a threat to the liberal order's foundational tenets, including democracy, the need to promote a more open global economy, and the value of alliances like NATO and with countries like South Korea and Japan. The post-war structure of international institutions developed and supported by the US was another target of the Trump administration as it challenges the liberal order. The Trump administration curtailed American financing for the UN. As a cornerstone of the liberal order, liberal internationalists in the US have long looked to NATO (Acharya, 2018, p. 293). As a cornerstone of the liberal order, liberal internationalists in the US have long looked to NATO. However, Trump's reaction was direct when asked about NATO. He called the organization obsolete (Parker, 2016). Although Trump is not the first president of the US to demand that a country's allies contribute more to their security, his approach goes beyond the typical burden-sharing rhetoric of previous American presidents. Many times, Trump displayed a deep mistrust in the strategic and normative value of US partnerships. During his first international tour as president in May 2017, to handle ties with NATO and Europe, he accused Germany and other NATO members of not paying their dues and threatened the foundations of the liberal system (Acharya, 2018, p. 293).

Furthermore, Trump thought NATO is a bad deal and stated outright that he did not believe NATO was worthwhile and threatened to break US treaty commitments to America's allies if they did not increase their defense spending (Walt, 2018b, pp. 100–101). He said it may not be so terrible if Japan or South Korea had missiles, he lauded Russian President Vladimir Putin as a good leader, and he didn't call out Russia for seizing Crimea, supporting the Bashar al-Assad dictatorship in Syria, or hacking the US (Smith, 2016). He threatened to start trade fights with China, Mexico, and Canada, and dubbed the pact curbing Iran's nuclear program "the worst deal ever negotiated" (Torbati, 2016). In an interview with *The New York Times*, Trump (2016a) considered NAFTA with Canada and Mexico as "the worst trade deal ever signed in the history of this country and one of the worst trade deals ever signed anywhere in the world." Hence, in his full acceptance Republican nomination speech published by Politico, Trump claimed that "making individual deals with individual countries" is a better strategy instead of multilateral trade talks (Full Text: Donald Trump, 2016). In this regard, Trump embraced what can be referred to as cost-benefit bilateralism in place of globalized multilateralism. This bilateralism is profoundly skeptical of regimes that it sees as obstructing or limiting American liberty of action and opposes a transformative foreign policy motivated by principles like human rights or democracy in favor of transactional ties. Instead, it favors dealing with foreign nations on an individual basis, basing decisions on how each relationship advances the US' deemed economic or political interests (Stokes, 2018, p. 137).

Trump was hardly the only new and disruptive force for the liberal international order or even its primary one. Because the US is not an exception, the threat that Trump posed to the liberal international order was amplified. Worldwide, faith in liberal democracies and the international system is eroding. It is probably no coincidence that his election coincided with other significant events such as the British people's decision to leave the EU (Brexit), the growth of right-wing populist movements in several European nations, and a rise in authoritarianism in several Eastern European nations as well as China and Russia (Jervis et al., 2018, p. 14). Arguments that the rise of populism in the US and other parts of the world heralds the end of the current age of international order and that turmoil may follow have virtually become accepted knowledge. Trump's victory and Britain's decision to quit the EU show that populist responses are widespread in Western democracies (Nye, 2017, p. 15).

Trump overcame vehement resistance from well-known politicians in both parties, with the US foreign policy elite's ranks issuing the loudest warnings. He triumphed despite fierce opposition from both major parties. It was to be expected that Democratic foreign policy professionals would oppose Trump, but it seemed likely that Republicans would oppose him even more fiercely. As an illustration, in March 2016, 122 former national security officials of the Republican Party published an open letter criticizing Trump's views on foreign policy and labeling him as "fundamentally dishonest" and "utterly unfitted for the office." In addition, Trump "lacks the temperament to be president," according to a second letter published in August and signed by 50 leading foreign policy specialists of the Republican Party (Walt, 2018b, pp. 99-100).

Trump had consistently contradicted several long-standing myths concerning US foreign policy. He was unconvinced by the argument that the US should work to protect and advance democratic ideals. He took a staunch anti-immigrant stance, singling out Mexicans, Muslims, and refugees, rather than praising these characteristics as assets. The construction of a wall on the southern border of the US, the cost of which Mexico, by some miracle, would agree to bear, was a fundamental pillar of his election platform (Daalder & Lindsay, 2018, p. 61). Hence, on January 25, 2017, Trump issued an executive order outlining his stance on the construction of a border wall. According to Executive Order 13767, the secretary of Homeland Security is responsible for "developing long-term funding requirements for the wall, including preparing Congressional budget requests for the current and upcoming fiscal years."

In addition, he advocated a "total and complete ban" on Muslims entering the US and hinted he would back the creation of a national register for all Muslims already in the US (as cited in Johnson & Hauslohner, 2017). Executive Order 13780 was issued by Trump on March 6, 2017, and it prohibited citizens of seven countries (Iran, Iraq, Libya, Somalia, Sudan, Syria, and Yemen) with a majority of Muslims from entering the US for at least the ensuing 90 days. In the executive order, it is proclaimed that "it is the policy of the US to protect its citizens from terrorist attacks, including those committed by foreign nationals" (Executive Order No. 13780, 2017).

In this regard, according to several analysts, Trump's presidency would put the strength and character of the American government and society to the test (Jervis, 2018, p. 35). Trump's ascent has brought to light an unsettling fact about world politics: the expansion of the liberal order was never more than a flimsy cover for American hegemony. It allowed all parties to accept the enormous American advantages in economic might and military might. But, as the post-war agreement grew less appealing, it became more conceivable that someone like Trump (or any of the noteworthy nationalist figures in contemporary Europe) would emerge (Jervis et al., 2018, pp. 17–18).

Trump has expressed a more limited understanding of the American national interest than any previous president by challenging the value of American alliances, at least as they are now constructed, and questioning the relevance of other international organizations. In addition, the main theme of his campaign, which was carried over into his speech as president, was that many of these agreements gave the US an unfair deal and that he could renegotiate them, particularly in the economic sphere (Jervis et al., 2018, p. 31). The development of democracy and human rights is one of the main tenets of the liberal international order. Trump's foreign policy, however, was distinguished by his tendency to ignore the human rights violations carried out by autocratic governments. Despite their oppressive practices, he respected leaders like Putin and Kim Jong Un of North Korea. This strategy damaged the US' standing as a supporter of democracy and human rights. During his campaign, Trump explicitly expressed that he did not have any intellectual or emotional adhesion to the alliances that the US had founded after the Second World War, to the multilateral trade system that had created global prosperity and removed millions out of poverty, or to America's position as the champion of democracy, human rights, and the rule of law. He believed that the allies of the US were just as dangerous as its enemies. The trade agreements and alliances that Presidents Clinton, Bush, and Obama thought were essential to American security and prosperity were actually part of the problem (Daalder & Lindsay, 2018, pp. 63–64).

Trump's campaign centered on his resistance to globalization, which he claimed had lost Americans millions of productive jobs, let dangerous immigrants into the country and weakened the US. These positions reveal a crucial perspective on global politics, and maybe on all human relations: Politics and relationships are transactional, depending on particular agreements rather than considering the long term and setting up circumstances that would be beneficial over time. Trump also viewed ties, even with allies, as a zero-sum game, unlike prior presidents (Jervis, 2018, p. 31).

In this respect, nearly every element of the liberal hegemony was contested by Trump, who repeatedly reminded Americans that it had been detrimental to the US (Posen, 2018). The most significant pledge he made was that the US would stop promoting democracy abroad if he were elected president. Trump believed that efforts to spread democracy were useless (Posen, 2018, p. 25). The US proposals were ignored elsewhere. In his foreign policy speech in 2016, published in *The New York Times*, he states that unrest in the Middle East was sparked since Washington supported "the dangerous idea that we could make western democracies out of countries that had no experience or interests in becoming a western democracy" (Trump, 2016b). Putin, the present nemesis of the liberal foreign policy elite, was specifically mentioned as someone with whom his government would have cordial ties.

Some scholars consider Trump's seeming opposition to democratization and humanitarian intervention as aligning with the advice of many realists. This is also the case for his conviction that earlier American policies that ignored Russian interests were partially to blame for the country's strained ties with the US (Jervis, 2018, pp. 32). For example, political scientist

Daniel Drezner (2016) defines Trump's period as "realism's moment in the foreign policy sun." Schweller (2018, p. 66) explains Trump's coming to power from a structural realist point of view. As the world moves from unipolarity to developing multipolarity, which, if and when it occurs, would be the first fully global multipolar system in history, competition, and tight connecting are intensifying. Americans have consistently had a more realist than liberal stance on foreign affairs, in sharp contrast to their leaders. Hence, the external situation of the US has been compelled enough to call for a foreign strategy that is more strictly self-interested (Schweller, 2018, p. 66). According to a Pew Research Center survey released in April 2016, Americans are equally skeptical of US involvement in the global economy and believe that the US contributes too much (41 percent) and too little (27 percent) to solving global issues. Just 28 percent believe that the US contributes the proper amount.

Trump did not initiate the transition away from a more realist American grand policy toward deep involvement, in both its liberal internationalist and neoconservative guises. American citizens chose Obama, who stood for "restraint and retrenchment," when the financial crisis hit and rumblings of growing multipolarity started. Obama's foreign policy sometimes straddled two stools because of his broad foreign policy perspective, which was a bit of a compromise between liberal internationalism and realism. Henry Kissinger gave an interview with a *National Interest* editor in 2015 and stated that on a practical level, Obama was a realist, but his goals were more ideological than practical (Heilbrunn & Kissinger, 2015).

Contrary to popular expectations, Trump's foreign policy choices have shown more consistency with past practice. According to Schweller (2018, p. 80), Trump's popular campaign themes—that the US needs its partners to share defense responsibilities, stronger trade agreements, and protection from currency manipulation—come from the political economics of realism, sometimes known as neomercantilism or, more correctly, economic nationalism. In addition, Schweller (2018, p. 89) claims that Trump's foreign policy strategy mainly adheres to the "offshore balancing" grand strategy. The concept was first introduced by Layne in a 1997 article in International Security and has since been embraced by several well-known realists. According to this strategy, Washington should allow other nations to take the lead in curbing growing powers in Europe, Northeast Asia, and the Persian Gulf, acting itself only when required rather than policing the world. Hence, offshore balancing has been seen as a strategy to uphold US primacy in the foreseeable future while ensuring the protection of domestic liberty. This approach involves the US fine-tuning its military posture in response to the power dynamics in three crucial regions. Additionally, it allows regional forces to act as the initial line of defense in the event of a potential emergence of a regional hegemon (Mearsheimer & Walt, 2016, pp. 71–73).

However, while it would be impossible to identify which alternative theory was supported, Trump's foreign policy that adheres to his campaign claims would be difficult to reconcile with realism, notwithstanding Trump's declaration in his first speech to the UN that he is adhering to "principled realism" (Jaffe & DeYoung, 2017). In addition, the concept of "principled realism" was the foundation of the 2017 NSS. A new geopolitical period necessitates a new worldview, described as "principled realism" in the NSS. Principled realism, according to the text, is a policy that is "guided by outcomes, not ideology," built on a state-centric worldview, and values "a world of strong, sovereign, and independent nations" (NSS, 2017, pp. 1–2). The strategy is based on realism since it acknowledges the key role of "power in international politics, affirms that sovereign states are the best hope for a peaceful world, and clearly defines our national interests." It is also principled in the sense that it is "grounded in the knowledge that advancing American principles spreads peace and prosperity around the globe. We are guided by our values and disciplined by our interests" (NSS, 2017, p. 55).

As it is also stated by Anton (2019), Trump is not a classic realist, a paleoconservative, or a liberal internationalist, which has led to a great deal of uncertainty. The same is true for the fact that he is not just a dove or a hawk and does not have an innate tendency toward isolationism or inter-ventionism. Although drawing from each of these categories, his foreign policy doesn't neatly fit into any of them (Anton, 2019). However, Anton claims that Trump had a consistent foreign policy: a Trump Doctrine. The issue is that, like other presidential theories, it is not possible to encapsu-late the Trump Doctrine in just two words. He stated at the APEC CEO Summit in Da Nang, Vietnam, in November 2017 that "There's no place like home." He made the same argument two months earlier when he spoke to the UN General Assembly and used the phrase "great reawakening of nations" (as cited in Anton, 2019). In these instances, the president was not only observing what was happening: a rise in nationalist or patriotic emotion in almost every region of the world, but particularly in sections of Europe and the US. Moreover, he said plainly that this tendency was favorable. He was urging nations already traveling this route to keep going and urging nations that weren't yet on it to do so (Anton, 2019).

Trump's initial steps in office were a dramatic departure from the policies of the previous three American administrations that contributed to the demise of the American hegemonic order. He started as president by filling key foreign policy positions with outsiders, leaving many others unfilled, and publicly criticizing the intelligence agency. The liberal international order is supported in large part by free trade. Yet, protectionism and a rejection of free trade accords characterized Trump's foreign policy. As promised, on his third day in office he pulled the US from the TPP, declared US allies would have to pay for American protection, and suggested a 30 percent decrease in the State Department budget. The Presidential Memorandum concerning the withdrawal of the US from the TPP Negotiations and Agreement stated that:

> Based on these principles, and by the authority vested in me as President by the Constitution and the laws of the US, I hereby direct you to withdraw the US as a signatory to the Trans-Pacific Partnership (TPP), to permanently withdraw the US from TPP negotiations, and to begin pursuing, wherever possible, bilateral trade negotiations to promote American industry, protect American workers, and raise American wages (Presidential Memorandum, 2017).

In addition, a unilateralist attitude to international affairs characterized Trump's foreign policy. He continued his administration's backing for long-standing Middle Eastern friends, and his controversial recognition of Jerusalem as Israel's capital was more an acknowledgment of America's long-standing "special relationship" with the Jewish state than a dramatic break from it. However, Trump's disorganized and even inept handling of crucial foreign policy matters had an impact. Important American allies like Germany, South Korea, Saudi Arabia, and Canada started to hedge (Walt, 2018b, pp. 106–107).

To sum up, Donald Trump's election in the US-led to increased skepticism over the survival of the liberal world order. The period in which Trump was the president of the US brought about a notable transformation in the realm of American foreign policy and the global system. Trump's "America First" policy posed a challenge to the established liberal international order that had been in place since the end of the Second World War. The cessation of the global liberal order, distinguished by unrestricted commerce, democratic governance, and collaborative decision-making, has been a topic of fervent discussion among decision-makers, scholars, and experts. Throughout his tenure as president, Trump contested the prevailing global liberal framework. He declined to support the concept of multilateralism and instead opted for a more nationalist stance in relation to matters of foreign policy. In this regard, the actions of President Trump represented a deviation from the customary position of the US as a global leader, which has historically been characterized by the advancement of democratic values, human rights, and open trade. Trump's repudiation of multilateralism had a detrimental effect on international institutions and resulted in a reduction of efficacy in the global governance system. In addition, his foreign policy strategy resulted in a state of unpredict-ability, disrupted worldwide economic stability, and instigated hostilities. His emphasis on economic nationalism, protectionism, and unilateralism posed a threat to the basic tenets of the order that the US had contributed to establishing. His foreign policy decisions against the foundations of the liberal international order damaged US leadership in the liberal interna-tional order and added to worldwide unrest.

4.4   FALL OF THE TRANSATLANTIC ORDER

Despite the fact that Donald Trump's election to the presidency intensified this issue, the US has been distancing itself from its allies for some time. The Obama administration's disrespect for friends and the unilateralism of the George W. Bush presidency both contributed to a significant crisis in the alliance system of the US. Hence, a serious number of observers contend that the fundamental nature of the transatlantic political system, which was formed after the Second World War, is in jeopardy. According to Petersson (2016, p. 43), from a European perspective, the US appears to be a "reluctant ally" more and more frequently. Due to the gravity of the most recent confrontation between the US and Europe, it is significant to consider the nature and potential future of the Atlantic alliance.

The North Atlantic community, the Atlantic political order, or the Western system are several names for the post-war regional political order that the US and Europe have constructed and operate within. Although the current form of the Atlantic order truly emerged after 1945, it has elements related to security, the economy, politics, and ideas. It has rules and structures that represent a functional, albeit disorganized political system. The Atlantic order is held together by networks of political and diplomatic governance as well as military alliances, economic integration, and similar ideals. It is also supported by democracy, economics, and a shared cultural history (Ikenberry, 2008, pp. 6–8). However, the transatlantic alliance has developed cracks in recent years.

The UK's choice to leave the EU, together with the strategic vacuum created by the Atlantic Alliance's deterioration and the instability of trade conflicts, have all intensified the effect of global unrest on European democracies. Russian and Chinese authoritarianism is no longer the only issue. The dilemma is now occurring in Western nations that pride them- selves on being the pillars of democracy. Global unrest feeds the crises of Western democracies, which in turn exacerbates international instability and the power struggle on a global scale (Duran, 2019, p. 13).

Transatlantic relations have worsened, especially after Trump took office. Trump despises practically all the organizations that make up the liberal international order, including NATO and the EU (Mearsheimer, 2019, p. 29). In this regard, the fundamental tenets of the post-Second World War Atlantic security arrangement have been challenged. Interests between the US and Europe have shifted, institutionalized collaboration can no longer be taken for granted, and the sense of shared Western iden- tity has waned (Kupchan, 2006, p. 77).

In his piece, "The End of the West," published in *The Atlantic*'s November 2002 issue Kupchan claims that the US and Europe will face off in the next clash of civilizations rather than the West and the rest of the world. He adds, "Europe is strengthening its collective consciousness and character and forging a clearer sense of interests and values that are quite distinct from those of the US" (Kupchan, 2002).

Transatlantic relations between the US and Europe were governed by the balance-of-power theory throughout the early stages (1776–1905) of the relationship. The major players engaged in militaristic competition under the Atlantic order. The rationale guiding Atlantic relations changed from a balance of power to a balance of threat in the early 1900s. The participants were no longer balancing against any concentration of power, just those that they perceived as dangerous. Cooperative security was the driving principle of transatlantic ties from the attack on Pearl Harbor to the fall of the Soviet Union (Kupchan, 2006, pp. 77–79). The transatlantic system is not only a shared political arena that spontaneously came into being. It is a created political system that is based on American hegemony, shared interests, political agreements, and established laws and standards. The Atlantic Charter of 1941, the Bretton Woods Agreements of 1944, the Charter of the UN of 1945, the Marshall Plan of 1947, and the Atlantic Pact of 1949 all contain principles that represent an Atlantic political community. These acts established many norms, institutions, and pledges that served as the cornerstones of the Atlantic order (Ikenberry, 2008, p. 9).

Soon after the collapse of the Soviet Union, US and European geopolitical interests began to diverge. Europe and the US were no longer dependent on one another to protect their first-order security interests in the absence of a shared external threat. As it switched its emphasis to objectives outside of its immediate area of operations, NATO has continued to exist as a military alliance only in name. Its provisions for collective defense are now meaningless (Kupchan, 2006, p. 80).

According to Ikenberry (2008, p. 9), the foundation of this Atlantic order is two significant agreements between the US and Europe. One stems from the American government's Cold War-era grand strategy and is a realist deal. In an open global economy, the US gives its European allies access to its markets, technology, and supplies as well as security protection. In exchange, these nations promise to help the US as it governs the larger post-war Western order by being dependable allies in the areas of diplomacy, commerce, and logistics. The end result has united Europe and the US, making peace "indivisible" on both sides of the Atlantic. Security relationships that are established offer outlets for communication and group decision-making. Threats to common security gave rise to unprecedented security cooperation, which was symbolized in the NATO alliance (Ikenberry, 2008, p.10). The other is a liberal deal that takes into account the ambiguities associated with US asymmetrical strength. States in East Asia and Europe consent to accept American leadership and function within a predetermined political-economic framework. In exchange, the US widens its horizons and commits to its allies. By improving its user-friendliness, the US effectively creates a formalized coalition of allies and strengthens the durability of these long-term, mutually beneficial relationships (Ikenberry, 2008, p. 10).

For Alcaro and Greco (2016, p. 271), "resilient" would be the term that best describes the relationship between the US and European countries. While there have been ups and downs in the partnership, it is noteworthy that a group of nations has maintained their commitment to collaboration over such a protracted period. This hitherto unheard-of occurrence has been made possible by the structure of the global economy, the distribution of resources, strong social ties, and perceptions shared by elites and the general public. The stability of their long-standing relationship has, however, been clouded in recent years by substantial systemic changes and internal developments in Europe and the US (Alcaro, 2020, p. 348).

The Cold War order's cornerstone of cooperative security is no longer the sole theory guiding transatlantic relations. Thinking from a balance of threat point of view is clearly resurfacing. While Europe is balancing, it is not against American force but rather against American behavior (Kupchan, 2006, p. 80). The transatlantic rift grew as a result of the EU's development. Europe's reliance on American power has decreased with the promotion of peace in Europe and the expansion of the EU. Hence, Europeans became more willing to show their independence and choose their own path, occasionally diverging from American positions on crucial policy matters like the Kyoto Protocol, the International Criminal Court (ICC), and the Iraq War. Expansion also increased Europe's influence eastward and southward, undermining the US' longstanding hegemony in the strategic core of Eurasia (Kupchan, 2006, p. 80).

Brexit triumphed in England with a sizable win, and Trump triumphed after being inspired by the Brexit result in June. Populism had reached the US and the UK, with repercussions that would be profoundly unsettling for the international order. Analysts began to consider the ramifications for the larger transatlantic relationship in particular. Americans were undoubtedly against Britain exiting the EU. American policymakers have favored the Brits being a critical element of the European project since the early 1960s (Cox, 2021, pp. 5–6). In his interview with the BBC's Jon Sopel, Obama (2015) articulated the official stance of the US by arguing that "having the UK in the EU gives us much greater confidence about the strength of the transatlantic union … and we want to make sure that the UK continues to have that influence … not just for ourselves but for Europe as a whole and the world as a whole." In this regard, with Brexit, the UK not only made a choice that might potentially diminish the US' standing in Europe but also lost a dependable major voice advocating policies in the EU with which it was broadly in agreement (Cox, 2021, p. 6).

In this regard, at least in part, the American-European conflict may be explained by the failure of major historical agreements and the intensifying antagonism between American and European aspirations. The security pact has deteriorated in the years after the end of the Cold War, despite NATO's expansion into Eastern Europe. The US' dedication to multi-lateral cooperation and consultative principles has also been called into doubt. Between now and then, there seems to be less harmony between the American and European projects after Brexit. Hence, it is simpler—and possibly even necessary—for the US to act alone and in ways that are at odds with Europe's security orientation as unipolarity grows and global threats change (Ikenberry, 2008, p. 11).

Trump's statement that, if elected president, he would leave Europe alone with its own problems and focus on his country's domestic prob-lems signaled a break in the ongoing US-Europe relations (Walt, 2017). European Council President Donald Tusk warned that Trump represented a severe threat to the viability of the EU in a letter to European leaders that was written soon after Trump took office (EU Leader Declares, 2017). A few months later, immediately following Trump's inauguration, German Chancellor Angela Merkel, an ardent supporter of the Atlantic Alliance, issued a dire warning that Europe could no longer rely on the US in the same way. She claimed Europe can no longer rely on allies after Trump and Brexit (Merkel: Europe Can No Longer, 2017). Since then, transat-lantic ties have only gotten worse, and it appears unlikely that anything will change in the near future (Mearsheimer, 2019, p. 29).

As mentioned above, the importance of multilateral institutions, the relevance of NATO, and the transatlantic alliance were just a few of the crucial elements of the liberal international order that the Trump admin-istration publicly questioned. As a result, the head of the liberal order became the source of internal conflict against it (Flockhart, 2020, p. 228). During his administration, US President Donald Trump sparked discus-sions over concerns about Washington's position in the world and raised concerns about the Atlantic Alliance's future (Duran, 2019, p. 9). He chas-tised Europe for defrauding the US in trade and for refusing to contribute fairly to the costs of keeping NATO in place. He became the first president to publicly doubt the value of NATO and the tight ties between Europe and North America that this global security organization was designed to maintain (Gerstle, 2022, p. 271).

The perception that the Trump administration fundamentally altered transatlantic relations with the US was felt in Europe the strongest (Daalder & Lindsay, 2018, p. 292). One of the major turning points in transatlantic relations was the US-led Iran nuclear deal. In a speech in Prague in

April 2009, Obama expressed his belief in dialog and his economic and political support for Iran's nuclear energy needs under strong international supervision (Obama, 2009b). On this understanding, a nuclear deal was reached between Iran and the international community during the Obama administration. However, Trump criticized his predecessor Obama's 2015 nuclear deal with Tehran. He called it "the worst deal ever" and suspended it (as cited in Collinson et al., 2017). After Trump's withdrawal from the Iran nuclear agreement, Merkel stated that there had been a "break in German-American and European-American relations" (as cited in Heilbrunn, 2018). Moreover, Donald Tusk, the head of the European Council, said, "Looking at the latest decisions of Donald Trump, someone could even think: With friends like that who needs enemies" (as cited in Birnbaum, 2018). These kinds of opinions were widely shared across the continent, with newspapers publishing articles claiming that the transatlantic alliance, a cornerstone of American and European foreign policy for more than 70 years, was coming to an end (Daalder & Lindsay, 2018, p. 293). Pierre Vimont, a former French ambassador to the US voiced the question, which even Europeans who weren't ready to give up on Washington were pondering: "How do we make it work with a US leadership that doesn't want to play the role of leader?" (as cited in Erlanger, 2018).

Once in office, Trump did not hesitate to put pressure on America's transatlantic allies to shoulder a greater share of the burden for their own defense, allowing the US to reallocate the freed-up resources to what appears to be his overarching goal of destroying the ISIS, al-Qaeda, and other jihadist groups in the Greater Middle East. He requested that the alliance's European members fulfill the stated minimum military budget of 2 percent of GDP. In addition, Article 5 of the North Atlantic Treaty, which deals with mutual defense, was not officially endorsed by Trump and NATO nations from Europe were lambasted by Trump for the financial load they have placed on the US (Keylor, 2018). Hence, American allies in Europe were growing more concerned that Trump was transforming the transatlantic alliance into a transactional alliance, where US commitment would be determined by how much some allies spent rather than by how serious the shared threat was or by what could be achieved through collective action to defend shared interests and promote shared values (Daalder & Lindsay, 2018, pp. 177–178).

In addition, Trump's decision to implement tariffs on the import of steel and aluminum from Europe and Canada, as well as his threats to put tariffs on autos, further weakened transatlantic solidarity (What you need to know about, 2018). In a similar vein, Trump's June 2018 tariffs on Chinese imports had no effect in getting Beijing to change its rapacious economic practices. Such an objective would have necessitated enlisting the aid of America's allies. Trump praised his tariffs as victories in the effort to correct unfair trade imbalances. But they were more likely to spark a trade war that would make everyone less fortunate (Daalder & Lindsay, 2018, p. 283).

In this regard, the international system has suffered significant repercussions as a result of the transatlantic order's collapse under the Trump administration. Authoritarian regimes like Russia and China have been able to increase their influence and threaten the liberal democratic system thanks to the void left by the US' retreat from the international scene. It is now more difficult for the US and Europe to cooperate to handle shared difficulties as a result of the growth of far-right populism in Europe, which has also damaged the solidarity and unity that had been the transatlantic relationship's cornerstone. Hence, the relationship between the US and Europe across the Atlantic Ocean was significantly impacted by the Trump administration. He undermined norms and institutions, rejected multilateralism, and assailed the foundations of the transatlantic order, which had been established on the common principles of democracy, human rights, and international cooperation. Wide-ranging effects of the collapse of the transatlantic order on the international system arose involving the development of authoritarianism and the demise of democratic norms.

To sum up, the fundamental basis of the liberal international order was the alliance between Europe and the US, which played a pivotal role in forming the worldwide economy and promoting democratic principles on a global scale. In recent years, the alliance between transatlantic partners has encountered several challenges such as divergent interests, increasing nationalism, and a decline in trust. The current state of affairs has led to a precarious situation for the liberal international order, which could have significant ramifications for the prospects of global governance and security. In this regard, as a political structure, the liberal international order has variously been conceptualized as including Europe, the Atlantic Alliance, the West, the free world, and the whole world (Ikenberry, 2020, p. 19). The previous grand strategic alliance between the US and Europe has been damaged in recent years. The EU and the US, whose partnership dates back to the First World War, are currently contending with significant conflicts and controversies. The cyclical and structural changes in US foreign policy changes have caused serious ruptures between the parties in transatlantic relations. At the same time, it has led to the emergence of significant changes. In this context, interrogating how transatlantic relations will be shaped based on foundations and balances has become important for understanding its trajectory. The end outcome won't be a total breakup of the transatlantic political community, but rather its evolution into a new category of Western political order. Hence, the long-term effects of this crisis are expected to change and modify the earlier post-war institutions, agreements, and rules of the Atlantic political system.

4.5   THE US AND THE INTERNATIONAL ORGANIZATIONS

The US has been a major player in the establishment and operation of international organizations. It has been actively involved in developing international policies and promoting global collaborations since the founding of the UN and the WTO. Hence, American influence on international institutions and their policies has been crucial.

Modern society's inherent interconnection motivates liberal internationalist goals for cooperation and drives governments to establish international institutions as instruments for balancing sovereignty and interdependence. Liberal democracies need to expand the globe to survive and grow since they cannot be safe or wealthy on their own (Ikenberry, 2020, p 33). In this sense, multilateralism, in Ruggie's (1993, p. 11) words, is an architectural style of the international organization that manages relationships between a number of nations in accordance with generalized standards of behavior.

The US was the primary creator and supporter of international multilateral governance in the 10 years after the Second World War. The US and the advanced industrial democracies built a wide range of international and regional institutions to handle economic, political, and security interactions during the Cold War. The UN, IMF, World Bank, NATO, and a wide range of other organizations and regimes were all founded as a result of this extraordinary surge of global institution-building. Washington tried to influence the environment in which other governments operated by pursuing a policy of order-building (Ikenberry, 2011, p. 155). These international institutions were expanded into a more comprehensively global multilateral system of governance after the Cold War. The world order was dominated by the US. However, it cemented its domination through institutions more so than powerful governments in earlier centuries. Hence, it was a liberal hegemonic regime under American leadership (Ikenberry, 2015, p. 399).

A liberal international order is defined by economic openness on a global scale, where ties between nations are governed by law and international organizations like the WTO, the Non-Proliferation Treaty, or multilateral alliances like NATO. Liberal institutionalism holds that robust international regimes can promote cooperation between nations, deter excessive rivalry, and reduce the likelihood that violent conflicts would arise or worsen. Together, these ideas suggested that the US might help create a wealthier and more peaceful world by advancing economic globalization, democratization, and the development, expansion, or strengthening of international institutions (Walt, 2018a, pp. 73–75).

In this regard, international organizations and multilateralism are seen by proponents of the liberal order as essential to preserving the legitimacy of the order and maintaining America's dominant position in world affairs. US centricity is at the heart of liberal multilateralism. Hence, the US is responsible for creating multilateralism's institutional structure, and institutions established by hegemonic powers are always capable of using coercive measures (Acharya, 2018, p. 145). Ikenberry (2001, pp. 51–57) believes that multilateralism and American hegemony go hand in hand because these institutions allow the US to gain the allegiance and obedience of lesser governments by pledging not to threaten them.

According to Mearsheimer (1994, p. 13), international organizations are vehicles used by governments to further their own interests, and as such, they invariably represent those of the most powerful states. Institutions and norms provide the ruling state with the means to exercise political power. Institutions and rules serve as both restraints on the exercise of hegemonic power and instruments of that power (Ikenberry, 2011, p. 188). For realists, liberal hegemony exaggerates how well international institutions can control interstate interactions and settle complex conflicts of interest. There is no doubt that laws are necessary to regulate interactions in a world of independent nations. International organizations can encourage cooperation when states have obvious incentives to do so, as multilateral institutions like NATO, the World Bank, or the WTO have repeatedly demonstrated, but they cannot prevent powerful states from acting independently, which means they cannot eliminate the threat of conflict and war. Because the US was by far their most influential member, the majority of current institutions have long adhered to American preferences. It is thus no surprise that China now wants to play a larger role in existing fora and, in some cases, is looking to establish its own rival institutions (Walt, 2018a, p. 94).

In this regard, Hillary Clinton stated in a speech at the Council on Foreign Relations Washington headquarters on September 8, 2010:

> So let me say it clearly: the US can, must, and will lead in this new century ... The world looks to us because America has the reach and resolve to mobilize the shared effort needed to solve problems on a global scale – in defense of our own interests, but also as a force for progress. In this we have no rival (Clinton, 2010).

However, as it is stated by Ikenberry (2015, p. 399), it appears that there is a problem in this hegemonic system of multilateral governance and concerns regarding the future of multilateralism are being raised. The US is no longer in a position to exercise the hegemonic power it once exercised. The non-Western nations that are rising to challenge American hegemony do so through participating in the post-war global order. Economic and security linkages are becoming more intense and complicated. Global warming, disease pandemics, nuclear proliferation, unstable financial conditions, and international terrorism are among the growing number of complex transnational threats. In addition, the US' standing within the global system has also shifted, which has lowered its capacity to exercise multilateral leadership (Ikenberry, 2015, pp. 408–410).

Acharya (2018) also states that the US has a selective and self-interested commitment to multilateralism. The most visible instance of this was the widespread unilateralism of the George W. Bush administration. To avoid being subject to the ICC, the US pledged to veto all UN peacekeeping deployments in 2002. Obama administration also urged that all decisions on ICC investigations be made with the agreement of the UNSC, which it may use the veto, endangering the court's independence. Although the Obama administration in theory favored the UNSC reform to improve the UN's overall performance, effectiveness, and efficiency to face the obstacles of the new century, it did not take the lead in achieving this aim (Acharya, 2018, pp. 145–146).

In this regard, according to Acharya (2018), the post-Second World War system of multilateral organizations has been under a lot of strain. These institutions are currently up against fierce competition since they are no longer the only players in global governance. There have been several regional and multilateral agreements, private sector-led efforts, and different types of partnerships including the public, commercial, and civil society sectors (Acharya, 2018, p. 156). The end consequence is a patchwork of international organizations with varying personalities, constituencies, geographic scopes, and subject matters (Biermann et al., 2009, p. 16).

In addition, the emergence of new institutions, particularly those driven by China, poses a threat to the US-led multilateralism system. These institutions include the New Development Bank (NDB), Contingency Reserve Arrangement (CRA), and the Asian Infrastructure Investment Bank (AIIB). It's conceivable that global governance will remain in its current state of disarray. It will result in a less US-centric system of global governance, as well as a modified or even a post-liberal order, which cannot absorb but must accept the rising powers and the developing nations, albeit maybe not on the conditions established by the Western powers (Acharya, 2018, pp. 162–163).

Robert Cox (1992, pp. 161–163) also presents new issues for multilateralism and promotes a more expansive understanding that acknowledges the importance of social movements as well as nations. In addition, it considers multilateral cooperation strategies as "post-hegemonic" since new approaches to multilateralism are independent of American power and objectives. In this regard, the post-Second World War structure of international institutions faces significant competition. Different types of initiatives, and arrangements, as well as public and private actors have emerged and a large number of these threaten the supremacy of US-led institutions, while others are neither the product of American initiatives nor under its control (Acharya, 2018, pp. 155–156).

The victory of Donald Trump "imperils the liberal international order," according to Stewart Patrick. As a candidate, Trump called into doubt enduring US alliances like NATO, lambasted global organizations like the UN and pledged to renege on significant trade, weapons control, and climate deals (Patrick, 2017). America's departure from multilateralism as an idea and a process is signaled by its withdrawal from several international accords. The harsh fact that the free trade regime has not benefitted is what the 45th president of the US understands very clearly, and what drove him into office (Duncombe & Dunne, 2018, pp. 27–28). The US has long worked to advance a global order based on rules, mostly by enticing other nations to join the multilateral organizations in which it has a key position. In keeping with his motto of "America First," Trump had frequently questioned the worth of these institutions, particularly in the economic sphere, which he saw as bad deals that restricted Washington's freedom of action, undermined American sovereignty, and severely hurt the US economy (Walt, 2018a, p. 295). President Trump's decision to pull the US out of the Paris Agreement in June 2017 is a prime example of the shifting dynamics of multilateralism in international politics. In addition, the US declared on June 19, 2018, that it was departing the UN Human Rights Council, as UN Ambassador Nikki Haley referred to the organization as "an organization that is not worthy of its name" (as cited in Lee & Lederman, 2018). In the remarks published by the Department of State, Secretary of State Pompeo (2018) stated that, "We have no doubt that there was once a noble vision for this council. But today, we need to be honest – the Human Rights Council is a poor defender of human rights."

Due to pressure from the US, the G20 summit's final statement reneged on its earlier pledge to resist all forms of protectionism. "We do have a new government and a different view on trade," Treasury Secretary Steven Mnuchin told reporters later (as cited in Jones & Fleming, 2017). Trump persisted in denouncing NAFTA as a "one-sided deal" that had resulted in a $60 billion trade imbalance (as cited in Ingraham, 2017). In addition, Trump vetoed fresh candidates to the WTO's seven-person appeals board, claiming that "the WTO was set up for the benefit of everybody but us." This action threatened to undermine the organization's capacity to settle future trade disputes (Trump Threatens to Pull, 2018).

According to *The New York Times* on January 25, 2017, the White House of President Donald J. Trump produced two draft executive orders that would reduce American contributions to the UN and halt the signing of any new international agreements. The first order headed "Auditing and Reducing US Funding of International Organizations" is the most troubling of them. The mandate urges the committee to cut voluntary donations to UN organizations by 40 percent, which is the most shocking instruction. The second order, those multilateral agreements that do not pertain to "national security, extradition, or international trade" are to be reviewed and perhaps withdrawn from (Fisher, 2017). The executive orders Trump drafted displayed a distrust of multilateral agreements that may be the most ingrained in Washington. Many of these treaties have long been disregarded by conservatives and proponents of isolationist foreign policy, who either see them as useless or, more sinisterly, as a way to bypass domestic political processes and codify a set of what they see as mostly liberal objectives (Bosco, 2017, p. 11).

In this regard, the reality that the Trump administration did not at all embrace the international pillars of the liberal order was obvious. This was also evident when US Secretary of State Mike Pompeo delivered a speech in Brussels praising nationalism and decrying multilateralism (Flockhart, 2020, p. 229). Pompeo stated that "international bodies" that limit national sovereignty "must be reformed or eliminated" (as cited in Stelzenmüller, 2019).

When the future of multilateral governance is concerned, a return to the golden age of multilateralism in the entire world is not expected. It is challenging to envision the creation of a cohesive and effective multilateral governance structure given the power dispersion and diversity of interests that characterize the current global system (Ikenberry, 2015, pp. 410–411). The political climate in the US has become more and more skeptical of multilateralism and international cooperation. International organizations, in particular during the Trump administration, were seen as encroaching on US sovereignty and impeding the country's capacity to further its interests.

To sum up, since the end of the Second World War, the US has played a significant role in various international organizations. These entities have afforded the US a forum to advance its principles and objectives and to collaborate with other nations on a variety of worldwide concerns. The US has had a multifaceted association with these entities, occasionally scrutinizing their efficacy and credibility. It has been a prominent advocate of international organizations, providing substantial financial support and assuming a pivotal role in their governing bodies. However, the US has maintained a complex relationship with these institutions, occasionally endorsing them while also scrutinizing their efficacy and credibility. In recent years, the US has displayed a growing inclination toward unilateralism, wherein its priorities are centered on advancing its interests at the expense of the global community. It has pursued unilateralist policies in different realms including trade and international security. The aforementioned policies have resulted in noteworthy ramifications for the international order, prompting apprehensions regarding the US' role in the global arena and the durability of the international system.

4.6   COVID-19 AND THE INTERNATIONAL SYSTEM

Many of the norms, institutions, and practices that supported the liberal international order and characterized American leadership with the end of the Second World War have been under immense pressure. The causes are numerous and interconnected: the reemergence of great-power political rivalry, exemplified by the deteriorating and increasingly hazardous relationship between the world's two largest powers, the US and China; the rise of populism and nationalism, as well as an apparent demise of democracy; the bewildering and disorienting impacts of new technology; and many others. These challenges have come to light as a polarized US becomes increasingly uncertain about its function in the world (Brands & Gavin, 2020, p. 2).

COVID-19 a "once-in-a-century global challenge" emphasized and exacerbated a number of pressures that were already straining the post-Cold War international system (Kahl & Berengaut, 2020). This outbreak was particularly disruptive because it erupted in a world that was becoming more and more chaotic. The question of how to recreate the international order following the COVID pandemic necessitates addressing not just the sickness, but also the underlying issues that it highlighted (Brands & Gavin, 2020, p. 5). Growing interdependence has made pandemics and other significant transnational shocks far more capable of upending the foundations of contemporary economies, communities, and international relations (Kahl & Wright, 2021, p. 103). The pandemic has presented numerous obstacles to international cooperation, coordination, and governance, revealing the shortcomings of the current international system. Global commerce and supply networks have been disrupted as a result of the COVID-19 outbreak. Essential medical supplies, food, and other products are in low supply because of the pandemic's impact on transportation, production, and distribution. The global nature of the economy has been brought into sharp focus, as has the necessity for more robust supply chains in the face of this upheaval. The pandemic has also prompted discussions on the impact of globalization on the spread of infectious illnesses and the need for improved response mechanisms during global health crises.

In addition, nationalism, protectionism, and xenophobia have all been exacerbated by the pandemic, heightening international tensions, and making international collaboration more difficult to achieve. Overly nationalistic responses to the epidemic have been condemned for putting domestic concerns before global health and collaboration. This has emphasized the importance of increased international collaboration and coordination to tackle global concerns.

The novel coronavirus was initially discovered in late December 2019 in the Hubei Province of China, near the city of Wuhan. Within a short period, adjacent nations reported their own instances, and it became evident that the virus had already spread throughout the whole planet. On January 30, 2020, the World Health Organization (WHO) issued a world-wide emergency declaration. On March 11, 2020, the WHO declared the crisis caused by the coronavirus a pandemic when the virus was quickly discovered across Africa and Europe (Timeline, 2020). A disease that killed more than 2.2 million people and left tens of millions very ill over the course of a year shocked the world (Tooze, 2021). A large portion of public life was suspended, schools were shuttered, families were split up, travel was halted, and the international economy was completely upended by the virus, which affected almost everyone's everyday activities. Social isolation, lockdowns, quarantines, and travel restrictions have all had negative impacts in addition to the disease's natural symptoms. It was claimed by different scholars that since the end of the Second World War, no one event has produced such widespread, rapid changes in human behavior. (Drezner, 2020, E18). While some theorists assert that the COVID-19 pandemic would accelerate the continuing wave of change in global politics (Haas, 2020), others argue that the individual repercussions of this catastrophe will not be as profound as previously believed (Drezner, 2020; Nye, 2020).

Early phases of the COVID-19 pandemic were marked by a life-threatening, rapidly spreading threat and persistent confusion over fundamental topics such as the nature of the virus and the effectiveness of reaction efforts. This pushed leaders to respond rapidly using ad hoc processes and made it challenging for citizens to build preferences about policy responses (Lipscy, 2020, E 106).

Unavoidably, many people have compared the COVID-19 outbreak with the strain of influenza that swept across 1918 and 1919. Possibly 500 million individuals worldwide were infected by the epidemic, which started in the closing months of the First World War, and 50 million died as a result (Kahl & Berengaut, 2020). The two decades after the global influenza epidemic were commonly referred to as the interwar years. These years were characterized by an increase in nationalism and xenophobia, the halting of globalization in favor of beggar-thy-neighbor policies, and the Great Depression (Kahl & Berengaut, 2020). According to Haas (2020), the COVID-19 pandemic and its repercussions are likely to "accelerate history" and return the globe to a much more perilous period. Although even before COVID-19, remnants of the interwar period had begun to reappear, the virus has highlighted these dynamics more clearly. COVID-19 is expected to intensify them significantly when economic and political turmoil ensues (Kahl & Berengaut, 2020) hence, COVID-19 has become the third significant crisis of the 21st century, following the 9/11 terrorist attacks, and the 2008 financial crisis.

COVID-19 has given governments additional opportunities to disrupt the politics and cohesiveness of democratic nations (Brands & Gavin, 2020, p. 15). The worldwide prestige of democracy has been harmed in different ways during the pandemic. First, the reaction of many democracies to the epidemic in terms of public health has been inadequate. Some of COVID-19's worst repercussions have been experienced by democracies such as Italy, Spain, France, the UK, Brazil, India, and—most notably—the US, and these damages have been exacerbated by governance failings. The delayed and vacillating responses of many of these nations' governments, the inadequacies in testing, tracking, and distributing medical supplies, and the overburdened hospital systems have all revealed democratic failings in the international community. Second, numerous autocrats have utilized the crisis to consolidate control and suppress opposition. From Belarus to Beijing to Brazil, dissidents have been subjected to rising official harassment. Other presidents, such as Hungary's Viktor Orbán, have suspended civil freedoms and implemented emergency legislation (Brands et al., 2020, p. 304).

The dominance of states, state sovereignty, state boundaries, and border restrictions appear to loom big as international politics got re-nationalized and the state acquired a more significant position. According to Kaplan (2020), great-power blocs with rising militaries and independent supply chains, the emergence of autocracies, social and socioeconomic gaps that have spawned nativism and populism, and middle-class anxiety in Western democracies resulted in a tale of new and reemerging global divisions.

Since it is conceivable that globalization and international collaboration will retreat, Kaplan (2020) called this new period "Globalization 2.0." He considers COVID-19 as "an economic and geopolitical shock," "the historical marker between the first phase of globalization and the second … In sum, it is a story about new and reemerging global divisions" (Kaplan, 2020).

The virus spread over the whole world very quickly. South Korea, Iran, and northern Italy all developed into new hot spots by March 11, 2020. The epidemic also spread to New York City, but on the eve of the breakout, the American president did nothing to prepare the nation and its citizens (Sheng, 2022, pp. 1–2). Trump was incompetent, and as a result of his inactivity and lack of a national policy, he served as an example of what not to do in a pandemic. By the end of the summer, the virus had spread from cities in the northeast to cities across the nation, rural regions, and every part of the country. As a result, by the beginning of April, the US was dominating the rest of the globe in both confirmed cases and fatalities. By the end of April, there were over 1 million confirmed cases in the country, making up almost one-third of all confirmed cases at that time worldwide (Sheng, 2022, p. 2).

The majority of governments, even the world's most powerful, adopted travel bans, implemented export controls, hoarded or obscured information, and marginalized the WHO and other multilateral organizations. COVID-19 appears to have exposed the liberal order and the international community as illusions while revealing the dire repercussions of deteriorating global collaboration (Patrick, 2020b). Regional collaboration and state-level solutions have become superior to worldwide cooperation in the battle against the virus. Once again, sovereign governments are the primary protagonists in the fight against the disease. Some academics predict that after the COVID-19 pandemic, sovereign nations will continue to play a major role in the international community, which might make them the center of international relations study once more (Sheng, 2022, p. 5). Hence, it may be noted that the COVID-19 crisis underlined the inadequacies of current international institutions in safeguarding people from natural and man-made disasters. Both the Group of 7 and the Group of 20 met virtually as a result of the epidemic. Neither group was able to move past hyperbole and take meaningful action to jointly attack the virus or lessen its effects on the global economy. While the UNSC was paralyzed by the blame game between the US and China, the organization was trying to finance its comparatively meager $2 billion COVID-19 response fund amid a "dire" liquidity crisis (Kahl & Berengaut, 2020). Hence, the pandemic has brought to light the need to reform and improve these organizations, as well as create new systems for coordinating efforts throughout the world.

In addition, the EU may be the international organization most in danger as a result of COVID-19. The 2008 financial crisis, the prolonged eurozone debt crisis that followed it, the 2015 wave of immigration, Brexit, the rise of right-wing and populist movements, the erosion of democracy in countries like Hungary, the intensifying transatlantic tensions with the Trump administration, and Russian efforts to sow discord and amplify Euroskepticism have all taken a toll on the EU in recent years. In this regard, some researchers worry that the simultaneous economic and health catastrophes caused by COVID-19 might drive the union into the dept. EU member states banned the export of some essential medical equipment and reverted to trends of self-help. Additionally, Italy's and Spain's requests for financial support have resurrected the scars of the eurozone crisis, with some Northern European nations blaming Southern European nations for repeatedly failing to manage their finances appropriately (Kahl & Berengaut, 2020).

When pandemic influenza attacked a globe devastated by war a century ago, there were few global organizations. Countries battled their shared microbial adversary on their own. Today, several international systems exist to manage global public health catastrophes and their economic, social, and political consequences. However, the availability of such institutions has not prevented the majority of governments from adopting a unilateral stance during the COVID-19 crisis (Patrrick, 2020). The WHO, the worldwide institution in charge of pandemic disease management, was prominent during the first epidemic in Wuhan but was subsequently overshadowed due to tensions between the US and China. Additionally, the EU did not meet the demands of its constituents. Governments undertook ad hoc, uncoordinated, and even competing methods to manage COVID-19, precipitating a virtual collapse of global cooperation. President Trump was the WHO's most vocal opponent. He froze US financing in April 2020 and later announced that the US will withdraw from the WHO altogether, a move that President Joe Biden eventually overturned (Jones & Hameiri, 2022).

Accordingly, the virus has significantly amplified trade-offs and highlighted the difficulties of leading in a highly interconnected environment. As a result, the global pandemic offers a helpful prism through which to examine, comprehend, and interact with the politics of international order. It should come as no surprise that the pandemic has sparked an abundance of assessments that claim that there will be changes in global politics. Kurt Campbell and Rush Doshi (2020) warned that the US may experience a "Suez moment" if it fails to respond effectively to the challenge. This phrase alludes to the 1956 Suez crisis, which served as a metaphor for the UK's eventual decline as a superpower (Sheng, 2022, pp. vi-vii).

According to Fukuyama (2020), when it comes to handling the COVID-19 disease, some nations have done better than others. No particular type of regime is relevant. Although some democracies succeeded well, others did not. State capability, social trust, and leadership have all contributed to effective pandemic responses. The damage that has been done to nations with all three—capable state machinery, a government that the populace trusts and pays attention to, and capable leaders—has been admirably contained. Countries that have failed have had their inhabitants and economies exposed and vulnerable due to their dysfunctional states or weak leadership (Fukuyama, 2020).

Fukuyama (2020) states that compared to Europe or the US, East Asia has handled the issue better. Beijing managed to retake control of the situation and moved on to the next difficulty to rapidly and sustainably speed up its economy. Contrarily, the US botched its reaction horribly and saw a significant decline in its reputation. The nation possesses a sizable amount of potential state capacity and an exceptional track record in dealing with epidemic emergencies, but its deeply divided population and inept leader prevented the state from operating efficiently. Instead of fostering unity, the president fostered conflict, politicized assistance distribution, shifted decision-making authority to governors while stirring unrest against them for defending public health, and attacked foreign organizations rather than energizing them (Fukuyama, 2020).

In this regard, COVID-19 has caused the US-led liberal international order to continue to deteriorate, the relative weakening of the US, and a rise of populist and isolationist policies. The progression of COVID-19 was hastened by a countervailing factor: the prevalence of populism and anti-globalization sentiment among key policy elites. In a more globalized society, however, it impeded and slowed the coordinated reaction that would have been required to prevent the spread of an aggressive illness. Initially, US leaders relied on border closures and travel restrictions as replacements for a full national and international response, rather than as components. Early in the year 2020, the world lacked the solidarity and cooperation required to handle the crisis effectively (Brands et al., 2020, p. 300).

According to Nye (2020), due to the pandemic, the economic gap between China and other big powers shifted substantially, as each struggles to control COVID-19. China is increasingly taking the lead in its political convenience marriage to Russia. Unsurprisingly, given its growing influence, China wants respect and deference. Not only are nearby partners influenced by the Belt and Road Initiative, but also those in Europe and Latin America. Voting against China within international organizations has become too expensive since doing so puts Chinese aid, investment, and access to the biggest market in the world at risk. Due to the pandemic's weakening of Western economies in comparison to China's, China's government and significant corporations could reform institutions and establish norms to their liking (Nye, 2020).

In addition, the coronavirus has further worsened transatlantic relations, which are already strained. The failure of the G7 to publish a statement was due to the Trump administration's insistence on mentioning the "China virus." A European diplomat argued that "What the State Department has suggested is a red line. You cannot agree with this branding of this virus and trying to communicate this" (as cited in Marquardt & Hansler, 2020). Leaders have warned that COVID-19 would be more damaging than Brexit, immigration, and the financial crisis. Jacques Delors, the former European Commission president, stated that the absence of solidarity presented "a mortal danger to the European Union" (as cited in Rankin, 2020). In addition, former Italian Prime Minister Enrico Letta stated that the pandemic poses a "deadly risk" to the EU, he then added that the EU's greatest threat was "the Trump virus." If everyone adopted the "Italy first," "Belgium first," or "Germany first" plan, he warned, "we will all sink together" (as cited in Rankin, 2020).

The global health system has also been severely tested by the COVID-19 pandemic, revealing its vulnerabilities and shortcomings. As a result of the pandemic, there is a pressing need for improved supply chain resilience, enhanced international collaboration and coordination, and the revision of current international institutions. Investment in health care and social welfare systems, as well as increased readiness for future global health catastrophes, have been highlighted by the pandemic. As the globe recovers from the COVID-19 pandemic, the lessons must be reflected upon and used to develop a more robust, sustainable, and equitable international order.

COVID-19 is not only a public health emergency. It is an unprecedented economic catastrophe. COVID-19 has had a disastrous impact on the world economy. Many nations' economies have suffered as a direct effect of COVID-19, and some have even gone into recession. The pandemic was responsible for the biggest economic downturn in modern times and nearly sparked a huge financial catastrophe in the US, which was only prevented thanks to the swift and decisive action taken by the Federal Reserve (Kahl & Wright, 2021, p. 21). The pandemic's economic impact has prompted debate over the proper function of international financial institutions during times of crisis. It has been brought to light that more funding for health care and social services is needed to reduce the potential effects of future pandemics. As a result of quarantines, shelter-in-place orders, and other limitations, the economy collapsed and unemployment spiked in the world (Brands & Gavin, 2020, p. 13). Travel and tourism were halted globally, trade has been affected, industries and businesses have closed, and billions of people were compelled into social isolation and shelter in place (Kahl & Berengaut, 2020). Moreover, according to the IMF, "the economic damage is mounting across all countries, tracking the sharp rise in new infections and containment measures implemented by governments," resulting in a global economic meltdown worse than the financial crisis of 2008 (Bluedorn et al., 2020). Moreover, the WTO forecasted in April 2020 that global commerce would shrink by around 32 percent in 2020, which was far higher than the fall forecast (Trade Set to Plunge, 2020).

Accordingly, the US hesitated to assume a leading position during pandemics. Extreme political division, exacerbated by the presidential impeachment story and election-year scheming, rendered Americans unable to even reach a shared sense of the threat. The main characteristics of contemporary American governance, including denigration of expertise, a propensity for trafficking in false or misleading information, resistance to systematic planning or preparation, and a hyper-transactional foreign policy, rendered the US uniquely ill-equipped to exercise global leadership and gave its response a unilateral value (Brands et al., 2020, p. 302).

In this regard, the pandemic undermined the US' and the Trump administration's credibility internationally and domestically. According to Fareed Zakaria (2020), due partly to the inefficiency of its administration, the US was on course to see the greatest coronavirus outbreak among affluent nations. Washington faced a lack of medical equipment, including ventilators, masks, and gloves, as there was no national emergency infrastructure to distribute new supplies swiftly. Hence, Zakaria (2020) characterized Washington as a "government ill executed."

The US implemented isolationist and nationalist policies during the pandemic. It has pulled away from its allies and international collaboration and was unsuccessful in helping other states cope with the crisis because of its America First policy agenda (Kahl & Berengaut, 2020). It will be difficult to forget the image of a hapless superpower with the world's largest economy and military caught with its trousers down and then brought to its knees by a forewarned virus. While Trump may not care about worldwide public opinion, many Americans across the political spectrum felt powerless (Acharya, 2020). All of this may contribute to another blow to the liberal international order, which is already suffering due to Trump's policies and the rise of Western populism. According to Acharya (2021), the fact that the US, the world's strongest nation in terms of (current) economic, military, and "soft" power, simultaneously had the worst infection and death rate in the whole globe, and by a significant margin, cannot be attributed just to Trump's bad leadership. Instead, systemically, a deficient public health system, racial inequity, and a political system were also to blame (Acharya, 2021, p. 12).

In this regard, the question of how the US-led international system will be shaped after COVID-19 has become significant. Notably, the post-pandemic global order will be different, but this does not necessitate the emergence of a new world after the coronavirus. Rather, it is contended that international order will enter a new epoch in which the worldwide distribution of power and the method and form of global governance will affect international order. Similar to past pandemics, which have influenced and transformed world orders, the new coronavirus is not only a catastrophe for global public health, but it will also cause a shift in world order (Acharya, 2020). The closure of national and provincial boundaries and the reassertion of state sovereignty has further debunked one of the most pervasive globalization clichés, that of a world without borders. Hence, in the long term, the crisis is anticipated to erode support for globalization, which was already damaged by increasing populism and the Trump administration's policies (Acharya, 2020). The pandemic may also have somewhat amplified pre-existing tendencies, including rising Chinese influence, domestic populism and division in the West, and the rise of authoritarian governments globally (Nye, 2020).

To sum up, the liberal international system is vulnerable to COVID-19 because it has necessitated some degree of closure while openness in politics and the economy is a hallmark of the liberal order. The liberal international order's advocacy of relatively open borders is undermined by the enforcement of border controls on foreigners and non-residents. Border closures, discrimination, and limitations on the right to privacy violate political liberties, which have been reduced in liberal democracies to address the issue (Norrlöf, 2020, pp. 808–811). Multilateral institutions and organizations have failed to mobilize a global response since nations have naturally been preoccupied with fighting the virus within their borders, particularly in the absence of American leadership. Hence, it would appear that COVID-19 poses an enormous threat to the international system. After all, it is not only a severe, multifaceted problem that calls for international cooperation. It also has the unfortunate effect of amplifying a number of pre-existing dynamics that are driving geopolitics in a less cooperative and more combative path (Kahl & Berengaut, 2020). The COVID-19 pandemic is anticipated to hasten the disintegration of the current liberal international order. COVID-19 does not indicate the demise of globalization or global governance, but it is conceivable that the pandemic will drive the globe further away from an international order dominated by the US and transport in a more pluralistic era.

4.7   RUSSIA-UKRAINE CONFLICT

After COVID-19, the Russia-Ukraine conflict has also contributed to interrogating the sustainability of the liberal international order. The Russian operation in Ukraine resulted in the greatest conflict between Russia and NATO since the end of the Cold War. The Ukraine-Russia War is seen by many military and political commentators as a turning moment in the development of global politics. A majority of analysts also concur that the Ukrainian state and its citizens serve as the principal actors in the ongoing international conflict, not as actors but more as objects on the negotiation table.

According to Kagan (2022), the invasion of Ukraine by Russia was a response to the US' growing post-Cold War hegemony. The conflict has occurred in a historical and geopolitical setting in which the US has had a starring role. The dissolution of the Soviet Union increased the US' global political influence. This was due to the appeal of the US' amalgamation of power and democratic principles, which offered a sense of security, prosperity, freedom, and autonomy to those seeking it. Hence, the US has represented a significant impediment to Russia's efforts to expand its sphere of influence (Kagan, 2022). Kagan claims that Eastern Europe's past three decades prove this. Washington didn't want regional dominance. After the Cold War, Eastern Europe's newly liberated countries, including Ukraine, looked to the US and its European allies because they felt joining the transatlantic community was the route to independence, democracy, and prosperity. Eastern Europeans wanted to escape decades of Russian and Soviet domination, and allying with Washington at a time of Russian weakness gave them an opportunity. Even if the US had denied their requests to join NATO and other Western institutions, the former Soviet satellites would have resisted Moscow's attempts to reintegrate them. As a result, Putin would have blamed the US for this anti-Russian activity because it attracted Eastern Europeans (Kagan, 2022).

In an interview in 2019, Putin stated, "The liberal idea has become obsolete" (as cited in Barber et al., 2019). As part of what Moscow referred to as an "objective process," Russia aspired to collaborate with China and other nations to oppose the American-led international system and forge a new multipolar world (Tierney, 2022). There is no doubt that the Russian invasion has effects that extend well beyond Ukraine's borders. Putin has stated his desire to rebuild as much of the old Soviet Union as he can, bringing Ukraine into Russia and establishing a sphere of influence that encompasses all the Eastern European nations that joined NATO starting in the 1990s (Fukuyama, 2022b). Hence, Putin has made it clear by invading Ukraine that he no longer accepts the tenet of the post-Second World War system, which is that international boundaries cannot be altered via the use of force alone (Brunk & Hakimi, 2022, p. 688). In a speech at the Munich Conference on Security Policy in 2007, Putin hinted at his desire to overturn the international order. He stated that "... we have reached that decisive moment when we must seriously think about the architecture of global security … the US, has overstepped its national borders in every way" (Putin, 2007). He also defined a unipolar world as "one type of situation, namely one center of authority, one center of force, one center of decision-making" where "no one feels safe" (Putin, 2007).

In addition, as his rhetoric toward Ukraine heated up in the summer of 2021, Putin openly defied this command. In an essay, he emphasized the shared history between Russia and Ukraine and accused the West of forcing Ukraine to change its identity (Putin, 2021). He described Ukraine as being protected and controlled by the Western powers and being a part of an "anti-Russia project." He also underlined that the "true sovereignty of Ukraine is possible only in partnership with Russia." An independent Ukraine that was free to sever ties with Moscow and align itself more closely with the West would no longer be tolerated by Russia (Brunk & Hakimi, 2022, p. 688).

In this respect, since the collapse of the Soviet Union, the Ukrainian-Russian relationship has been marked by abnormality, instability, and conflict (Mbah & Wasum, 2022, p. 145). The origins of war can be traced back to the dissolution of the Soviet Union in 1991. The concept of Ukraine as a sovereign nation with a distinct national identity was challenging for a significant number of Russians to conceive. Putin perceived the division of the two states as an unnatural occurrence, which generated an artificial disharmony that lacked rationality in the context of their shared past. Putin also expressed concern regarding the potential escalation of Ukraine's perceived threat to Russia as it aligns itself more closely with Western nations. This scenario would particularly apply if the nation were to align itself with Western organizations, such as the EU and NATO. Additionally, it could also occur if the nation was regarded as an exemplar of a democratic society that exhibits limited tolerance for authoritarian leaders (Freedman, 2022, p. 361).

Accordingly, examining the chronology of events that preceded the Russian invasion of Ukraine holds great importance regarding international politics. Especially for the last 15 years, Russia evolved as a belligerent revisionist force. Russia's leadership is determined to make up for some of the losses of the 1990s, expand its territory, and create strong zones of influence, as evidenced by its war in Georgia in 2008, the annexation of Crimea, intervention in the Donbas in 2014, and invasion of Ukraine in 2022 (Lehne, 2023).

In the year 2014, Putin exerted significant influence over the political landscape of Russia. He leveraged the conflicts in Kosovo and the Second Chechen War to advance their political career, subsequently utilizing these events to assert that Russia had regained its strategic prowess. The country of Ukraine was a matter of particular significance. The protests and popular revolt known as the Euromaidan that occurred in Ukraine in 2014 resulted in the removal of President Viktor Yanukovych, who was known to be aligned with Russia's interests (Freedman, 2022, p. 364). Following this, the interim government, which was pro-Western in its orientation, signed a trade agreement with the EU, marking the initial step toward membership. In April of the same year, Russia seized control of Crimea. During the period spanning from 2014 to 2015, the Minsk Accord, which pertains to a cease-fire, was ratified by Russia, Ukraine, France, and Germany. Subsequently, in April 2019, Volodymyr Zelenskyy was democratically elected as the president of Ukraine (Mbah & Wasum, 2022, p. 145). In January 2021, President Zelenskyy requested Ukraine join NATO, which subsequently led to Russia amassing troops at Ukraine's border under the guise of conducting training exercises. This development resulted in escalating tensions between Western countries, Russia, and Ukraine, culminating in Russia's invasion of Ukraine on February 24, 2022. In the initial weeks of February 2022, satellite imagery revealed a significant concentration of Russian military personnel along its border with Belarus, marking the most substantial deployment of Russian troops in the region since the end of the Cold War (Balmforth et al., 2022). The negotiations among the US, Russia, and European nations, comprising France and Germany, were unsuccessful in achieving a resolution. The US issued a warning in late February 2022, indicating that Russia had intentions to invade Ukraine. This warning was based on Russia's increasing military presence at the border shared by Russia and Ukraine. Subsequently, troops were dispatched by President Putin to Luhansk and Donetsk under the pretext of serving a "peacekeeping" role (Center for Preventive Action, 2023).

The US has implemented a multifaceted and ongoing response to Russia's invasion of Ukraine, which commenced in 2014. Executive Order 13660 was signed by President Obama on March 6, 2014. It granted authorization for the imposition of sanctions on individuals and entities found to be responsible for encroaching upon the sovereignty and territorial integrity of Ukraine, or for misappropriating the assets of the

Ukrainian populace. The aforementioned sanctions imposed limitations on the mobility of specific individuals and officials (Executive Order No. 13660, 2014). Similarly, following the recent attacks Biden administration announced sanctions against Russia. In the US NSS adopted in October 2022, it is stated:

> America maintains our fundamental commitment to the pursuit of a Europe that is whole, free, and at peace. Russia's further invasion of Ukraine poses a grave threat to this vision, which is why we are determined to support Ukraine in defending its sovereignty and territorial integrity while imposing severe costs on Moscow for its aggression ... We have joined with allies and partners in Europe and around the globe to impose sanctions and export controls that will degrade Russia's ability to wage future wars of aggression.

Following the recent attack, Ukraine's US-led Western allies have implemented significant financial sanctions against Russia, including limitations on the central bank and the removal of key banks from the primary global payments system (Aloisi & Daniel, 2022). The Nord Stream 2 gas pipeline project has been suspended by Germany. The 2022 aggression of Russia toward Ukraine and the consequential imposition of severe financial sanctions resulted in a significant economic impact not only on President Vladimir Putin's Russia but also on the country's overall financial stability. The consequences are also posing a threat to the worldwide economy, destabilizing financial markets and increasing the level of risk for all individuals (Wiseman & McHugh, 2022). Russia and Ukraine play a significant role in the global market as exporters of commodities such as oil, natural gas, coal, wheat, and other goods. According to Mark Zandi, the chief economist at Moody's Analytics, both nations are responsible for producing 70 percent of the world's neon, which is a crucial commodity in the manufacturing of semiconductors (Wiseman & McHugh, 2022). This has caused concern during the current crisis, particularly among nations and automakers who are already experiencing a shortage of computer chips. Zandi notes that both nations contribute equally to 13 percent of the worldwide supply of titanium, a crucial component in the production of commercial aircraft, and 30 percent of global palladium, which is utilized in the manufacturing of automobiles, mobile devices, and dental restorations. As a result, the ramifications of this crisis on the global supply chain are significant (Wiseman & McHugh, 2022).

Accordingly, the Russia-Ukraine conflict can be attributed to underlying tensions between the two nations, stemming from their deep-rooted historical and cultural connections spanning several centuries. In recent times, similar to the Syrian crisis, the conflict between Russia and Ukraine has been converted into a proxy war due to the involvement of various regional and global actors to protect their respective interests in the region. The Kremlin has alleged that the US is engaged in a proxy conflict against Russia, following the latter's decision to augment military aid to Ukraine and extend an invitation to Zelenskyy for a momentous diplomatic visit (Russia Accuses US, 2022). Subsequently, Moscow has further strengthened its political and economic relations with China while also establishing partnerships with significant powers in the Middle East. The aforementioned situation has resulted in significant geopolitical tensions that are likely to result in intense rivalry among major global powers.

Allegations have been made that Russia has furnished military and monetary assistance to separatist insurgents in the eastern region of Ukraine, whereas Ukraine has garnered backing from Western nations, such as the US and the European countries. The conflict has transformed into a proxy war due to the significant involvement of Russia and Ukraine in the region, as well as the vested interests of other nations in the outcome. Russia perceives Ukraine as a constituent element of its sphere of influence and endeavors to uphold its status as a preeminent force in the area. Conversely, the US perceives Ukraine as a significant partner and endeavors to impede Russia's efforts to extend its sphere of influence.

With the rise of regional powers and the changing nature of warfare, the world has witnessed an increase in the frequency of proxy wars in global politics. The concept of a proxy war differs from both a conventional war, in which a state assumes responsibility for its own defense or offense, and an alliance, in which major and minor powers collaborate and contribute significantly according to their respective capabilities. Proxies are utilized by states for various purposes. In the context of the US, the matter at hand frequently pertains to financial expenses, as individuals residing in a particular area engage in combat and ultimately lose their lives to spare American citizens from such sacrifices (Byman, 2018). Hence, it is comparatively convenient for nations to extend assistance to proxy forces instead of directly engaging in a conflict. This enables individual states to pursue their interests without jeopardizing their own military personnel or assets. Thus, the Russia-Ukraine crisis is a prime example of a proxy war. The conflict has attracted outside actors such as the US and the EU, who have imposed sanctions on Russia and provided military support to Ukraine. This has further escalated the conflict and turned it into a proxy war between the Russia-China alliance and the Western bloc led by the US. During the Russia-Ukraine conflict, the Ukrainian government has received military and financial assistance from the US, enabling Washington to combat separatist rebels without deploying its own military personnel.

In this regard, the US engagement in proxy war reveals that the post-Cold War international order based on US hegemony is altering and the US is not the absolute power in world politics. In recent years, Washington has started to use proxies for regional balances of power instead of directly engaging alone and using its power to solve conflicts. The US continues to implement a regional balance of power policies mentioned in the NSS issued by the White House in December 2017. Accordingly, it is stated in the document that, "We will promote a balance of power that favors the US, our allies, and our partners ... Sustaining favorable balances of power will require a strong commitment and close cooperation with allies and partners because allies and partners magnify US power and extend US influence" (NSS, 2017, pp. ii-45). Hence, through a proxy war, the US has implemented balance of power policies in the Russia-Ukraine conflict to rally the liberal international order and take action against Russia. This reveals that the hegemonic power of the US is in decline.

In addition, instead of actively engaging in the Russia-Ukraine conflict, the US prefers to support Ukraine by providing economic and security assistance. Washington does not aspire to constitute a peacekeeping force led by the US and put an end to the conflict. Instead, it aims to share the burden by making alliances with European countries. In the current conflict, a large group of nations has banded together to assist a victim of blatant aggression.

Furthermore, the ongoing conflict between Russia and Ukraine has a significant effect on the international political landscape, but international organizations established in the US-led liberal order are often incapable of resolving worldwide or local conflicts. The increasing influence of China and Russia is a contributing factor to the lack of effectiveness exhibited by international institutions. These two nations are at the forefront of advocating for the redistribution of political and economic power among international and regional entities. China is progressively extending its sphere of influence. The military incursion has resulted in a significant increase in economic sanctions, ranging from the exclusion of a majority of Russian financial institutions from the SWIFT communication network to prohibitions and substantial restrictions on the exportation of energy resources. The imposition of economic sanctions by Western nations on Russia has resulted in an escalation of international trade between Russia and China. In the previous year, the bilateral trade between China and Russia reached an unprecedented volume of $190 billion (Gao et al., 2023). Hence, China has been endeavoring to occupy the power vacuum in global politics that has arisen due to the absence of Western nations. The Russia-Ukraine war is hardly independent of the global power struggle and US efforts to balance China.

Similarly, according to a text of the speech to a forum advocating for the partnership between the US and Europe, held at Ditchley Park, 100 kilometers west of London, former British Prime Minister Tony Blair stated, "The Ukraine war shows that the West's dominance is coming to an end as China rises to superpower status in partnership with Russia at one of the most significant inflection points in centuries" (as cited in Faulconbridge, 2022). He also added, "The world is going to be at least bi-polar and possibly multi-polar," and that, "The biggest geo-political change of this century will come from China not Russia" (as cited in Faulconbridge, 2022). Thus, the Russia-Ukraine conflict reveals that American supremacy has weakened and that US power has fallen behind in maintaining liberal international order.

In this regard, the protracted conflict between Russia and Ukraine has persisted for a number of years and exhibited a trend of intensification in the year 2022. The ramifications of the conflict have been significant. Thousands of people have lost their lives or sustained injuries, while a significant number have been compelled to evacuate their residences. The ongoing conflict between the two nations has resulted in noteworthy economic repercussions, as the imposition of sanctions and trade limitations have inflicted considerable harm on their respective economies.

Biden promised at the early stages of his administration that the US would "again lead not just by the example of our power but the power of our example" (Biden, 2022). However, when the recent Russia-Ukraine conflict is considered, it is obvious that the era of post-Cold War optimism regarding the US-led international order has almost passed. The conflict raised questions about American supremacy in world politics. The US' dream of a global order based on democracy, the rule of law, and multilateral collaboration, which had already begun to look implausible in recent years, now appears to be completely illusory (Lehne, 2023). The projected outcomes were not produced by globalization or the fall of the Iron Curtain, but the fact that some of these confrontations started and have persisted is more concerning. There are still a number of unanswered concerns regarding the future role of the US in the global arena and the nature of the transatlantic partnership in the coming years that are brought up by the conflict in Ukraine. The conflict has raised questions about the durability of the US-led liberal international order. Likwise, the future of the international political system will be significantly impacted by the Russian offensive in Ukraine and the escalating US-China conflict.

4.8   CYBERTERRORISM AND THE LIBERAL ORDER

In contemporary times, there has been a surge in apprehension regarding technological advancements in global politics. The emergence of the internet during the 20th century is widely regarded as a significant technological advancement, having originated at the heart of the liberal international order. The significant correlation between liberalism and technological advancement has played a pivotal role in the development of liberal democracies and the liberal international system (Kanevskiy, 2023, pp. 3–4). The liberal order in the latter half of the 20th century was propelled by globalization, which involved the internationalization of production chains and enhanced connectivity between capitalist centers worldwide, facilitated by technological advancements. However, the potential for liberalization offered by the internet was jeopardized by political entities in both authoritarian and democratic nations, as well as various forms of populist and illiberal groups (Kanevskiy, 2023, pp. 3–4).

The information sector has been a significant driver of growth and interconnectedness, owing to profound technological changes. While previously this technological revolution was viewed as almost entirely beneficial to humanity, some of its dark sides have become more apparent. The proliferation of disinformation campaigns has contributed to the exacerbation of political polarization within democratic societies. The fields of artificial intelligence, robotics, machine learning, and biotechnology hold great potential for significant advancements that could benefit humanity. However, these same fields also pose potential risks and dangers that must be taken into consideration (Brands & Gavin, 2020, p. 14).

Similar to how the introduction of advanced weaponry and contemporary combat techniques were brought about by the First World War in the 20th century, the information age is presently transforming the nature of warfare in the 21st century. Globally, there is a growing prevalence of information technology in various aspects, such as weapons systems, defense infrastructures, and national economies. Consequently, cyberspace has emerged as a novel arena for international conflict. The utilization of information attacks has emerged as a form of terrorism in the current era. In contrast to the traditional approach of achieving military triumphs through direct combat involving soldiers and weaponry, contemporary information warfare is characterized by cyberattacks, perpetrated by hackers who represent either private entities or governments (Adams, 2001, p. 98).

Greater international connectivity and an improvement in information sharing and presentation have both been made possible by the digital revolution. Digital communication has been widely acknowledged for its potential to affect change in society, whether at the local, national, or global level. Hence, digital communication is a significant factor in both maintaining and challenging the existing international system. It effectively neutralizes the conventional limitations of geopolitical factors by minimizing the significance of spatial and temporal considerations, and by facilitating the establishment of worldwide networks and associations (Simons, 209, p. 108).

The digital realm is currently being utilized to challenge and disrupt the liberal world order led by the US. The act of intentionally providing false information to deceive, commonly known as disinformation, has been a longstanding practice throughout history. However, with the advancement of the internet, widespread global connectivity, and the prevalence of social media, the effectiveness of disinformation has grown exponentially (Matthews, 2019, p. 86). The employment of social media has become a potent tool, and its malevolent utilization presents a grave danger to democratic societies that lack the necessary measures to safeguard against it. The utilization of weaponized social media as a means to disseminate disinformation poses a distinct menace to the existing international order. Thus, social media is utilized by disinformation campaigns to undermine the US, posing a threat to the US-led international order through the dissemination of false information, fostering division, incitement of instability, and erosion of national determination (Matthews, 2019, p. 86).

The geographical scope of the internet is limitless. The realm of cyberspace transcends geographical boundaries, traversing various legal domains and posing distinct complexities in ascertaining account-ability and purpose. Cyberterrorism takes advantage of online activities, including social media campaigns or online propaganda campaigns and hacking activities. It pertains to the utilization of digital technology to instill fear, inflict harm, or exert pressure on individuals or governing bodies. Cyberterrorists employ a range of tactics, including but not limited to hacking, spreading viruses, and other forms of malware, to illicitly access confidential data, disrupt computer networks, and inflict harm. The employment of fake news by cyberterrorists serves as a mechanism to disseminate false information, exert influence over the perceptions of the general populace, and foment societal turmoil. Cyberterrorists employ diverse tactics to disseminate disinformation, such as leveraging social media platforms, websites, and virtual discussion boards.

Leon Edward Panetta, the former director of the US Central Intelligence Agency (CIA) and then US Defense Secretary, stated, "Cyber-attacks are every bit as real as the more well-known threats like terrorism, nuclear weapons proliferation and the turmoil that we see in the Middle East" (as cited in Conway, 2018, p. 105). Accordingly, the significance of cyberse-curity has increased considerably recently and has become a fundamental aspect of national security policies in numerous countries globally. This development has garnered the attention of various stakeholders such as utilities, regulators, energy markets, and government entities. The employ-ment of cyber warfare is rapidly emerging as a prominent mode of warfare and a pivotal instrument for military strategists (Dawson, 2015, p. 1).

Terrorism persists as a societal affliction and is progressively facili-tated by the dissemination of information and technology. Both state and non-state actors can cause disruptions in cyberspace without the need for advanced military capabilities (Lissner & Rapp-Hooper, 2018, p. 14). Furthermore, there is a lack of established regulations regarding cyber violations, and a precise delineation of cyber warfare remains elusive. The detection and prevention of cyberterrorism pose a significant challenge due to its elusive nature. The efficacy of conventional counterterrorism techniques, such as intelligence gathering and surveillance, is diminished in the digital domain. Cyberterrorists can conduct their operations from any location globally, and their assaults can be executed expeditiously and covertly.

Several contemporary threats are not instantly existential and lack direct implications for the territorial integrity of sovereign states, rendering the identification and anticipation of aggression more challenging. In addition, a significant portion of this conduct is transpiring within sectors that lack well-established regulations and standards, thereby exacerbating the challenge of achieving a coordinated and efficacious response from nation-states (Lissner & Rapp-Hooper, 2018, p. 15).

Cyberterrorism can be used to undermine democratic institutions and values. The proper functioning of democracies is contingent upon the presence of communication that is both free and open. The potential for cyberterrorists to disseminate disinformation and propaganda via social media and other digital platforms is a concern. In addition, they can interfere with crucial infrastructure, such as financial systems and power grids, thereby generating disorder and instability.

The potential for cyberterrorism poses a global threat that surpasses geographical limits. The impact of this phenomenon is observed worldwide, and it has implications for democratic systems around the world. The proliferation of authoritarian regimes globally has intensified the perceived danger. Frequently, these political regimes employ cyberterrorism as a means to stifle opposition and uphold their authority.

In this regard, the topic of cybersecurity has emerged as a significant area of concern with implications for national and international affairs, as well as economic and societal domains, impacting multiple nations. Since the early 1990s, there has been a trend of exploiting vulnerabilities by users to gain unauthorized access to networks with malicious intent. Since cybercriminals and other digital offenders are continually coming up with new ways to attack systems and access private information, many new challenges and threats come along with this new ease of communication and access. The frequency of cyberattacks on the networks of nations has been increasing at an exponential pace in recent times. This encompasses the presence of malevolent embedded programming, the utilization of preexisting vulnerabilities, and additional methods of unauthorized access. Cyberattacks have the potential to be launched globally from any location, utilizing a computer with an obscured Internet Protocol (IP) address (Dawson, 2015, p. 1).

Following the end of the Cold War, the US military emerged as an unchallenged superpower in both conventional and nuclear capabilities. The US, despite its significant military might and technological advancements in information technology, paradoxically finds itself at the highest risk of cyberattacks (Adams, 2001, p. 98). The US' reliance on cyberspace has grown significantly, encompassing the facilitation of goods and services, the maintenance of crucial infrastructure (including electricity, water, banking, communication, and transportation), and the operation of military systems. Simultaneously, there has been a rise in malevolent conduct within the realm of cyberspace perpetrated by both nation-states and nonstate actors possessing advanced capabilities. It is paradoxical that the US' leadership in the development of cyber technology and the internet has resulted in a disproportionate vulnerability to damage caused by cyber instruments (Nye, 2016, p. 44).

As the decades passed, the post-Cold War liberal order encountered different challenges. The growing dangers posed by cyber threats call into question the sustainability of the liberal international order. The proliferation of technology in various domains of human existence has engendered a novel susceptibility for democratic systems globally in recent times. The US' responsibility within the liberal international order is to offer guidance and maintain stability, which is essential for facilitating economic and informational exchange. However, concerning transnational security, the US has not been successful in fulfilling its role as the leader of collective hegemony (Kiggins, 2014, p. 161). Despite Washington's efforts to establish and manage a cohesive approach to address cyber threats to global security, it remains unable to avert their detrimental impact on the liberal order. The US faces challenges in adopting a proactive stance toward cybersecurity in the context of countering cyberterrorism. This includes the need to invest in novel technologies and training programs, enhance information sharing and coordination among various entities, and devise more efficacious deterrence strategies. It is important to note that the actions of the US are not motivated by an altruistic or benevolent concept of global leadership. Hence, the US has no intention to guide cyberspace stakeholders in the development of norms and rules for global cybersecurity governance regimes and institutions. Such regimes and institutions would aim to impart to states the necessary norms and rules for ensuring a stable and secure cyber domain, which would facilitate the continued flourishing of global information and economic exchange (Kiggins, 2014, p. 161).

Conclusion

The 1920s and 1930s interwar years saw a great deal of social, political, and economic turmoil. International organizations unable to handle great-power rivalry conflicted with the rising nationalism and the revisionist goals of authoritarian powers. The community of democracies broke apart as a result of the US' inward orientation. When recent developments of the international order are considered, it might be claimed that there are some unsettling similarities between today's world politics and that chaotic and conflict-prone period.

The American grand strategy objective, which was formerly stated as worldwide democracy, victory for all mankind, and a worldwide victory for freedom, now appears curiously out of date and out of step with reality. Given that many countries have adopted other forms of governance that do not adhere to Western principles, the notion that advancing democracy represents a global victory for freedom also seems obsolete. Furthermore, the US' advocacy of democracy has frequently been criticized as hypo-critical, fueling claims that the US is more concerned with advancing its own interests.

During his campaign, Joe Biden pledged to advance democracy and human rights around the globe, along with rebuilding alliances and working with multilateral organizations. However, he neglected to mention restoring globalization because that depends on how strong the US economy is, which is still extremely flimsy and unreliable. Hence, it is important to be aware of the fact that the mix of ongoing toxic domestic politics and rivalry overseas makes it difficult for Biden to restore the US' global leadership.

Based on the aforementioned chapters in the book, this study suggests that in recent years, the US foreign policy decisions are against the founda-tions of the liberal international order, which damaged US leadership and added to worldwide unrest. In other words, Washington's foreign policy choices regarding recent issues have shown the erosion of American supremacy and exposed the weaknesses of the US-led liberal order. The US no longer rules the world as it once did. Middle-power nations have started ascending to the top. By analyzing theoretical discussions in the literature regarding the international system and by scrutinizing primary sources, including the NSS, executive orders, archives of the White House office, interviews, and remarks by the US presidents, the book has elaborated on the factors underlying the current crisis of the liberal international order. In addition, the positions and stances of the rising powers, which are assumed to have the potential to establish order, were discussed.

Accordingly, the liberal order led by the US is coming to an end over the power projection and the US is experiencing a breakdown of its power. The seats vacated by the Soviet Union during the Cold War are being filled by rising powers that are getting stronger by not adopting the liberal order. Thus, as the unipolar world order in the post-Cold War era comes to an end, new powers are emerging. It can be argued that today's world is post-American, in which the US' relative influence and power have been steadily declining. The post-American international order refers to how the US' position as the leading powerhouse in the world is eroding. Hence, many have started to question America's supremacy and the role it will play in the future, the emergence of new economic powers, and the shifting global landscape. With the emergence of new actors and power structures as a result of this change, the political and economic landscape of the world has been reconfigured. The US influence and its reputation abroad have decreased as a result of its foreign policy choices. Its position as a global leader was also further weakened by Donald Trump's election and his "America First" agenda.

One potential result of this decline is that the rest gain more power and influence as a result of the US losing its leadership role in the world order. This leads to a multipolar world where various states battle for resources and influence and have significant sway. In other words, a multipolar world, in which no one country or group of countries can control world politics, is the result of a shift in global power dynamics. As nations fight to defend their interests and express their power, this shift has also intensified competition and conflict between them. Countries are increasingly employing their economic and military strength to further their interests in sectors like commerce, security, and technology as a result of this competition.

Another potential outcome is that the US might go through a period of political and economic unrest as it gets used to a new reality in which its authority is no longer absolute. Domestic unrest, political divisiveness, and other issues could result from this, which could potentially destabilize the nation.

In this regard, the future of the US-led liberal international order is a contentious topic. It is not just debated in academic circles. It is publicly mentioned in US government papers as well, such as those by the National Intelligence Council (2012), which encouraged the US government to get ready for the reemergence of multipolarity by 2030. Although most observers concur that the US' relative influence is waning, there is much disagreement over what this means for the country's future and the state of world peace.

With the erosion of the US' leadership role in the international system, the US won't be able to accomplish many of its foreign objectives acting alone. For instance, international financial stability is essential to Americans' prosperity, but the US requires other countries' cooperation to guarantee it. Additionally, the quality of life will be impacted by global warming and increasing sea levels, but Americans cannot solve these issues on their own.

Accordingly, the US stands at risk of losing respect and becoming an unpopular global leader that is lurching dangerously in an uncontrollable state of disarray. The reduction in confidence and credibility, the emergence of new rising powers, and the failure to address urgent global problems are all contributors to this demise.

In this respect, as it is argued by Acharya (2021, p. 6), liberal hegemony has passed its prime. In a world of increasing complexity and interconnection, the liberal international order will be merely one of many crosscutting systems that must contend or converge with other concepts. International relations experts should be skeptical of traditional thinking and open to new ideas and theories, as well as historically unprecedented prospects for the future of the international order.

There is little doubt that the US and China will play a significant role in determining how globalization will develop in the future. A multipolar system is emerging as the US hegemony is eroding and power is shifting toward China. One of the most notable aspects of China's ascent has been often referred to as a "heterodox" brand of capitalism. China's strategy prioritizes governmental intervention and communal values more than the traditional model of capitalism, which lays more of a focus on free markets and individuality. This strategy has its roots in Chinese history and culture, which emphasizes societal harmony and stability. The conventional rules of the international order, which were influenced by Western notions of liberalism and free-market capitalism, have been called into question by

China's unorthodox approach to capitalism. Some have criticized China's state-led economic model as unfair and anti-competitive because it involves significant governmental involvement and regulation.

In this respect, the liberal international order is being threatened by rising powers in several ways. They are advancing alternative forms of government, clamoring for more power in organizations that oversee international affairs, and advancing their own economic and strategic objectives. By advocating alternative forms of governance that are not founded on liberal democratic principles, rising nations are posing a threat to the liberal international order. For instance, China has been advancing its own version of authoritarian capitalism, which has been effective in generating economic growth. This has prompted several nations to consider alternate forms of governance and to interrogate the utility of the liberal democratic model.

By requesting more influence in global governance organizations like the UN, the World Bank, and the IMF, rising powers are also challenging the liberal international order. They contend that these institutions must be reformed to better represent the interests of all countries because they fail to accurately depict the shifting global balance of power.

Several issues, notably in terms of maintaining stability and managing conflict, are presented by the advent of multipolarity. Different players will have conflicting interests and agendas in a multipolar globe, which might cause tensions and possibly conflict. A power vacuum that prevents a clear leader from directing world affairs from arising is another possibility with the risk of the US leaving the international scene.

The transition to multipolarity, however, also offers tremendous potential. Greater invention and creativity may result from a more diversified global environment as many viewpoints and strategies are applied to challenging issues. Additionally, as several players cooperate to accomplish common objectives, it might promote increased collaboration and cooperation. Because of the increasing complexity, it is possible that soon countries may not have complete control over world politics. Individuals and private organizations, including businesses, NGOs, terrorist organizations, and social movements, are becoming more powerful, and informal networks will challenge the conventional bureaucracies' monopoly on power. Governments will still be able to exert influence because of their wealth and power, but as the playing field gets more crowded, they will lose some of their control.

In this regard, today, a new multipolar balance not led solely by the US is sought by the entire world, where rising powers also have responsibilities. There is no doubt rising powers are looking for possibilities for a new international order. Thus, in today's multipolar world, newcomers tend to exert pressure for change inside the key institutional frameworks of the current international order. There is a growing understanding that a new, multipolar equilibrium is required to preserve security and prosperity for all as global power dynamics change and new players appear on the international scene. Hence, the shift to a new, multipolar balance, is considered an indispensable reflection of the altering world order.

A new world order might be more multipolar, inclusive, or democratic than the current order. It might also be founded on ideals like mutual respect, equality, and fairness rather than on the hegemony of a few superpowers. A more inclusive world order would need to be founded on a bigger set of values that take into account the variety of cultures and political structures around the globe. This might entail putting more focus on cooperation and economic progress, as well as an increased acceptance of non-Western traditions and values. Although there is a rising awareness that the current order may no longer be sufficient, there is little consensus on what a new order should look like. The question of whether a new international order is feasible and desirable will ultimately depend on a variety of variables, including geopolitical developments, internal politics, and the willingness of nations to cooperate to find common ground.

Bibliography

1950s America, (2023). Khan Academy. Available at: https://www.khanacademy. org/humanities/us-history/post-warera/1950s-america/a/the-start-of-the-space-race (accessed on 15 July 2023).

2017 Donald Trump Inauguration Speech Transcript, (2017). Politico. Available at: https://www.politico.com/story/2017/01/full-text-donald-trump-inauguration-speech-transcript-233907#:~:text=We%20the%20citizens%20of%20America,will%20get%20 the%20job%20done (accessed on 1 August 2023).

Abele, R. P., (2009). *The Anatomy of a Deception: A Reconstruction and Analysis of the Decision to Invade Iraq*. Maryland, University Press of America.

Ables, K., (2018). *What Happens When China's State-run Media Embraces AI?* Columbia Journalism Review. Available at: https://www.cjr.org/analysis/china-xinhua-news-ai.php (accessed on 15 July 2023).

Acharya, A., (2017). After liberal hegemony: The advent of a multiplex world order. *Ethics & International Affairs, 31*(3), 271–285. https://doi.org/10.1017/S089267941700020X.

Acharya, A., (2018). *The End of American World Order* (p. 64). Cambridge, UK; Medford, MA: Polity Press.

Acharya, A., (2020). *How Coronavirus May Reshape the World Order*. The National Interest. Available at: https://nationalinterest.org/feature/how-coronavirus-may-reshape-world-order-145972 (accessed on 15 July 2023).

Acharya, A., (2021). Back to the future or a brave new world?—Reflections on how the COVID-19 pandemic is reshaping globalization. In: Huiyao, W., & Alistair, M., (eds.), *Consensus or Conflict?: China and Globalization in the 21st Century* (pp. 3–15). Singapore: Springer.

Açıkalın, Ş. N., & Bölücek, C. A., (2014). Understanding of Arab spring with chaos theory—uprising or revolution. In: *Chaos Theory in Politics* (pp. 29–47). Springer, Dordrecht.

Adams, J., (2001). Virtual defense. *Foreign Affairs, 80*(3), 98–112. https://www.jstor.org/stable/20050154?origin=crossref (accessed on 15 July 2023).

Akıllı, E., (2016). *Türkiye'de Devlet Kimliği ve Dış Politika*. Ankara: Nobel Yayıncılık.

Akkurt, M., (2005). *Afganistan'ın Yapılanmasında Siyasi ve Ekonomik Stratejiler*. İstanbul: IQ Kültür Sanat Yayıncılık.

Albert, E. (2018). *China's Big Bet on Soft Power*. Council on Foreign Relations. Available at: https://www.cfr.org/backgrounder/chinas-big-bet-soft-power (accessed on 30 July, 2023).

Albright, M. K., (1993). *Yes, There Is a Reason to Be in Somalia*. The New York Times. Available at: https://www.nytimes.com/1993/08/10/opinion/yes-there-is-a-reason-to-be-in-somalia.html (accessed on 15 July 2023).

Albright, M. K., (1997a). *American Principle and Purpose in East Asia*. 1997 Forrestal Lecture, U.S. Naval Academy. Available at: https://1997-2001.state.gov/statements/970415.html (accessed on 15 July 2023).

Albright, M. K., (1997b). *Finding the Path to Lasting Peace in Bosnia.* US Department of State Archive. Available at: https://1997-2001.state.gov/publications/dispatch/May1997. pdf (accessed on 15 July 2023).

Albright, M. K., (1998). *NBC's The Today Show.* Madeleine K. Albright, interview by Matt Lauer. Available at: https://1997-2001.state.gov/statements/1998/980219a.html (accessed on 15 July 2023).

Albright, M. K., (2003). *Madam Secretary* (p. 391). New York: Miramax Books.

Alcaro, R., & Greco, E., (2016). Beyond resilience. The case for transatlantic leadership. In: John, P., & Ettore, G., (eds.), *The West and the Global Power Shift: Transatlantic Relations and Global Governance* (pp. 271–288). Basingstoke and New York: Palgrave Macmillan.

Alcaro, R., (2018). Contestation and transformation. Final thoughts on the liberal international order. *The International Spectator, 53*(1), 152–167. https://doi.org/10.108 0/03932729.2018.1429533.

Alcaro, R., (2020). The fraying transatlantic order and Europe's struggle in a multipolar world. In: Justin, M., & Jonathan, P., (eds.), *America's Allies and the Decline of U.S. Hegemony* (pp. 348–393). London and New York: Routledge.

Alfonsi, C., (2006). *Circle in the Sand: Why We Went Back to Iraq* (pp. 154–162). New York: Doubleday.

Allison, G., (2017). *Destined for War: Can America and China Escape Thucydides's Trap?* Houghton Mifflin Harcourt.

Allison, R., (2014). Russian 'deniable' intervention in Ukraine: How and why Russia broke the rules. *International Affairs, 90*(6), 1255–1297.

Al-Matter, T., (2016). *Saudi Arabia and the Arab Spring: Five Years of Influence and Action.* Asia Pacific Institute of Advanced Research. Available at: https://apiar.org.au/ wp-content/uploads/2016/10/8_APCAR_July_BRR734_Social-Sciences-448-454.pdf (accessed on 15 July 2023).

Altun, F. (2021). *Türkiye as a Stabilizing Power in an Age of Turmoil.* Washington, Academica Press.

Aloisi, S., & Daniel, F. J., (2022). *Timeline: The Events Leading up to Russia's Invasion of Ukraine.* Reuters. Available at: https://www.reuters.com/world/europe/events-leading-up-russias-invasion-ukraine-2022-02-28/ (accessed on 30 July 2023).

Alvesson, M., & Sköldberg, K., (2009). *Reflexive Methodology: New Vistas for Qualitative Research.* London: SAGE Publications Ltd.

Andreas, P., (2004). The clandestine political economy of war and peace in Bosnia. *International Studies Quarterly, 48*(1), 29–51. https://doi.org/10.1111/j.0020-8833.2004.00290.x.

Anthony, L., (1993). *From Containment to Enlargement.* U.S. Department of State Dispatch 4. Available at: http://academic.brooklyn.cuny.edu/history/johnson/lake.htm (accessed on 15 July 2023).

Anton, M., (2019). *An Insider Explains the President's Foreign Policy.* Foreign Policy. Available at: https://foreignpolicy.com/2019/04/20/the-trump-doctrine-big-think-america-first-nationalism/ (accessed on 15 July 2023).

Ardovini, L., & Mabon, S., (2019). Egypt's unbreakable curse: Tracing the state of exception from Mubarak to Al Sisi. *Mediterranean Politics, 25*(4), 456–475. doi: 10.10 80/13629395.2019.1582170,1.

Arı, T., (2004). *Irak, İran ve ABD/ Önleyici Savaş, Petrol ve Hegomanya*. İstanbul: Alfa Yayınları.

Armaoğlu, F., (2010). *20. Yüzyıl Siyasi Tarihi (1914–1995)*. Alkım Yayınevi: İstanbul.

Arnove, A., (2003). *ABD'nin Irak Savaşı (Çev. Taylan Doğan)*. İstanbul: Aram Yayıncılık.

Ataman, P. E., (2009). *Chronology of Global Crises and Actions Taken by Countries* (Vol. 68, pp. 85–89). Bankacılar Dergisi.

Ateş, A., (2022). Understanding US foreign policy: A theoretical analysis. *Novus Orbis: Siyaset Bilimi ve Uluslararası İlişkiler Dergisi, 4*(1), 4–27.

Awery, W. P., & Rapkin, D. P., (1982). *America in a Changing World Political Economy*. New York: Longman.

Bachman, J. (2017). Libya: a UN Resolution and NATO failure to protect. In: Makdisi, K. & Prashad, V., (eds.), *Land of Blue Helmets: The United Nations in the Arab World* (pp. 212-230). Los Angeles, University of California Press.

Baig, M. A., & Muhammad, S. S., (2020). Redefining terrorism: An offshoot of military strategy. *IPRI Journal, 20*(1), 44–71.

Balcı, A., (2004). Afganistan: Ulus devlet ve kabilecilik arasinda. In: İnat, K., Duran, B., & Ataman, M., (eds), *Dünya Çatışma Bölgeleri* (pp. 258, 259). Ankara: Nobel Yayın Dağıtım.

Balmforth, T., Tsvetkova, M., & Kerry, F., (2022). *Satellite Images Show Troop Deployment to Belarus Border with Ukraine Ahead of Russian Drills*. Reuters. Available at: https://www.reuters.com/world/satellite-images-show-troop-deployment-belarus-border-with-ukraine-ahead-russian-2022-02-06/ (accessed on 15 July 2023).

Banai, H., (2013). Democratic solidarity: Rethinking democracy promotion in the new Middle East. *Security Dialogue, 44*(5, 6), 411–429.

Barber, L., Foy, H., & Barker, A., (2019). *Vladimir Putin Says Liberalism has 'Become Obsolete.'* Financial Times. Available at: https://www.ft.com/content/670039ec-98f3-11e9-9573-ee5cbb98ed36 (accessed on 15 July 2023).

Barboza, D. (2008). *China unveils $586 billion stimulus plan*. The New York Times. Available at: https://www.nytimes.com/2008/11/10/world/asia/10iht-10china.17673270.html (accessed on 30 July 2023)

Barboza, D. (2010). *China Passes Japan as Second-Largest Economy*. The New York Times. Available at: https://www.nytimes.com/2010/08/16/business/global/16yuan.html (accessed on 30 July 2023).

Barnett, M. N., (2018). What is international relations theory good for? In: Jervis, R., Gavin, F. J., Rovner, J., Labrosse, D. N., & Fujii, G., (eds.), *Chaos in the Liberal Order: The Trump Presidency and International Politics in the 21st Century* (pp. 38–64). Columbia University Press.

Barnett, M., (2021). International progress, international order, and the liberal international order. *The Chinese Journal of International Politics, 14*(1), 1–22.

Becker, J., & Schmitt, E., (2018). *As Trump Wavers on Libya, an ISIS Haven, Russia Presses On*. The New York Times. Available at: https://www.nytimes.com/2018/02/07/world/africa/trump-libya-policy-russia.html (accessed on 15 July 2023).

Bejesky, R., (2011). Politico-international law, *Loy. L. Rev., 57*, 29.

Biden, J. R., (2021). *Remarks by President Biden on America's Place in the World*. The White House. Available at: https://www.whitehouse.gov/briefing-room/speeches-remarks/2021/02/04/remarks-by-president-biden-on-americas-place-in-the-world/ (accessed on 15 July 2023).

Biermann, F., Pattberg, F., Van, A. H., & Zelli, F., (2009). The fragmentation of global governance architectures: A framework for analysis. *Global Environmental Politics, 9*(4), 14–40.

Biersack, J., & O'lear, S., (2014). The geopolitics of Russia's annexation of Crimea: Narratives, identity, silences, and energy. *Eurasian Geography and Economics, 55*(3), 247–269.

Bin Laden calls Sept. 11 attacks 'blessed terror'. (2001). CNN. Available at: http://edition. cnn.com/2001/WORLD/asiapcf/central/12/26/ret.bin.laden.statement/ (accessed on 30 July, 2023).

Binder, M., & Heupel, M., (2015). The legitimacy of the UN security council: Evidence from recent general assembly debates. *International Studies Quarterly, 59*, 238–250.

Birnbaum, M., (2018). *E.U. Leader Lights into Trump: 'With Friends Like That, Who Needs Enemies?'* Washington Post. Available at: https://www.washingtonpost.com/news/worldviews/wp/2018/05/16/e-u-leader-lights-into-trump-with-friends-like-that-who-needs-enemies/ (accessed on 15 July 2023).

Blair, T. (2001). *Coalition against International Terrorism.* UK Parliament. Available at: https://publications.parliament.uk/pa/cm200102/cmhansrd/vo011004/debtext/11004-01.htm (accessed on 30 July 2023).

Bluedorn, J., Gopinath, G., & Sandri, D., (2020). *An Early View of the Economic Impact of the Pandemic in 5 Charts.* IMF blog. Available at: https://www.imf.org/en/Blogs/Articles/2020/04/06/blog-an-early-view-of-the-economic-impact-of-the-pandemic-in-5-charts (accessed on 15 July 2023).

Bommakanti, K., (2017). *China's Military Modernization: Recent Trends* (p. 2). ORF Occasional Paper.

Bonner, R., & Shanker, T., (2003). *U.S. Military Officer Dies in Rocket Barrage at Baghdad Hotel.* The New York Times. Available at: https://www.nytimes.com/2003/10/26/international/worldspecial/us-military-officer-dies-in-rocket-barrage-at.html (accessed on 15 July 2023).

Bosco, D., (2017). We've been here before: The durability of multilateralism. *Journal of International Affairs, 70*(2), 9–15. https://www.jstor.org/stable/90012616 (accessed on 15 July 2023).

Bowker, M., (1998). The wars in Yugoslavia: Russia and the international community. *Europe-Asia Studies, 50*(7), 1245–1261 https://doi.org/10.1080/09668139808412593.

Börzel, T., & Zürn, M., (2021). Contestations of the liberal international order: From liberal multilateralism to postnational liberalism. *International Organization, 75*(2), 282–305.

Brandl, B., & Benchter, B., (2011). The hybridization of national collective bargaining systems: The impact of the economic crisis on the transformation of collective bargaining in the European Union. In: Brandl, B., & Traxler, F., (eds.), *Labor History* (pp. 1–22). Durham: Durham University Business School.

Brands, H., & Gavin, F. J., (2020). COVID-19 and world order. In: H. Brands, F., & Gavin, J., (eds.), *COVID-19 and World Order: The Future of Conflict, Competition, and Cooperation* (pp. 1–20) Baltimore: Johns Hopkins University Press.

Brands, H., Feaver, P., & Inboden, W., (2020). Maybe it won't be so bad a modestly optimistic take on COVID and world order. In: Brands, H., & Gavin, F. J., (eds.), *COVID-19 and World Order* (pp. 297–315) Baltimore: Johns Hopkins University Press.

Brooks, S., & Wohlforth, W., (2008). *World Out of Balance: International Relations and the Challenge of American Primacy*. Princeton, NJ: Princeton University Press.

Broz, J., Frieden, J., & Weymouth, S., (2021). Populism in place: The economic geography of the globalization backlash. *International Organization, 75*(2), 464–494.

Bruce, G., (2013). Definition of terrorism social and political effects. *Journal of Military and Veterans' Health, 21*(2), 26–30.

Brunk, I. W., & Hakimi, M., (2022). Russia, Ukraine, and the future world order. *American Journal of International Law, 116*(4), 687–697. https://doi.org/10.1017/ajil.2022.69.

Brzezinski, Z., (1992). *The Cold War and Its Aftermath*. Foreign Affairs. Available at: https://www.foreignaffairs.com/articles/russia-fsu/1992-09-01/cold-war-and-its-aftermath (accessed on 15 July 2023).

Brzezinski, Z., (2010). From hope to audacity: Appraising Obama's foreign policy. *Foreign Affairs, 89*(1), 16–30. http://www.jstor.org/stable/20699780 (accessed on 15 July 2023).

Buckley, C., (2009). *China Official Says 20 Million Migrants Lost Jobs*. Reuters. Available at: https://www.reuters.com/article/us-china-economy-migrants-sb-idUKTRE51117920090202 (accessed on 15 July 2023).

Bueno De, M. B., (2009). *Principles of International Politics*. Washington, DC: CQ Press.

Bumiller, E., & MacFarquhar, N., (2011). *Gates Arrives in Bahrain Amid Huge Protests*. The New York Times. Available at: https://www.nytimes.com/2011/03/12/world/middleeast/12unrest.html (accessed on 15 July 2023).

Burchill, S., Linklater, A., Devetak, R., Paterson, M., & True, J., (1996). *Theories of International Relations*. London: MacMillan Press Ltd.

Bush, G. H. W., (1990). *Address Before a Joint Session of the Congress on the Persian Gulf Crisis and the Federal Budget Deficit*. George Bush Presidential Library & Museum. Available at: https://bush41library.tamu.edu/archives/public-papers/2217 (accessed on 15 July 2023).

Bush, G. H. W., (1991). *Address Before a Joint Session of the Congress on the Cessation of the Persian Gulf Conflict*. Public Papers of the Presidents of the US Bush. Available at: https://www.govinfo.gov/content/pkg/PPP-1991-book1/html/PPP-1991-book1-doc-pg218-3.htm (accessed on 15 July 2023).

Bush, G. H. W., (1992). *Address to the Nation on the Situation in Somalia*. Public Papers of the Presidents of the United States: George H. W. Bush (1992–1993, Book II). Available at: https://www.govinfo.gov/content/pkg/PPP-1992-book2/html/PPP-1992-book2-doc-pg2174-3.htm (accessed on 15 July 2023).

Bush, G. W., (2001a). *The Global War on Terrorism: The First 100 Days*. The White House Archives. Available at: https://2001-2009.state.gov/s/ct/rls/wh/6947.htm (accessed on 15 July 2023).

Bush, G. W. (2001b). *Statement by the President in His Address to the Nation.The White House*. Available at: https://georgewbush-whitehouse.archives.gov/news/releases/2001/09/20010911-16.html (accessed on 30 July 2023).

Bush, G. W. (2001c). *Address to a Joint Session of Congress and the American People*. The White House. Available at: https://georgewbush-whitehouse.archives.gov/news/releases/2001/09/20010920-8.html (accessed on 30 July, 2023).

Bush, G. W., (2002). *The National Security Strategy of the United States of America*. The White House Archives. Available at: https://georgewbush-whitehouse.archives.gov/nsc/nssall.html (accessed on 15 July 2023).

Bush, G. W. (2003). President Discusses the Future of Iraq. The White House. Available at: https://georgewbush-whitehouse.archives.gov/news/releases/2003/02/20030226-11. html (accessed on 31 July 2023)

Búzás, Z., (2021). Racism and antiracism in the liberal international order. *International Organization, 75*(2), 440–463.

Byman, D. L., (2018). *Why Engage in Proxy War? A State's Perspective.* Brookings. Available at: https://www.brookings.edu/blog/order-from-chaos/2018/05/21/ why-engage-in-proxy-war-a-states-perspective/ (accessed on 15 July 2023).

Cameron, F., (2005). *US Foreign Policy After the Cold War: Global Hegemon or Reluctant Sheriff?* (p. 35) London & New York: Routledge.

Campbell, K., & Doshi, R., (2020). *The Coronavirus Could Reshape Global Order. Foreign Affairs.* Retrieved from https://www.foreignaffairs.com/articles/china/2020-03-18/coronavirus-could-reshape-global-order (accessed on 15 July 2023).

Campbell, D. (2001). *The US will hunt down and punish those responsible for these attacks.* The Guardian. Available at: https://www.theguardian.com/world/2001/sep/12/ september11.usa15 (accessed on 30 July, 2023).

Caplan, R., (2000). Assessing the Dayton accord: The structural weaknesses of the general framework agreement for peace in Bosnia and Herzegovina. *Diplomacy & Statecraft, 11*(2), 213–232. https://doi.org/10.1080/09592290008406163.

Carroll, J., (2022). Courage under fire: Re-evaluating black hawk down and the battle of Mogadishu. *War in History, 26*(3), 704–726.

Center for Preventive Action, (2023). *War in Ukraine.* Global Conflict Tracker. Available at: https://www.cfr.org/global-conflict-tracker/conflict/conflict-ukraine (accessed on 15 July 2023).

China overtakes Germany as biggest exporter (2010). NBC News. Available at: https:// www.nbcnews.com/id/wbna34793064 (accessed on 30 July 2023).

Chollet, D., & Goldgeier, J. (2008). *America Between the Wars: From 11/9 to 9/11: The Misunderstood Years Between the Fall of the Berlin Wall and the Start of the War on Terror* (pp. 147, 148). New York: Public Affairs.

Chomsky, N., (1997). *World Orders: Old and New* (p. 19). London: Pluto Press.

Chomsky, N., (2002). 11 Eylül, Çev. Dost Körpe, İstanbul, Om Yayınevi, 2, 84.

Chronology of Events in Iraq, August 2003. (2003). UNHCR. Available at: https://www. refworld.org/pdfid/403225cd1.pdf (accessed on 30 July 2023).

Clinton, B., (1995). *Transcript of President Clinton's Speech on Bosnia.* CNN, http:// edition.cnn.com/US/9511/bosnia_speech/speech.html (accessed on 15 July 2023).

Clinton, H. R., (2009). *Foreign Policy Address at the Council on Foreign Relations.* US Department of State. Available at: https://2009-2017.state.gov/secretary/20092013clinton/ rm/2009a/july/126071.htm (accessed on 15 July 2023).

Clinton, H. R., (2010). *A Conversation with U.S. Secretary of State Hillary Rodham Clinton.* Council on Foreign Relations. Available at: https://www.cfr.org/event/conversation-us-secretary-state-hillary-rodham-clinton-2 (accessed on 15 July 2023).

Clinton, W. J., (1999). *A Just and Necessary War.* The New York Times. Available at: https://www.nytimes.com/1999/05/23/opinion/a-just-and-necessary-war.html (accessed on 15 July 2023).

Cohen, E. A., & McGrath, B., (2016). *Open Letter on Trump from GOP National Security Leaders.* War on the Rocks. Available at: https://warontherocks.com/2016/03/

open-letter-on-donald-trump-from-gop-national-security-leaders/ (accessed on 15 July 2023).

Colgan, J. D., & Keohane, R. O., (2017). The liberal order is rigged. *Foreign Affairs, 96*(3), 36–44.

Collinson, S., Liptak, K., & Merica, D., (2017). *Trump Says Iran Violating Nuclear Agreement, Threatens to Pull Out of Deal.* CNN Politics. Available at: https://edition.cnn.com/2017/10/13/politics/iran-deal-decertify/index.html (accessed on 15 July 2023).

Colucci, L., (2012). *The National Security Doctrines of the American Presidency.* Prager, Santa Barbara.

Connah, L., (2021). US intervention in Afghanistan: Justifying the unjustifiable? *South Asia Research, 41*(1), 70–86.

Conway, M., (2018). Is cyberterrorism a real threat?: Yes: Why we should start from this assumption. In: Jackson, R., & Pisoiu, D., (eds.), *Contemporary Debates on Terrorism,* (pp. 102–107). Abingdon, OX: Routledge.

Cooper, R., (2013). *China to Overtake America by 2016. The Telegraph.* Available at: https://www.telegraph.co.uk/finance/china-business/9947825/China-to-overtake-America-by-2016.html?WT.mc_id=tmgoff_psc_ppc_us_news_performancemax_dsa&gclid=Cj0KCQjw8qmhBhClARIsANAtbocPTpazJ3rqL1UpvcK6H0KWUumNvLUbvHne1kfTcS1ebI5KO6p6Bw4aAit0EALw_wcB (accessed on 15 July 2023).

Cortright, D., (2011). *Ending Obama's War: Responsible Military Withdrawal from Afghanistan.* Boulder: Paradigm.

Cox, M., (2017). The rise of populism and the crisis of globalization: Brexit, Trump and beyond. *Irish Studies in International Affairs, 28,* 9–17.

Cox, M., (2021). *Brexit, and the Crisis of the Transatlantic Relationship* (pp. 1–14). DCU Brexit Institute Working Paper N.8. Available at: http://dx.doi.org/10.2139/ssrn.3798458.

Cox, R., (1992). Multilateralism and world order. *Review of International Studies, 18*(2), 161–180.

Crabb, C. V., (1982). *The Doctrines of American Foreign Policy: Their Meaning, Role, and Future.* Baton Rouge: Louisiana State University Press.

Crawford, N. C., (2003). Just war theory and the U.S. counterterror war. *Perspectives on Politics, 1*(1), 5–25.

Crowley, P. J., (2017). *Red Line* (p. 285). (e-publication), Maryland: Rowman & Littlefield.

Cyrus, B., (2022). *Globalization and the Decline of American Power: The Political Economy of the American Fall.* Routledge.

Daalder, I., & Lindsay, J. M., (2018). *The Empty Throne: America's Abdication of Global Leadership.* New York: Public Affairs.

Daalder, I., & O'Hanlon, M., (2000). *Winning Ugly.* Washington, DC: Brookings Institution Press.

Danner, M., (1997). *The US and the Yugoslav Catastrophe* (Vol. 44, No. 18, pp. 56–64). New York Review of Books.

Dashti, Z., (2022). Afghan external migration movements in the historical process. *Asian Studies-Academic Social Studies, 6*(20), 301–314.

David, A., Lake, D. A., Martin, L. L., & Risse, T., (2021). Challenges to the liberal order: Reflections on international organization. *International Organization, 75*(2), 225–257.

Dawson, M., (2015). A brief review of new threats and countermeasures in digital crime and cyber terrorism. In: Dawson, M., & Omar, M., (eds.), *New Threats and Countermeasures in Digital Crime and Cyber Terrorism* (pp. 1–7). Hershey, PA: Information Science Reference.

De Vries, C., Hobolt, S., & Walter, S., (2021). Politicizing international cooperation: The mass public, political entrepreneurs, and political opportunity structures. *International Organization, 75*(2), 306–332.

Deibel, T. L., (1991). Bush's foreign policy: Mastery and inaction. *Foreign Policy, 84,* 3–23.

Denek, S., (2016). *Balance of Power in Central Asia After the US-led Intervention in Afghanistan 2001* (pp. 305–323). Gazi Üniversitesi Sosyal Bilimler Dergisi, Özel Sayı.

Di, D., (2007). Continuity and changes: A comparative study on China's new grand strategy. *Historia Actual Online, 12,* 7–18.

Diamond, L. (2010). Liberation Technology. *Journal of Democracy,* 21(3), 69–83.

Dilanian, K., (2012). *U.S. Intelligence Official Acknowledges Missed Arab Spring Signs.* Los Angeles Times. Available at: https://www.latimes.com/archives/blogs/world-now/story/2012-07-19/u-s-intelligence-official-acknowledges-missed-arab-spring-signs#:~:text=WASHINGTON%20%2D%2D%20U.S.%20intelligence%20agencies,senior%20U.S.%20intelligence%20official%20said.&text=%E2%80%9CWe%20missed%20that.%E2%80%9D (accessed on 15 July 2023).

Doyle, M. W., (1983). Kant, liberal legacies, and foreign affairs. *Philosophy & Public Affairs, 12*(3), 213–235.

Doyle, M., (1997). *The Ways of War and Peace: Realism, Liberalism, and Socialism.* New York: Norton.

Dragneva, R., & Wolczuk, K., (2016). Between dependence and integration: Ukraine's relations with Russia. *Europe-Asia Studies, 68*(4), 678–698.

Drehle, D. V., (2001). *World War, Cold War Won. Now, the Gray War.* Washington Post. Available at: https://www.washingtonpost.com/archive/politics/2001/09/12/world-war-cold-war-won-now-the-gray-war/52a2b151-cb90-4a53-9092-d7e999069654/ (accessed on 15 July 2023).

Dreyfuss, R., (2012). *Obama on Petraeus, Iran and Syria.* The Nation. Available at: http://www.thenation.com/blog/i7i2Ó4/obama-petraeus-iran-and-syria (accessed on 15 July 2023).

Drezner, D. W., (2016). *So When Will Realists Endorse Donald Trump?* Washington Post. Available at: https://www.washingtonpost.com/posteverything/wp/2016/02/01/so-when-will-realists-endorse-donald-trump/ (accessed on 15 July 2023).

Drezner, D. W., (2020). The song remains the same: International relations after COVID-19. *International Organization, 74*(S1), E18–E35 doi: https://doi.org/10.1017/S0020818320000351.

Drozdiak, W. (2001). *EU Leaders Back Attacks on Afghanistan.* The Washington Post. Available at: https://www.washingtonpost.com/archive/politics/2001/10/20/eu-leaders-back-attacks-on-afghanistan/fb12b220-966b-4829-ad55-52e0c1fdad2f/ (Accessed on 30 July 2023)

Dumbrell, J., (1997). *The Making of US Foreign Policy.* New York, NY: Manchester University Press.

Duncombe, C., & Dunne, T., (2018). After liberal world order. *International Affairs, 94*(1), 25–42.

Dunmire, P. L., (2009). "9/11 changed everything": On intertextual analysis of the bush doctrine. *Discourse & Society*, *20*(2), 195–222. http://www.jstor.org/stable/42889254 (accessed on 15 July 2023).

Dunne, C. W., (2011). Iraq: Policies, politics, and the art of the possible. In: Shahram, A., (ed.), *America's Challenges in The Greater Middle East, The Obama Administration's Policies* (pp. 11–31) New York: Palgrave Macmillan.

Dunne, M., & Hamzawy, A., (2017). *Egypt's Secular Political Parties: A Struggle for Identity and Independence*. Carnegie Endowment for International Peace. Available at: https://carnegieendowment.org/2017/03/31/egypt-s-secular-political-parties-struggle-for-identity-and-independence-pub-68482 (accessed on 15 July 2023).

Dunne, M., (2014). *A U.S. Strategy Toward Egypt Under Sisi*. Carnegie Endowment for International Peace. Available at: https://carnegieendowment.org/files/us_strategy_under_sisi.pdf (accessed on 15 July 2023).

Dunne, T., & Schimit, B., (2019). "Realism." In: John, B., Steve, S., & Patricia, O., (eds.), *The Globalization of World Politics* (pp. 130–144). Oxford University Press: New York.

Duran, B., (2019). The crisis of the liberal world order and turkey's resistance. *Insight Turkey, 21*(3), 9–21. https://www.insightturkey.com/file/1181/the-crisis-of-the-liberal-world-order-and-turkeys-resistance; doi: 10.25253/99.2019213.01 (accessed on 15 July 2023).

Eğilmez, M., (2013). Küresel krizin neresindeyiz. *Kendime Yazılar*. Available at: http://www.mahfiegilmez.com/2013/04/kuresel-krizin-nere-sindeyiz.html (accessed on 15 July 2023).

Ellison, M., (2000). *Bill Clinton Reveals How He Smiled Through Tough Times*. The Guardian. Available at: https://www.theguardian.com/world/2000/oct/09/michaelellison (accessed on 15 July 2023).

Endaylalu, G. A., (2022). The implication of the rise of China to the US-led liberal international order: The case of one belt and one road initiatives. *Chinese Journal of International Review*, *4*(1), 2250002.

Erlanger, S., (2018). *Europe, Again Humiliated by Trump, Struggles to Defend Its Interests*. The New York Times. Available at: https://www.nytimes.com/2018/05/09/world/europe/europe-iran-trump.html (accessed on 15 July 2023).

Erlanger, S., (2019). *Macron Says NATO is Experiencing 'Brain Death' Because of Trump*. The New York Times. Available at: https://www.nytimes.com/2019/11/07/world/europe/macron-nato-brain-death.html (accessed on 15 July 2023).

Esmer, C., (2005). Yeniden ayağa kalkmaya çalişan ülke: Afganistan. *TİKA Avrasya Bülteni*, 32, 33. Mart/Nisan s. 34.

Esposito, J. L., (2002). *İslam Tehdidi Efsanesi* (Çev. Ömer Baldık, vd.). İstanbul: Ufuk Kitapları.

EU Leader Declares Trump a "Threat" to European Union, (2017). CBS News. Available at: https://www.cbsnews.com/news/european-union-donald-tusk-donald-trump-threat-eu-future-highly-unpredictable/ (accessed on 15 July 2023).

Exec. Order No. 13660 79 (46) 3.C.F.R 13493, (2014). https://www.govinfo.gov/content/pkg/FR-2014-03-10/pdf/2014-05323.pdf (accessed on 15 July 2023).

Exec. Order No. 13767 82 Fed. Reg. 18, (2017). https://www.govinfo.gov/content/pkg/FR-2017-01-30/pdf/2017-02095.pdf (accessed on 15 July 2023).

Exec. Order No. 13780 82 Fed. Reg. 45, (2017). https://www.govinfo.gov/content/pkg/FR-2017-03-09/pdf/2017-04837.pdf (accessed on 15 July 2023).

Faulconbridge, G., (2022). *Ukraine war Shows West's Dominance is Ending as China Rises, Blair Says.* Reuters. Available at: https://www.reuters.com/world/europe/ukraine-war-shows-wests-dominance-is-ending-china-rises-blair-says-2022-07-17/ (accessed on 15 July 2023).

FCIC, (2011). *Financial Crisis Inquiry Commission Report.* Washington: U.S. Government Printing Office.

Federal Bureau of Investigation, (2006). *Terrorism 2002/2005.* Available at: https://www.fbi.gov/stats-services/publications/terrorism-2002-2005 (accessed on 15 July 2023).

Finlan, A., (2005). *Essential Histories the Gulf War 1991,* Taylor & Francis.

Finnemore, M., Scheve, K., Schultz, K. A., & Voeten, E., (2021). Preface. *International Organization, 75*(2), iii–iv.

Fisher, M., (2017). *Trump Prepares Orders Aiming at Global Funding and Treaties.* The New York Times. Available at: https://www.nytimes.com/2017/01/25/us/politics/united-nations-trump-administration.html (accessed on 15 July 2023).

Fitzgerald, M., & Ugolini, M., (2015). *Mapping Libya's Factions* (pp. 2–4). European Council on Foreign Relations.

Flaherty, T., & Rogowski, R., (2021). Rising inequality as a threat to the liberal international order. *International Organization, 75*(2), 495–523.

Flanagan, S. J., & Michael, E. M., (2003). *The People's Liberation Army and China in Transition.* Washington DC: National Defense University, Inst for National Strategic Studies.

Flockhart, T., (2016). The coming multi-order world. *Contemporary. Security Policy, 37*(1), 3–30.

Flockhart, T., (2020). Is this the end? Resilience, ontological security, and the crisis of the liberal international order. *Contemporary Security Policy, 41*(2), 215–240. doi: 10.1080/13523260.2020.1723966.

Forsythe, D. P., (2011). US foreign policy and human rights: Situating Obama. *Human Rights Quarterly, 33*(3), 767–789.

Fravel, M. T., (2008). China's search for military power. *Washington Quarterly, 31*(3), 125–141.

Frederick, B., Povlock, M., Watts, S., Priebe, M., & Geist, E., (2018). *Assessing Russian Reactions to US and NATO Posture Enhancements.* RAND Cooperation. Available at: https://www.rand.org/pubs/research_reports/RR1879.html (accessed on 15 July 2023).

Freedman, L., & Karsh, E., (1993). *The Gulf Conflict, 1990–1991: Diplomacy and War in the New World Order* (p. XXX). Princeton, New Jersey: Princeton University Press.

Freedman, L., (1991). The Gulf war and the new world order. *Survival: Global Politics and Strategy, 33*(3), 195–209.

Freedman, L., (2022). *Command: The Politics of Military Operations.* Dublin: Penguin Random House Ireland.

Fukuyama, F., (1989). *The End of History?* (No. 16). The National Interest.

Fukuyama, F., (1992). *The End of History and The Last Man.* New York, NY: The Free Press.

Fukuyama, F., (2020). *The Pandemic and Political Order.* Foreign Affairs. Available at: https://www.foreignaffairs.com/articles/world/2020-06-09/

pandemic-and-political-order?check_logged_in=1&utm_medium=promo_
email&utm_source=lo_flows&utm_campaign=registered_user_welcome&utm_
term=email_1&utm_content=20230325 (accessed on 15 July 2023).

Fukuyama, F., (2022a). *Liberalism and its Discontents*. New York: Farrar, Straus and Giroux.

Fukuyama, F., (2022b). *Francis Fukuyama: Putin's War on the Liberal Order.* Financial Times. Available at: https://www.ft.com/content/d0331b51-5d0e-4132-9f97-c3f41c7d75b3 (accessed on 15 July 2023).

Full Text: Donald Trump 2016 RNC Draft Speech Transcript, (2016). Politico. Available at: https://www.politico.com/story/2016/07/full-transcript-donald-trump-nomination-acceptance-speech-at-rnc-225974 (accessed on 15 July 2023).

Gao, L., Cash, J., Yan, S., Aizhu, C., Coghill, K., & Mallard, W., (2023). *China's 2022 Trade with Russia Hit Record $190 Bln – Customs*. Reuters. Available at: https://www.reuters.com/world/china-customs-says-trade-with-russia-hit-new-high-2022-2023-01-13/ (accessed on 15 July 2023).

Gardner, H., (2015). *Crimea, Global Rivalry, and the Vengeance of History*. Springer.

Gardner, H., (2016). The Russian annexation of Crimea: Regional and global ramifications. *European Politics and Society, 17*(4), 490–505.

Garthoff, R. L., (1994). *The Great Transition: American–Soviet Relations and the End of the Cold War*. Washington DC, The Brooking Institution Press.

Gerges, F. A., (2013). The Obama approach to the middle east: The end of America's moment? *International Affairs, 89*(2), 299–323.

Gerges, F., (2005). *The far Enemy: Why Jihad Went Global*. Cambridge and New York: Cambridge University Press.

German Leader Reiterates Solidarity with US (2001). The White House. Available at: https://georgewbush-whitehouse.archives.gov/news/releases/2001/10/20011009-13.html (accessed on 30 July, 2023).

Gerrits, A. W. M., & Bader, M., (2016) Russian patronage over Abkhazia and South Ossetia: Implications for conflict resolution, *East European Politics, 32*(3), 297–313.

Gerstein, J., & Epstein, J., (2011). *Obama to Draw Down Surge Troops*. Politico. Available at: https://www.politico.com/story/2011/06/obama-to-draw-down-surge-troops-057595 (accessed on 15 July 2023).

Gerstle, G., (2022). *The Rise and Fall of the Neoliberal Order*. New York: Oxford University Press.

Gilpin, R., (1981). *War and Change in World Politics*. New York: Cambridge University Press.

Giusti, S., & Penkova, T., (2008). From ideology to pragmatism: The new course of Russian foreign policy. *World Affairs: The Journal of International Issues, 12*(4), 14–53. https://www.jstor.org/stable/48505029 (accessed on 15 July 2023).

Glaser, C. L., (2014). Realists as optimists: Cooperation as self-help. In: Elman, C., &. Jensen, M., (eds.), *Realism Reader* (pp. 157–166). London: Routledge.

Glaser, C. L., (2019). A flawed framework: Why the liberal international order concept is misguided. *International Security, 43*(4), 51–87. https://doi.org/10.1162/isec_a_00343.

Global Financial Stability Report, April 2009: Responding to the Financial Crisis and Measuring Systemic Risks, (2009). International Monetary Fund. Available at: https://www.imf.org/en/Publications/GFSR/Issues/2016/12/31/

Global-Financial-Stability-Report-April-2009-Responding-to-the-Financial-Crisis-and-22583 (accessed on 15 July 2023).

Global Trends 2025: A Transformed World, Office of the Director of Intelligence, (2008). *National Intelligence Council.* Available at: https://www.dni.gov/files/documents/Newsroom/Reports%20and%20Pubs/2025_Global_Trends_Final_Report.pdf (accessed on 15 July 2023).

Gold, H. (2020). *Chinese state TV breached UK media rules over Hong Kong protests.* CNN. Available at: https://edition.cnn.com/2020/05/27/media/cgtn-ofcom-china-breach/index.html (accessed on 30 July 2023).

Goldstein, J., & Gulotty, R., (2021). America and the trade regime: What went wrong? *International Organization, 75*(2), 524–557.

Gompert, D., (1996). The US and Yugoslavia's wars. In: Ullman, R. H., (ed.), *The World and Yugoslavia's Wars* (pp. 122–144). New York: Council on Foreign Relations Press.

Goodman, S., & Pepinsky, T., (2021). The exclusionary foundations of embedded liberalism. *International Organization, 75*(2), 411–439.

Gordon, M. R., & Lander, M., (2013). *Senate Hearing Draws out a Rift in U.S. Policy on Syria.* The New York Times. Available at: http://www.nytimes.com/2013/02/08/us/politics/panetta-speaks-to-senate-panel-on-benghazi-attack.html?ref=marklandler (accessed on 15 July 2023).

Gordon, P. H., (2002). *Iraq: The Transatlantic Debate.* Occasional Papers No. 39. European Union Institute for Security Studies. The European Union Institute for Security Studies. Available at: https://www.iss.europa.eu/sites/default/files/EUISSFiles/occ39.pdf (accessed on 15 July 2023).

Gözen, R., (2006). ABD'nin irak savaşi: Yeni muhafazakar demokratik emperyalist bir proje. In: Şahin, M., & Taştekin, M., (eds.), *2. Körfez Savaşı* (pp. 29–66). Ankara: Platin Yayınları.

Grant, T. D., (2015). Annexation of crimea. *American Journal of International Law, 109*(1), 68–95.

Green, C., & Ruhleder, K., (1995). Globalization, borderless worlds, and the tower of Babel: Metaphors gone awry. *Journal of Organizational Change Management, 8*(4), 55–68.

Güdek, Ş., (2017). ABD'nin zora dayali diş politikasinda söylemsel bir değişim: 11 Eylül Terörü. *Ömer Halisdemir Üniversitesi İktisadi ve İdari Bilimler Fakültesi Dergisi, 10*(4), 143–158.

Gunaratna, R., & Jayasena, K., (2011). *Global Support For Al Qaeda and Osama Bin Laden: An Increase or Decrease?* UNISCI Discussion Papers No 25.

Gürseler, C., (2016). Yeni Olgusu: 100. Yılında Sykes-Picot Antlaşması, Orta Doğu ve Türkiye. *Akademik Bakış, 9*(18), 79–92.

Haas, R. N., (2002). *Defining US Foreign Policy in a Post-Post-Cold World, Arthur Ross Lecture: Remarks to Foreign Policy Association.* US Department of State Archive. Available at: https://2001-2009.state.gov/s/p/rem/9632.htm (accessed on 15 July 2023).

Haass, R. N., (2020). *The Pandemic Will Accelerate History Rather than Reshape It, Not Every Crisis Is a Turning Point.* Foreign Affairs. Available at: https://www.foreignaffairs.com/articles/united-states/2020-04-07/pandemic-will-accelerate-history-rather-reshape-it (accessed on 15 July 2023).

Halatçı, Ü., (2006). 11 eylül terörist saldirilari ve afganistan operasyonunun bir değerlendirilmesi. *Uluslararası Hukuk ve Politika, 2*(7), 80–98.

Hale, H., (2014). *Russian Nationalism and the Logic of the Kremlin's Actions on Ukraine.* The Guardian. Available at: https://www.theguardian.com/world/2014/aug/29/russian-nationalism-kremlin-actions-ukraine (accessed on 15 July 2023).

Hamlett, J. C., (2017). The constitutionality of russia's undesirable NGO law. *UCLA Journal of International Law and Foreign Affairs, 21*(2), 246–310.

Hartwig, R. E., (2008). *Winning is Everything: The Presidency of George W. Bush* (Vol. 4, No. 7, pp. 87–101.). Confines De Relaciones Internacionales Y Ciencia Política.

Heilbrunn, J., & Kissinger, H., (2015). *A Conversation with Henry Kissinger* (Vol. 139, pp. 12–17). The National Interest.

Heilbrunn, J., (2018). *Trump Isn't Fighting American Decline. He's Speeding It Up.* Washington Post. Available at: https://www.washingtonpost.com/news/global-opinions/wp/2018/05/25/trump-isnt-fighting-american-decline-hes-speeding-it-up/ (accessed on 15 July 2023).

Hemment, J., (2012). Nashi, youth voluntarism, and Potemkin NGOs: Making sense of civil society in post-soviet Russia. *Slavic Review, 71*(2), 234–260.

Heydemann, S., (2014). America's response to the Arab uprisings: US foreign assistance in an era of ambivalence. *Mediterranean Politics, 19*(3), 299–317.

Hinnebusch, R., (2007). *The American Invasion of Iraq: Causes and Consequences* (Vol. 12, No. 1, pp. 9–27). Perceptions.

Hirschman, A. O., (1980). *National Power and the Structure of Foreign Trade.* Berkeley and Los Angeles: Univ of California Press.

Hobbes, T. (1996). *Leviathan* (R. Tuck, Ed.). Cambridge: Cambridge University Press, 1996.

Hobsbawm, E., (1995). *The Age of Extremes: 1914–1991.* Abacus: New Ed.

Holbrooke, R., (1998). *To End a War.* New York: Random House.

Hook, S. W., (2016). *U.S. Foreign Policy: The Paradox of World Power.* CQ Press.

Hook, S., & Spanier, J., (2016). *Amerikan Dış Politikas: İkinci Dünya Savaşı'ndan Günümüze* (p. 340). Özge Zihnioğlu (çev.), İstanbul: İnkılap.

Hooker, R. D. Jr., (2014). *The Grand Strategy of the US.* INSS Strategic Monograph, Washington D.C: NDU Press.

Hooper, J., & McCharty, R., (2003). *26 Killed in Suicide Attack on Italian Base.* The Guardian. Available at: https://www.theguardian.com/world/2003/nov/13/italy.iraq (accessed on 15 July 2023).

Huntington, S. P., (1993). The clash of civilizations? *Foreign Affairs, 72*(3), 99–118.

Huntington, S. P., (1996). *The Clash of Civilizations and the Remaking of World Order.* Penguin Books: London.

Hyndman, J., (1999). A post-cold war geography of forced migration in Kenya and Somalia. *The Professional Geopgrapher, 51*(1), 104–114.

Ikenberry, G. J., (1989). Rethinking the origins of American hegemony. *Political Science Quarterly, 104*(3), 375–400.

Ikenberry, G. J., (2006). *Liberal Order and Imperial Ambition.* Cambridge, UK: Polity Press.

Ikenberry, G. J., (2008). The rise of China and the future of the west: Can the liberal system survive? *Foreign Affairs, 87*(1), 23–37.

Ikenberry, G. J., (2009). Liberal internationalism 3.0: America and the dilemmas of liberal world order. *Perspectives on Politics*, *7*(1), 71–87. doi: 10.1017/S153.759.2709090112.

Ikenberry, G. J., (2011). *Liberal Leviathan: The Origins, Crisis and Transformation of American World Order* (p. 122). Princeton, NJ: Princeton University Press.

Ikenberry, G. J., (2015). The future of multilateralism: Governing the world in a post-hegemonic era. *Japanese Journal of Political Science*, *16*(3), 399–413. doi: 10.1017/S1468109915000158.

Ikenberry, G. J. (2016). *Between the Eagle and the Dragon: America, China, and Middle State Strategies in East Asia.* Political Science Quarterly, 131(1), 9–43

Ikenberry, G. J., (2017). *The Plot Against American Foreign Policy: Can the Liberal Order Survive?* (Vol. 96, No. 3, pp. 1–7) Foreign Affairs.

Ikenberry, G. J., (2018a). The end of liberal international order? *International Affairs*, *94*(1), 7–23. https://doi.org/10.1093/ia/iix241.

Ikenberry, G. J., (2018b). Why the liberal world order will survive. *Ethics & International Affairs*, *32*(1), 17–29. https://doi.org/10.1017/S0892679418000072.

Ikenberry, G. J., (2020). *A World Safe for Democracy: Liberal Internationalism and the Crises of Global Order*. New Haven and London: Yale University Press.

Ingraham, C., (2017). *The Smart Way to Think About that Trade Deficit with Mexico.* The Washington Post. Available at: https://www.washingtonpost.com/news/wonk/wp/2017/01/26/the-smart-way-to-think-about-that-trade-deficit-with-mexico/ (accessed on 15 July 2023).

İnat, K., (2004). *ABD'nin "Haydut Devletler"i.* Değişim.

ISAF's mission in Afghanistan. (2022). NATO. Available at: https://www.nato.int/cps/en/natolive/topics_69366.htm (accessed on 30 July 2023)

Jackson, P., (2021). *11 Eylül Saldırıları: 2001'de Nasıl Düzenlendi, Kaç Kişi Öldü, Sonrasında ne Oldu?* BBC News. Available at: https://www.bbc.com/turkce/haberler-dunya-58462900 (accessed on 15 July 2023).

Jackson, R., (2020). *War on Terrorism.* Encyclopedia Britannica. Available at: https://www.britannica.com/topic/war-on-terrorism (accessed on 15 July 2023).

Jacobson, G., (2010). A tale of two wars: Public opinion on the U.S. military interventions in Afghanistan and Iraq. *Presidential Studies Quarterly*, *40*(4), 585–610.

Jaffe, G., & DeYoung, K., (2017). *In Trump's U.N. Speech, Emphasis on Sovereignty Echoes His Domestic Agenda.* Washington Post. Available at: https://www.washingtonpost.com/world/national-security/in-trumps-un-speech-an-emphasis-on-sovereignty-jostled-with-threats-of-intervention/2017/09/19/98a7a13e-9d3b-11e7-8ea1-ed975285475e_story.html?utm_term=.65f23770dd62 (accessed on 15 July 2023).

Jahn, B., (2018). Liberal internationalism: Historical trajectory and current prospects. *International Affairs*, *94*(1), 43–61.

Jakhar, P., (2019). *Confucius Institutes: The Growth of China's Controversial Cultural Branch.* BBC News. Available at: https://www.bbc.com/news/world-asia-china-49511231 (accessed on 15 July 2023).

Jang, J., McSparren, J., & Rashchupkina, Y., (2016). Global governance: Present and future. *Palgrave Communications*, *2*(1), 1–5.

Jawad, P., (2008). Conflict resolution through democracy promotion? The Role of the OSCE in Georgia. *Democratization*, *15*(3), 611–629.

Jentleson, B. W., (2011). *Beware the Duck Test* (Vol. 34, No. 3, pp. 137–149). The Washington Quarterly.

Jervis, D., (2017). Obama and the middle East. *TEKA of Political Science and International Relations, 12*(2), 31–57.

Jervis, R., (2003). Understanding the bush doctrine. *Political Science Quarterly, 118*(3), 365–388.

Jervis, R., (2006). *The Remaking of a Unipolar World* (Vol. 29, No. 3, pp. 7–19). Washington Quarterly.

Jervis, R., (2009). Unipolarity: A structural perspective. *World Politics, 61*(1), 188–213.

Jervis, R., (2018). President trump and international relations theory. In: Jervis, R., Gavin, F. J., Rovner, J., Labrosse, D. N., & Fujii, G., (eds.), *Chaos in the Liberal Order: The Trump Presidency and International Politics in the Twenty-First Century* (pp. 28–37). Columbia University Press.

Jervis, R., Gavin, F. J., Rovner, J., Labrosse, D. N., & Fujii, G., (2018). *Chaos in The Liberal Order: The Trump Presidency and International Politics in the 21st Century.* Columbia University Press. https://www.jstor.org/stable/10.7312/jerv18834 (accessed on 15 July 2023).

Johnson, J., & Hauslohner, A., (2017). *I Think Islam Hates Us': A Timeline of Trump's Comments About Islam and Muslims.* Washington Post. Available at: https://www. washingtonpost.com/news/post-politics/wp/2017/05/20/i-think-islam-hates-us-a-timeline-of-trumps-comments-about-islam-and-muslims/ (accessed on 15 July 2023).

Joint Statement by the President of the US and the President of the Russian Federation, (2017). U.S. Department of State. Available at: https://2017-2021.state.gov/background-briefing-on-the-joint-statement-by-the-president-of-the-united-states-and-the-president-of-the-russian-federation-on-syria/index.html (accessed on 15 July 2023).

Jones, C., & Fleming, S., (2017). *G20 Drops Vow to Resist all Forms of Protectionism.* Financial Times. Available at: https://www.ft.com/content/241cdf2a-0be9-11e7-a88c-50ba212dce4d (accessed on 15 July 2023).

Jones, L., & Hameiri, S., (2022). Explaining the failure of global health governance during COVID-19. *International Affairs, 98*(6), 2057–2076. doi: 10.1093/ia/iiac231.

Jørgensen, K. E., & Ergül, J. F. A., (2021). Realist theories in search of realists: The failure in Europe to advance realist theory. *International Relations, 35*(1), 3–22.

Kagan, R., (2017). *The Twilight of the Liberal World Order.* Brookings Institution. Available at: https://www.brookings.edu/research/the-twilight-of-the-liberal-world-order/ (accessed on 15 July 2023).

Kagan, R., (2021). *A Superpower, Like it or Not: Why Americans Must Accept Their Global Role* (Vol. 100, No. 2, pp. 28–38). Foreign Affairs.

Kagan, R., (2022). *The Price of Hegemony Can America Learn to Use Its Power?* Foreign Affairs. Available at: https://www.foreignaffairs.com/articles/ukraine/2022-04-06/russia-ukraine-war-price-hegemony (accessed on 15 July 2023).

Kahl, C., & Berengaut, A., (2020). *Aftershocks: The Coronavirus Pandemic and The New World Disorder.* War on the Rocks. Available at: https://warontherocks.com/2020/04/aftershocks-the-coronavirus-pandemic-and-the-new-world-disorder/ (accessed on 15 July 2023).

Kahl, C., & Wright, T., (2021). *Aftershocks: Pandemic Politics and the End of the Old International Order.* New York, NY: St. Martin's Press.

Kan, K., (2011). *Globalleşmenin Uluslararası İlişkilere Etkileri* (Vol. 13, No. 20, pp. 1–10). Karamanoğlu Mehmetbey Üniversitesi Sosyal ve Ekonomik Araştırmalar Dergisi.

Kanet, R. E., & Moulioukova, D., (2021). *Russia and the World in the Putin Era: From Theory to Reality in Russian Global Strategy*. Routledge.

Kanevskiy, P., (2023). Digital illiberalism and the erosion of the liberal international order. In: Berghofer, J., Futter, A., Häusler, C., Hoell, M., & Juraj, N., (eds.), *The Implications of Emerging Technologies in the Euro-Atlantic Space: Views from the Younger Generation Leaders Network* (pp. 3–21). Cham: Springer International Publishing.

Kaplan, R. D., (2020). *Coronavirus Ushers in the Globalization We Were Afraid Of. Bloomberg*. Available at: https://www.bloomberg.com/opinion/articles/2020-03-20/coronavirus-ushers-in-the-globalization-we-were-afraid-of (accessed on 15 July 2023).

Karakoç-Dora, Z., (2021). The US-led "War on Terror" in Afghanistan: 2001–2021. *MANAS Journal of Social Studies*, *10*, 172–185.

Katulis, B. & Juul, T. (2021). *The Lessons Learned for U.S. National Security Policy in the 20 Years Since 9/11*. Center for American Progress. Available at:https://www.americanprogress.org/article/lessons-learned-u-s-national-security-policy-20-years-since-911/ (accessed on 30 July 2023)

Keylor, W., (2018). The future of the Atlantic alliance under president trump. In: Jervis, R., Gavin, F. J., Rovner, J., Labrosse, D. N., & Fujii, G., (eds.), *Chaos in the Liberal Order: The Trump Presidency and International Politics in the Twenty-First Century* (pp. 629–640). Columbia University Press.

Khurami, H., (2023). Afghanistan and US foreign relation after September 11th 2001. *Technium Business and Management (TBM), 3*, 1–14.

Kiggins, R. D., (2014). US leadership in cyberspace: Transnational cyber security and global governance. In: Kremer, J. F., & Müller, B., (eds.), *Cyberspace and International Relations: Theory, Prospects and Challenges* (pp. 161–180). Berlin: Springer.

Kindleberger, C. P., (1973). *The World in Depression, 1929–39*. Berkeley: University of California Press.

Kindleberger, C. P., (1981). Dominance and leadership in the international economy: Exploitation, public goods, and free rides. *International Studies Quarterly, 25*(2), 242–254.

Kissinger, H., (1995). *Diplomacy*. Simon & Schuster.

Kissinger, H., (2002). *Diplomacy*. Simon & Schuster.

Kissinger, H., (2014). *World Order: Reflections on the Character of Nations and the Course of History*. New York: Penguin Press.

Klare, M., (1995). *Rogue States and Nuclear Outlaws: America's Search for a New Policy* (p. 67). New York: Hill and Wang.

Klitzman, S., & Freudenberg, N., (2003). Implications of the world trade center attack for the public health and health care infrastructures. *Am. J. Public Health, 93*(3), 400–406.

Kostyuchenko, E., (2015). *Invisible Army: The Story of a Russian Soldier Sent to Fight in Ukraine* | Ukraine the Guardian. Available at: https://www.theguardian.com/world/2015/mar/25/russia-ukraine-soldier (accessed on 15 July 2023).

Kotkin, S., (2016). *Russia's Perpetual Geopolitics: Putin Returns to the Historical Pattern* (Vol. 95, No. 3, pp. 2–9). Foreign Affairs.

Kramer, M., (2002). NATO, the Baltic states and Russia: A framework for sustainable enlargement. *International Affairs, 78*(4), 731–756.

Krasner, S. D., (1982). American policy and global economic stability. In: Avery, W. P., & Rapkin, D. P., (eds.), *America in a Changing World Political Economy* (pp. 29–48). New York: Longman.

Krasniqi, N., (2019). Kosovo: The development of interest groups in a fragile democracy. *Journal of Public Affairs, 19*(2), 1–10. https://doi.org/10.1002/pa.1721.

Krauthammer, C., (1990/91). *The Unipolar Moment* (Vol. 70, No. 1, pp. 23–33). Foreign Affairs.

Krugman, P., (2009). *The Return of Depression Economics and the Crisis of 2008*. W. W. Norton & Company.

Kupchan, C. A., (2002). *The End of the West*. The Atlantic. Available at: https://www.theatlantic.com/magazine/archive/2002/11/the-end-of-the-west/302617/ (accessed on 15 July 2023).

Kupchan, C. A., (2006). *The Fourth Age: The Next Era in Transatlantic Relations* (Vol. 85, pp. 77–83). The National Interest. http://www.jstor.org/stable/42897767 (accessed on 15 July 2023).

Kupchan, C. A., (2018). *Trump's Nineteenth-Century Grand Strategy*. Foreign Affairs. Available at: https://www.foreignaffairs.com/articles/united-states/2018-09-26/trumps-nineteenth-century-grand-strategy (accessed on 15 July 2023).

Kurtbağ, Ö., (2020). ABD liderliğindeki liberal uluslararasi düzenin sonu tartişmasi: Liberalizmin krizi ve geleceği. *Marmara Üniversitesi Siyasal Bilimler Dergisi., 8*(2), 379–403.

Lake, D., Martin, L. L., & Risse, T., (2021). Challenges to the liberal order: Reflections on international organization. *International Organization, 75*(2), 225–257.

Lake, T., (2001). *Lake Interview in PBS Frontline: The Clinton Years*. PBS. Available at: www.pbs.org/wgbh/pages/frontline/shows/clinton/interviews/lake.html (accessed on 15 July 2023).

Langan, J., (2004). *Bush's Iraq Project*. Commonweal. Available at: https://www.commonwealmagazine.org/bushs-iraq-project (accessed on 15 July 2023).

Laqueur, W., (1999). *The New Terrorism: Fanaticism and the Arms of Mass Destruction*. New York: Oxford University Press.

Laruelle, M., (2015). Russia as a "Divided nation," from compatriots to Crimea: A contribution to the discussion on nationalism and foreign policy. *Problems of Post-Communism, 62*(2), 88–97.

Lauterbach, T., (2011). Constructivism, strategic culture, and the Iraq war. *Air & Space Power Journal-Africa and Francophonie, 2*(4), 61–93.

Layne, C., (1993). The unipolar illusion: Why new great powers will rise. *International Security, 17*(4), 5–51.

Layne, C., (1994). Kant or cant: The myth of the democratic peace. *International Security, 19*(2), 5–49.

Layne, C., (1997). From preponderance to offshore balancing: America's future grand strategy. *International Security, 22*(1), 86–124.

Layne, C., (2006). The unipolar illusion revisited. *International Security, 31*(2), 7–41.

Lebow, R. N., (1994). The long peace, the end of the cold war and the failure of realism. *International Organization, 48*(2), 249–77.

Lee, M., & Lederman, J., (2018). *Trump Administration Pulls US out of UN Human Rights Council*. AP News. Available at: https://apnews.com/article/

united-nations-north-america-ap-top-news-international-news-politics-9c5b1005f06447 4f9a0825ab84a16e91 (accessed on 15 July 2023).

Lehne, S., (2023). *After Russia's War Against Ukraine: What Kind of World Order?* Carnegie Europe. Available at: https://carnegieeurope.eu/2023/02/28/after-russia-s-war-against-ukraine-what-kind-of-world-order-pub-89130 (accessed on 15 July 2023).

Licklider, R. E., (1970). The missile gap controversy. *Political Science Quarterly, 85*(4), 600–615.

Limited Benefits of US Ties to Egypt's Military, (2011). CBS. Available at: https://www. cbsnews.com/news/limited-benefits-of-us-ties-to-egypts-military/ (accessed on 15 July 2023).

Lin, K. J., Xiaoyan Lu, J. Z., & Ying, Z., (2020). State-owned enterprises in China: A review of 40 years of research and practice. *China Journal of Accounting Research, 13*(1), 31–55.

Lind, J., & Wohlforth, W. C., (2019). *The Future of the Liberal Order Is Conservative* (Vol. 98, No. 2, pp. 70–80). Foreign Affairs.

Lind, M., (2014). *The American Century is Over: How Our Country Went Down in a Blaze of Shame.* Salon. Available at: https://www.salon.com/2014/07/12/the_american_century_is_over_how_our_country_went_down_in_a_blaze_of_shame/ (accessed on 15 July 2023).

Lippit, V., (1981). The people's communes and China's new development strategy. *Bulletin of Concerned Asian Scholars, 13*(3), 19–30.

Lipscy, P. L., (2020). COVID-19 and the politics of crisis. *International Organization, 74*(S1), E98–E127. doi: 10.1017/S0020818320000375.

Lissner, R. F., & Rapp-Hooper, M., (2018). The day after trump: American strategy for a new international order. *The Washington Quarterly, 41*(1), 7–25 https://doi.org/10.1080 /0163660X.2018.1445353.

Luce, E., (2017). *The Retreat of Western Liberalism.* Atlantic Monthly Press.

Lute, D., & Burns, N., (2019). *NATO at 70: An Alliance in Crisis.* Belfer Center Report. Available at: https://www.belfercenter.org/publication/nato-seventy-alliance-crisis (accessed on 15 July 2023).

Lutter, K., (2015). *Soft Power and Cultural Exchange: The Obama Administration and the Impact of US Public Diplomacy on the Beliefs of Estonians.* Degree of Bachelor of Arts, Bucknell University. Available at: https://core.ac.uk/download/pdf/216950285.pdf (accessed on 15 July 2023).

Lynch, C., (2015). *Rwanda Revisited.* Foreign Policy. Available at: https://foreignpolicy. com/2015/04/05/rwanda-revisited-genocide-united-states-state-department/ (accessed on 15 July 2023).

Lyon, D., (2003). *Surveillance After September 11.* Polity Press.

Mahbubani, K., (2020). *Has China Won? The Chinese Challenge to American Primacy.* Public Affairs.

Mahesar, P. A., Ghumro, A. K., & Ali, I., (2021). A crisis of status quo or power transition amidst China. *Global Social Sciences Review,* (VI-I), 281–286. http://dx.doi. org/10.31703/gssr.2021(VI-I).28.

Malik, S., (2004). US war in Iraq in the light of the major and minor powers conflict. *The Turkish Yearbook, 35*, 83–106. doi: 10.1501/Intrel_0000000101.

Mandelbaum, M., (1999). A perfect failure: NATO's war against Yugoslavia. *Foreign Affairs*, *78*(5), 2–8. https://doi.org/10.2307/20049444.

Mandelbaum, M., (2016). *Mission Failure* (p. 138). New York: Oxford University Press.

Marquardt, A., & Hansler, J., (2020). *US Push to Include 'Wuhan Virus' Language in G7 Joint Statement Fractures Alliance*. CNN. Available at: https://edition.cnn.com/2020/03/25/politics/g7-coronavirus-statement/index.html (accessed on 15 July 2023).

Marshall, K., (2012). Youth neither enrolled nor employed. *Perspectives on Labor and Income*, *24*(2), 1–15.

Martin-Ortega, O., (2013). Building peace and delivering justice in Bosnia and Herzegovina: The limits of externally driven processes. In: Sriram, C. L., García-Godos, J., Herman, J., Martin-& Ortega, O., (eds.), *Transitional Justice and Peacebuilding on the Ground: Victims and Ex-Combatants* (pp. 139–158). Newyork, NY: Routledge.

Mastanduno, M., (1999). A realist view: Three images of the coming international order. In: Paul, T. V., & Hall, J. A., (eds.), *International Order and the Future of World Politics* (pp. 19–40). New York: Cambridge University Press.

Mastanduno, M., (2019). Liberal hegemony, international order, and US foreign policy: A reconsideration. *The British Journal of Politics and International Relations*, *21*(1), 47–54.

Matthews, J. P., (2019). Defending liberal democracies against disinformation. *American Intelligence Journal*, *36*(2), 86–94. https://www.jstor.org/stable/27066376 (accessed on 15 July 2023).

Mazarr, M. J., (2007). The Iraq war and agenda setting. *Foreign Policy Analysis*, *3*(1), 1–23.

McFaul, M., & Goldgeier, J. M., (1992). A tale of two worlds: Core and periphery in the post–cold war era. *International Organization*, *46*(2), 467–492.

McKinsey Global Institute, (2019). *China and the World Inside the Dynamics of a Changing Relationship*. McKinsey & Company. Available at: https://www.mckinsey.com/featured-insights/china/china-and-the-world-inside-the-dynamics-of-a-changing-relationship (accessed on 15 July 2023).

McNeill, D., (2018). Why was Iraq invaded in 2003? *Undergraduate Journal of Politics and International Relations*, *1*(1), 1–16. doi: https://doi.org/10.22599/ujpir.14.

Mearsheimer, J. J., & Walt, S. M., (2016). The case for offshore balancing: A superior US grand strategy. *Foreign Affairs*, 70–83.

Mearsheimer, J. J., (1990). Back to the future: Instability in Europe after the cold war. *International Security*, *15*(1), 5–55.

Mearsheimer, J. J., (1992). Disorder restored. In: Allison, G., & Treverton, G., (eds.), *Rethinking America's Security* (pp. 213–237). New York: Norton.

Mearsheimer, J. J., (1994). The false promise of international institutions. *International Security*, *19*(3), 5–49. https://doi.org/10.2307/2539078.

Mearsheimer, J. J., (2001). *The Tragedy of Great Power Politics* (p. 40). New York: W.W. Norton.

Mearsheimer, J. J., (2014). Why the Ukraine crisis is the west's fault: The liberal delusions that provoked Putin. *Foreign Affairs*, *93*(5), 77–89. https://www.jstor.org/stable/24483306 (accessed on 15 July 2023).

Mearsheimer, J. J., (2018). *The Great Delusion: Liberal Dreams and International Realities*. New Haven, CT: Yale University Press.

Mearsheimer, J. J., (2019). Bound to fail: The rise and fall of the liberal international order. *International Security, 43*(4), 7–50.

Mearsheimer, J. J., (2020). *Liberalism and Nationalism in Contemporary America*. The James Madison Lecture, University of Chicago. Available at: https://www.mearsheimer. com/wp-content/uploads/2020/09/Madison-Lecture.September-10-2020.pdf (accessed on 15 July 2023).

Mearsheimer, J. J., (2021). Liberalism and nationalism in contemporary America. *PS: Political Science & Politics, 54*(1), 1–8. doi: 10.1017/S1049096520001808.

Merkel: Europe 'Can no Longer Rely on Allies' After Trump and Brexit, (2017). BBC News. Available at: https://www.bbc.com/news/world-europe-40078183 (accessed on 15 July 2023).

Miller, L. H., (1964). The contemporary significance of the doctrine of just war. *World Politics, 16*(2), 256–257.

Miller, P. D., (2012). Five pillars of American grand strategy. *Survival, 54*(5), 7–44. doi: 10.1080/00396338.2012.728343.

Milner, H., & Tingley, D., (2012). The choice for multilateralism: Foreign aid and American foreign policy. *The Review of International Organizations, 8*(3), 313–341.

Mirza, M., (2018). Enduring legacy of realism and the us foreign policy: Dynamics of prudence, national interest, and balance of power. *Orient Research Journal of Social Sciences, 3*(2), 163–176.

Mishkin, F., (2017). *Financial Policies and the Prevention of Financial Crises in the Emerging Market Countries*. NBER Working Paper Series. Available at: http://www. nber.org/papers/w8087 (accessed on 15 July 2023).

Mishra, P., (2017). *Age of Anger: A History of the Present*. New York: Farrar, Straus & Giroux.

Misra, A., (2004). *Afghanistan: The Labyrinth of Violence*. Cambridge: Polity.

Morey, D. S., Thyne, C. L., Hayden, S. L., & Senters, M. B., (2012). Leader, follower, or spectator? The role of president Obama in the Arab spring uprisings. *Social Science Quarterly, 93*(5), 1185–1201.

Morgan, M. J., (2009). *The Impact of 9/11 on Politics and War: The Day That Changed Everything?* New York: Palgrave Macmillan.

Morrison, W. M., (2013). *China's Economic Rise: History, Trends, Challenges, and Implications for the US*. Congressional Research Service. Available at: https://www. refworld.org/pdfid/52cfef6b4.pdf (accessed on 15 July 2023).

Mueller, J., (1995). The perfect enemy: Assessing the gulf war. *Security Studies, 5*(1), 77–117. https://doi.org/10.1080/09636419508429253.

Mueller, J., (2004). *The Remnants of War* (p. 121). Ithaca, NY: Cornell University Press.

National Intelligence Council, (2012). *Global Trends 2030: Alternative Worlds*. Available at: https://www.dni.gov/files/documents/GlobalTrends_2030.pdf (accessed on 15 July 2023).

National Security Strategy of the United States of America, (1994). White House. Available at: https://history.defense.gov/Portals/70/Documents/nss/nss1994.pdf (accessed on 15 July 2023).

National Security Strategy of the United States of America, (2010). White House. Available at: https://obamawhitehouse.archives.gov/sites/default/files/rss_viewer/national_security_strategy.pdf (accessed on 15 July 2023).

National Security Strategy of the United States of America, (2017). White House. Available at: https://trumpwhitehouse.archives.gov/wp-content/uploads/2017/12/NSS-Final-12-18-2017-0905.pdf (accessed on 15 July 2023).

National Security Strategy of the United States of America, (2022). White House. Available at: https://www.whitehouse.gov/wp-content/uploads/2022/10/Biden-Harris-Administrations-National-Security-Strategy-10.2022.pdf (accessed on 15 July 2023).

NATO, (2022). *Collective Defense and Article 5*. Available at: https://www.nato.int/cps/en/natohq/topics_110496.htm (accessed on 15 July 2023).

Nau, H. R., (2002). *At Home Abroad: Identity and Power in American Foreign Policy*. Cornell University Press.

Nazir, M., (2006). Democracy, Islam and insurgency in Iraq. *Pakistan Horizon, 59*(3), 47–65.

Neil, M., (2019). *Outrage Grows as Russia Grants Passports to Ukraine's Breakaway. The New York Times*. Available at: https://www.nytimes.com/2019/04/25/world/europe/russia-citizenship-ukraine.html (accessed on 15 July 2023).

Niblett, R., (2017). Liberalism in retreat: The demise of a dream. *Foreign Affairs, 96*(1), 17–24.

Noonan, J., (2020). Trump and the liberal international order. *International Critical Thought, 10*(2), 182–199.

Noortmann, M., (2009). *Understanding Non-State Entities in the Contemporary World Order* (). Working Paper Presented at Non-State Actor Research Seminar, Leuven, Belgium. Available at: https://ghum.kuleuven.be/ggs/research/non_state_actors/publications/noortmann.pdf (accessed on 15 July 2023).

Norris, P., (2020). *Measuring Populism Worldwide* (pp. 1–40). HKS Faculty Research Working Paper Series RWP20-002. Harvard Kennedy School.

Norrlöf, C., (2020). Is COVID-19 a liberal democratic curse? Risks for liberal international order. *Cambridge Review of International Affairs, 33*(5), 799–813. https://doi.org/10.1080/09557571.2020.1812529.

Nowland, M. C., (2001). *Eliminating the Rhetoric: An Evaluation of the Halt-Phase Strategy*. Air University Press. Maxwell Air Force Base, Alabama. Available at: https://media.defense.gov/2017/Dec/27/2001861493/-1/-1/0/T_0012_NOWLAND_ELIMINATING_RHETORIC.PDF (accessed on 15 July 2023).

Nye, J. S. Jr., (1992). What new world order? *Foreign Affairs, 71*(2), 83–96.

Nye, J. S. Jr., (2015). Is the American century over? *Political Science Quarterly, 130*(3), 393–400.

Nye, J. S. Jr., (2016). Deterrence and dissuasion in cyberspace. *International Security, 41*(3), 44–71. doi: 10.1162/ISEC_a_00266.

Nye, J. S. Jr., (2017). Will the liberal order survive? The history of an idea. *Foreign Affairs, 96*(1), 10–16.

Nye, J. S. Jr., (2020). *Post-Pandemic Geopolitics*. Project Syndicate. Available at: https://www.project-syndicate.org/commentary/five-scenarios-for-international-order-in-2030-by-joseph-s-nye-2020-10; https://www.project-syndicate.org/commentary/

five-scenarios-for-international-order-in-2030-by-joseph-s-nye-2020-10 (accessed on 15 July 2023).

Obama Urges Egyptian Leader to Protect Democratic Principles, (2013). Reuters. Available at: https://www.reuters.com/article/us-egypt-usa-obama-idUSBRE91P0ZA20130226 (accessed on 15 July 2023).

Obama, B., (2009a). *Remarks by the President at Cairo University*. White House. Available at: https://obamawhitehouse.archives.gov/the-press-office/remarks-president-Cairo-university-6-04-09 (accessed on 15 July 2023)

Obama, B., (2009b). *Remarks By President Barack Obama in Prague as Delivered*. White House. Available at: https://obamawhitehouse.archives.gov/the-press-office/remarks-president-barack-obama-prague-delivered (accessed on 15 July 2023).

Obama, B., (2011). *Remarks by the President on the Middle East and North Africa*. The White House. Available at: https://obamawhitehouse.archives.gov/the-press-office/2011/05/19/remarks-president-middle-east-and-north-africa%20 (accessed on 15 July 2023).

Obama, B., (2014). *Remarks by the President at the US Military Academy Commencement Ceremony*. Washington, D.C.: White House.

O'Connor, B., & Cooper, D., (2021). Ideology and the foreign policy of Barack Obama: A liberal-realist approach to international affairs. *Presidential Studies Quarterly, 51*(3), 635–666.

OECD, (2022). *China Economic Snapshot*. OECD. Available at: https://www.oecd.org/economy/china-economic-snapshot/#:~:text=Economic%20Outlook%20Note%20%2D%20China,2023%20and%204.1%25%20in%202024 (accessed on 15 July 2023).

Onea, T. A., (2013). *US Foreign Policy in the Post-Cold War Era: Restraint Versus Assertiveness from George H. W. Bush to Barack Obama Series*. Palgrave MacMillan.

Over 1.3 Million Ukrainian Refugees Remain in Poland One Year Since Russia's Invasion, (2023). Notes From Poland. Available at: https://notesfrompoland.com/2023/02/23/over-1-3-million-ukrainian-refugees-remain-in-poland-one-year-since-russias-invasion/ (accessed on 15 July 2023).

Önel, E., (2020). The first and the only option: The war analysis of Bush's personality and decision-making process of Iraq War. *Contemporary Research in Economics and Social Sciences, 4*(1), 65–88.

Özdemir, H., (2002). *11 Eylül: Post Modern Savaşın Miladı ya da Dış Politika Mücadelelerinin Görünmeyen Boyutu* (Vol. 7, No. 1, pp. 153–173). Süleyman Demirel Üniversitesi İktisadi ve İdari Bilimler Fakültesi.

Özdemir, Ç. (2018). *Amerikan Grand Stratejisi: Obama'nın Ortadoğu Mirası*. İstanbul, SETA.

Özlük, E., (2015). Adil savaş ve irak savaşi: Anakronik bir öğretiyi 21. Yüzyılda yeniden okumak. *Sosyal Ekonomik Araştırmalar Dergisi, 15*(30), 15–38.

Öztürk, S., (2019). Küresel terör örgütü el-kaide'nin gelişimi ve ön plana çıkan liderleri bağlamında "cihad" anlayişinin geçirdiği değişimler. *Türkiye Ortadoğu Çalışmaları Dergisi, 6*(2), 185–186.

Packer, G., (2014). *The Unwinding*. Farrar, Straus and Giroux.

Paine, T., (2008). In: Foner, E., (ed.), *The Rights of Man*. New York, NY: Cosimo, Inc.

Parker, A., (2016). *Donald Trump Says NATO Is 'Obsolete,' UN Is a Political Game*. The New York Times. Available at: https://archive.nytimes.com/www.nytimes.com/

politics/first-draft/2016/04/02/donald-trump-tells-crowd-hed-be-fine-if-nato-broke-up/ (accessed on 15 July 2023).

Patil, V., (2017). *Libyan Army Commander Signs $2 Billion Arms Deal with Russia Despite UN Sanction.* Defense Mirror.com. Available at: https://www.defensemirror.com/ news/18245/Libyan_Army_Commander_Signs__2_Billion_Arms_Deal_With_Russia_ Despite_UN_Sanctions#.ZDfAHexBxQI (accessed on 15 July 2023).

Patrick, S. M., (2017a). Trump and world order: The return of self-help. *Foreign Affairs, 96*(2), 52–57.

Patrick, S. M., (2017b). An open world is in the balance: What might replace the liberal order?' *World Politics Review.* Available at: https://www.worldpoliticsreview.com/ an-open-world-is-in-the-balance-what-might-replace-the-liberal-order/ (accessed on 15 July 2023).

Patrick, S. M., (2020a). The world order after COVID-19 hinges on what kind of America emerges. *World Politics Review.* Available at: https://www.worldpoliticsreview.com/ the-world-order-after-covid-19-hinges-on-what-kind-of-america-emerges/?one-time-read-code=51608168073423972931 (accessed on 15 July 2023).

Patrick, S. M., (2020b). *When the System Fails: COVID-19 and the Costs of Global Dysfunction.* Foreign Affairs. Available at: https://www.foreignaffairs.com/articles/ world/2020-06-09/when-system-fails (accessed on 15 July 2023).

Paul, J. A., (2002). *Oil in Iraq: The Heart of the Crisis.* Global Policy Forum. Available at: https://archive.globalpolicy.org/component/content/article/185-general/40510-oil-in-iraq-the-heart-of-the-crisis.html (accessed on 15 July 2023).

Petersson, M., (2016). The US as the reluctant ally. *Parameters, 46*(1), 43–50. Available at: https://ssi.armywarcollege.edu/pubs/parameters. doi: 10.55540/ 0031-1723.2823. (accessed on 15 July 2023).

Peterson, N. (2017). *CNN American Coal Miners Undermine Putin's Energy Weapon Against Ukraine.* Newsweek. Available at: https://www.newsweek.com/american-coal-miners-undermine-putins-energy-weapon-against-ukraine-708358 (accessed on 30 July 2023).

Pfiffner, J. P., (2004). Did president bush mislead the country in his arguments for war with Iraq? *Presidential Studies Quarterly, 34*(1), 25–46.

Ping, X. & Li, W., (2015). The China model vs. American soft power: Going global and peaceful. *İstanbul Gelişim Üniversitesi Sosyal Bilimler Dergisi, 2*(2), 153–170.

Piper, E., (2013). *Why Ukraine Spurned the EU and Embraced Russia.* Reuters. Available at: https://www.reuters.com/article/us-ukraine-russia-deal-special-report-idUSBRE9BI0DZ20131219 (accessed on 15 July 2023).

Pompeo, M. R., (2018). *Remarks on the UN Human Rights Council.* US Department of State. Available at: https://2017-2021.state.gov/remarks-on-the-un-human-rights-council/index.html (accessed on 15 July 2023).

Posen, B. R., (2000). The war for Kosovo: Serbia's political-military strategy. *International Security, 24*(4), 39–84.

Posen, B. R., (2003). Command of the commons: The military foundation of U.S. hegemony. *International Security, 28*(1), 5–46.

Posen, B. R., (2013). *Pull Back: The Case for a Less Activist Foreign Policy* (Vol. 92, No, 1, pp. 116–128). Foreign Affairs.

Posen, B. R., (2018). *The Rise of Illiberal Hegemony: Trump's Surprising Grand Strategy* (Vol. 97, No. 2, pp. 20–27). Foreign Affairs.

Posen, B. R., & Ross, A., (1996/1997). Competing visions for US grand strategy. *International Security, 21*, 5–53. https://doi.org/10.2307/2539272.

President Barack Obama's Inaugural Address, (2009). The White House. Available at: https://obamawhitehouse.archives.gov/blog/2009/01/21/president-Barack-obamas-inaugural-address (accessed on 30 July 2023).

President Bush's Second Inaugural Address, (2005). NPR. Available at: https://www.npr.org/templates/story/story.php?storyId=4460172 (accessed on 15 July 2023).

Presidential Memorandum Regarding Withdrawal of the US from the Trans-Pacific Partnership Negotiations and Agreement, (2017). The White House. Available at: https://trumpwhitehouse.archives.gov/presidential-actions/presidential-memorandum-regarding-withdrawal-united-states-trans-pacific-partnership-negotiations-agreement/ (accessed on 15 July 2023).

Press, D. G., (2001). The myth of air power in the Persian Gulf war and the future of warfare. *International Security, 26*(2), 5–44.

Public Uncertain, Divided Over America's Place in the World, (2016). Pew Research Center. Available at: http://www.people-press.org/2016/05/05/public-uncertain-divided-over-americas-place-in-the-world/ (accessed on 15 July 2023).

Putin, V., (2007). *Speech and the Following Discussion at the Munich Conference on Security Policy*. President of Russia. Available at: http://en.kremlin.ru/events/president/transcripts/copy/24034 (accessed on 15 July 2023).

Putin, V., (2021). *Article by Vladimir Putin "On the Historical Unity of Russians and Ukrainians*. President of Russia. Available at: http://en.kremlin.ru/events/president/news/66181 (accessed on 15 July 2023).

Qianming, S., (2021). *How Should China Build a Modernized Superpower?* CSIS Interpret. Available at: https://interpret.csis.org/translations/how-should-china-build-a-modernized-superpower/ (accessed on 15 July 2023).

Qin, J. Y., (2019). Forced technology transfer and the US–China trade war: Implications for international economic law. *Journal of International Economic Law, 22*(4), 743–762.

Ramsbotham, O., Woodhouse, T., & Miall, H., (2011). *Contemporary Conflict Resolution: The Prevention, Management and Transformation of Deadly Conflicts*. Cambridge: Polity.

Rankin, J., (2020). *Coronavirus Could be Final Straw for EU, European Experts Warn*. The Guardian. Available at: https://www.theguardian.com/world/2020/apr/01/coronavirus-could-be-final-straw-for-eu-european-experts-warn (accessed on 15 July 2023).

Rapoport, D., (2001). The fourth wave: September 11 and the history of terrorism. *Current History, 100*(650), 419–424.

Rapoport, D., (2002). The four waves of rebel terror and September 11. *Anthropoetics, 8*(1), 33.

Rapoport, D., (2013). The four waves of modern terror: International dimensions and consequences. In: Hanhimaki, J. M., & Blumenau, B., (2013). *An International History of Terrorism: Western and Non-Western Experiences* (pp. 282–310). New York: Routledge.

Rashid, A., & Ghouri, A., (2021). Liberal international order: Competing trends and narratives. *Strategic Studies, 41*(2), 16–31.

Ratnesar, R., (2011). *Obama's Mission: Talk to Some Enemies, Don't Kill Them*. Time. Available at: https://content.time.com/time/nation/article/0,8599,2071658,00.html (accessed on 15 July 2023).

Ratrout, E., & Köprülü, N., (2022). International dimensions of authoritarian persistence in the MENA region: Revisiting US foreign aid to Egypt in the post-2011 Arab uprisings Era. *Uluslararası İlişkiler Dergisi, 19*(75), 45–63. doi: 10.33458/uidergisi.1163569.

Rayburn, J. D., & Sobchak, F. K., (2019). *The US Army in the Iraq War*. New York: US Press Regions.

Redd, S. B., & Mintz, A., (2013). Policy perspectives on national security and foreign policy decision making. *Policy Studies Journal, 41*(S1), 11–37.

Resolution 1368, (2001). *Adopted by the Security Council at its 4370th Meeting*. United Nations Security Council. Available at: https://digitallibrary.un.org/record/448051?ln=en (accessed on 15 July 2023).

Resolution No 63/303, (2009). *Outcome of the Conference on the World Financial and Economic Crisis and Its Impact on Development, 63rd Session*. United Nations General Assembly. Available at: https://www.un.org/esa/ffd/wp-content/uploads/2014/09/Outcome_2009.pdf (accessed on 15 July 2023).

Reuters, (1992). *The 1992 Campaign; Excerpts from Speech by Clinton on U.S. Role*. The New York Times. Available at: https://www.nytimes.com/1992/10/02/us/the-1992-campaign-excerpts-from-speech-by-clinton-on-us-role.html (accessed on 15 July 2023).

Richardson, L., (2006). *What Terrorists Want? Understanding the Terrorist Threat*. London: John Murray.

Riddell, P. G., (2001). *Blair Can Count on Support for the Time Being* (p. 231). The Times.

Roberts, J. M., (1999). *The Penguin History of the Twentieth Century*. Penguin Books Ltd.

Rolland, N., (2020). *China's Vision for a New World Order (NBR Special Report. 83)*. The National Bureau of Asian Research. Available at: https://www.nbr.org/wp-content/uploads/pdfs/publications/sr83_chinasvision_jan2020.pdf (accessed on 15 July 2023).

Rosati, J., & Twing, S., (1998). The presidency and US foreign policy after the cold war. In: Scott, J. M., (ed.), *After the End: Making U.S. Foreign Policy in the Post-Cold War World* (pp. 29–56). Duke University Press.

Rose, G., (1998), Neoclassical realism and theories of foreign policy. *World Politics, 51*(1), 144–172.

Rose, G., (2019). The fourth founding: The US and the liberal order. *Foreign Affairs, 98*(1), 10–21.

Ross, R. S., (2006). Balance of power politics and the rise of China: Accommodation and balancing in East Asia. *Security Studies, 15*(3), 355–395.

Rourke, J. T., Carter, R. G., & Boyer, M. A., (1996). *Making American Foreign Policy* (pp. 111–113). Madison, Wise: Brown and Benchmark.

Rousseau, D., (2005). *Democracy and War: Institutions, Norms, and the Evolution of International Conflict*. Standford: Stanford University Press.

Ruggie, J., (1982). International regimes, transactions, and change: Embedded liberalism in the post-war economic order. *International Organization, 36*(2), 379–415.

Ruggie, J. G., (1993). Multilateralism: The Anatomy of an Institution. In: Ruggie, (ed.), *Multilateralism Matters: The Theory and Praxis of an Institutional Form* (pp. 3–47). New York: Columbia University Press.

Ruggie, J. G., (1998). What makes the world hang together? neo-utilitarianism and the social constructivist challenge. *International Organization, 52*(4), 855–885.

Runningen, R., & Nichols, H., (2010). *Obama Strategy Puts Emphasis on Economics, Alliances.* Bloomberg. Available at: https://www.bloomberg.com/news/articles/2010-05-26/obama-s-security-strategy-to-put-focus-on-economic-diplomatic-alliances#xj4y7vzkg (accessed on 15 July 2023).

Russia Accuses US of Fighting Proxy War in Ukraine, (2022). Aljazeera. Available at: https://www.aljazeera.com/news/2022/12/22/russia-accuses-us-of-fighting-proxy-war-in-ukraine (accessed on 15 July 2023).

Ryan, J., (2019). *Education in China: Philosophy, Politics and Culture.* John Wiley & Sons.

Sander, O., (2010). *Siyasi Tarih (1918–1994).* Ankara: İmge Yayınevi.

Scanlon, K., (2019). *Effects of Terrorism on the U.S. Stock Market: Evidence from High Frequency Data.* Honors College (Capstone Experience/Thesis Projects Paper 781). Available at: https://core.ac.uk/reader/212147190 (accessed on 15 July 2023).

Schulenberg, R., (2019). *Obama and 'Learning' in Foreign Policy: Military Intervention in Libya and Syria.* Available at: from https://www.e-ir.info/2019/09/05/obama-and-learning-in-foreign-policy-military-intervention-in-libya-and-syria/ (accessed on 15 July 2023).

Schunz, S., & Didieri, B., (2019). The European Union's evolving role in response to U.S. waning hegemony. In: Massie, J., & Paquin, J., (eds.), *America's Allies and the Decline of U.S. Hegemony* (pp. 176–193). NY: Routledge.

Schweller, R. L., (2018). Why trump now: A third image explanation. In: Jervis, R., Gavin, F. J., Rovner, J., Labrosse, D. N., & Fujii, G., (eds.), *Chaos in the Liberal Order: The Trump Presidency and International Politics in the Twenty-First Century* (pp. 65–98). Columbia University Press.

Schwenninger, S. R., (1999). *World Order Lost: American Foreign Policy in the Post-Cold War World, 16*(2), 42–71. Duke University Press.

Scott, J. M., (1998). *After the End: Making U.S. Foreign Policy in the Post-Cold War World.* Duke University Press.

Sever, M., & Kılıç, E., (2001). *Düşmanını Arayan Savaş.* İstanbul: İmge Yayınları.

Shanker, T., (2003). *Wolfowitz's Hotel Is Attacked in Baghdad.* The New York Times. Available at: https://www.nytimes.com/2003/10/26/world/wolfowitz-s-hotel-is-attacked-in-baghdad.html (accessed on 15 July 2023).

Sheng, L., (2022). *How COVID-19 Reshapes New World Order: Political Economy Perspective.* Singapore: Springer Nature Singapore Pte Ltd.

Shepherd, A. J. K., (2009). "A milestone in the History of the EU": Kosovo and the EU's international role. *International Affairs (Royal Institute of International Affairs 1944), 85*(3), 513–530.

Shipoli, E. A., (2018). Theoretical approaches to US foreign policy. *Islam, Securitization, and US Foreign Policy,* 13–70.

Shveda, Y., & Park, J. H., (2016). Ukraine's revolution of dignity: The dynamics of Euromaidan. *Journal of Eurasian Studies, 7*(1), 85–91.

Simmons, B., & Goemans, H., (2021). Built on borders: Tensions with the institution liberalism (thought it) left behind. *International Organization, 75*(2), 387–410.

Simons, G., (2019). Digital communication disrupting hegemonic power in global geopolitics: New media shape new world order. *Russia in Global Affairs, 17*(2), 108–130. doi: 10.31278/1810-6374-2019-17-2-108-130.

Singh, R. S., (2012). *Barack Obama*. Oxford University Press.

Smith, A., (1776). *The Wealth of Nations*. London: Printed for W. Strahan and T. Cadell, London.

Smith, A., (2016). *Donald Trump Praised Putin on the National Stage Again—Here's What It All Means*. Business Insider. Available at: http://www.businessinsider.com/donald-trump-vladimir-putin-strong-leader-obama-2016-9 (accessed on 15 July 2023).

Snauwaert, D., (2004). The buch doctrine and just war theory. *The Online Journal of Peace and Conflict Resolution*, 123–124.

Soder, K., (2009). *The Supreme Court, the Bush Administration and Guantánamo Bay*. SIPRI.

Sopel, J., (2015). *Full Transcript of BBC Interview with President Barack Obama*. BBC News. Available at: https://www.bbc.com/news/world-us-canada-33646542 (accessed on 15 July 2023).

Sönmezoğlu, F., (1996). *Uluslararası İlişkiler Sözlüğü*. İstanbul: Der Yayınları.

Spechler, D. R., & Spechler, M. C., (2019). *Putin and His Neighbors: Russia's Policies Toward Eurasia*. Lexington Books.

Spencer, J., (2005). *The 2005 Quadrennial Defense Review: Strategy and Threats*. The Heritage Foundation. Available at: https://www.heritage.org/defense/report/the-2005-quadrennial-defense-review-strategy-and-threats (accessed on 15 July 2023).

Starr, S. F., & Cornell, S. E., (2014). *Putin's Grand Strategy: The Eurasian Union and its Discontents*. Central Asia-Caucasus Institute & Silk Road Studies Program, Joint Transatlantic Research and Policy Center, Johns Hopkins University, School of Advanced International Studies (SAIS).

Statement by Former National Security Officials, (2016). *In "A Letter from G.O.P. National Security Officials Opposing Donald Trump."* The New York Times. Available at: https://www.nytimes.com/interactive/2016/08/08/us/politics/national-security-letter-trump.html (accessed on 15 July 2023).

Stelzenmüller, C., (2019). *America's Policy on Europe Takes a Nationalist Turn*. Financial Times. Available at: https://www.ft.com/content/133ef614-23b3-11e9-b20d-5376ca5216eb (accessed on 15 July 2023).

Stent, A. E., (2008). Restoration and revolution in Putin's foreign policy. *Europe-Asia Studies, 60*(6) 1089–1106.

Stewart, P., & Zengerle, P., (2013). *Pentagon Backed Plan for U.S. to Arm Syrian Rebels*. Reuters. Available at: https://www.reuters.com/article/uk-usa-syria-pentagon-idUKBRE91613720130207 (accessed on 15 July 2023).

Stiglitz, J., (2011). Macroeconomics, monetary policy, and the crisis. *IMF Conference on Macro and Growth Policies in the Wake of the Crisis*. Washington: IMF.

Stojanoavic, D., (2022). *Explainer: Why do Kosovo-Serbia Tensions Persist?* Associated Press News. Available at: https://apnews.com/article/politics-serbia-kosovo-european-union-aleksandar-vucic-cce01ee269c5a2a4a7e216936fd4a4a5 (accessed on 15 July 2023).

Stokes, D., (2018). Trump, American hegemony and the future of the liberal international order. *International Affairs, 94*(1), 133–150. https://doi.org/10.1093/ia/iix238.

Stoltenberg, J. (2021). *Joint press point.* NATO. Available at: https://www.nato.int/cps/en/natohq/opinions_181350.htm?selectedLocale=en (accessed on 30 July 2023).

Stout, D., (2001). *Bush Says He Wants Capture of Bin Laden 'Dead or Alive.'* The New York Times. Available at: https://www.nytimes.com/2001/09/17/national/bush-says-he-wants-capture-of-bin-laden-dead-or-alive.html (accessed on 15 July 2023).

Stradiotto, G. A., (2004). Democratızıng Iraq: Regime transition and economic development in comparative perspective. *International Journal on World Peace, 21*(2), 3–36.

Strong, J., (2017). *Public Opinion, Legitimacy and Tony Blair's War in Iraq.* London: Routledge.

Suri, J., (2017). *How Trump's Executive Orders Could Set America Back 70 Years.* The Atlantic. Available at: https://www.theatlantic.com/politics/archive/2017/01/trumps-executive-orders-will-set-america-back-70-years/514730/ (accessed on 15 July 2023).

Sweeney, M., (2020). *Assessing Chinese Maritime Power.* Defense Priorities. Available at: https://www.defensepriorities.org/explainers/assessing-chinese-maritime-power (accessed on 15 July 2023).

Syria's War: Aid Agencies Suspend Cooperation with UN, (2016). Al Jazeera. Available at: https://www.aljazeera.com/news/2016/9/8/syrias-war-aid-agencies-suspend-cooperation-with-un (accessed on 15 July 2023).

Talbott, S., (1995). Why NATO should grow. *New York Review of Books, 27,* 28.

Taliban Government in Afghanistan: Background and Issues for Congress, (2001). Congressional Research Service. Available at: https://crsreports.congress.gov/product/pdf/R/R46955 (accessed on 15 July 2023).

Tayal, U., (2003). Public health at risk as aid agencies pull out of Iraq. *BMJ, 327*(7414), 522. doi: 10.1136/bmj.327.7414.522-d. PMID: 12958106; PMCID: PMC1150329.

Tek kişi kalsak da Ladin'i vermeyiz. (2001). Hürriyet. Available at: https://www.hurriyet.com.tr/gundem/tek-kisi-kalsak-da-ladin-i-vermeyiz-20336 (accessed on 30 July, 2023).

Tellis, A. J., (2004). Assessing America's war on terror: Confronting insurgency, cementing primacy. *NBR Analysis, 15*(4), 1–104.

The 9/11 Commission Report, (2002). *Final Report of the National Commission on Terrorist Attacks Upon the US.* Government Printing Office. Available at: https://www.govinfo.gov/content/pkg/GPO-911REPORT/pdf/GPO-911REPORT.pdf (accessed on 15 July 2023).

The U.S. War in Afghanistan, (n.d.). Council on Foreign Relations. Available at: https://www.cfr.org/timeline/us-war-afghanistan (accessed on 15 July 2023).

Tierney, D., (2012). *The Obama Doctrine and The Lessons of Iraq* (p. 3). Foreign Policy Research Institute, E-Notes. Available at: https://www.files.ethz.ch/isn/146469/2012_05_tierney_obama_iraq.pdf (accessed on 15 July 2023).

Tierney, D., (2022). *The Ukraine War and the New Global Liberal Order.* The National Interest. Available at: https://nationalinterest.org/feature/ukraine-war-and-new-global-liberal-order-205561 (accessed on 15 July 2023).

Timeline: How the New Coronavirus Spread, (2020). Al Jazeera. Available at: https://www.aljazeera.com/news/2020/12/31/timeline-how-the-new-coronavirus-spread (accessed on 15 July 2023).

Timeline: Political Crisis in Ukraine and Russia's Occupation of Crimea, (2014). Reuters. Available at: https://www.reuters.com/article/us-ukraine-crisis-timeline-idUSBREA270PO20140308 (accessed on 15 July 2023).

Tooze, A., (2021). *Has Covid Ended the Neoliberal Era?* The Guardian. Available at: https://www.theguardian.com/news/2021/sep/02/covid-and-the-crisis-of-neoliberalism (accessed on 15 July 2023).

Torbati, Y., (2016). *Trump Election Puts Nuclear Deal on Shaky Ground.* Reuters. Available at: https://www.reuters.com/article/us-usa-election-trump-iran-idUSKBN13427E (accessed on 15 July 2023).

Trade Set to Plunge as COVID-19 Pandemic Upends Global Economy, (2020). World Trade Organization. Available at: https://www.wto.org/english/news_e/pres20_e/pr855_e.htm (accessed on 15 July 2023).

Trial is Adjourned After Americans Fail to Appear in Cairo Court, (2012). CNN. Available at: https://edition.cnn.com/2012/02/26/world/africa/egypt-ngos/index.html (accessed on 15 July 2023).

Truman Doctrine, (1947). National Archives. Available at: https://www.archives.gov/milestone-documents/truman-doctrine (accessed on 15 July 2023).

Trump Threatens to Pull US out of World Trade Organization, (2018). BBC News. Available at: https://www.bbc.com/news/world-us-canada-45364150 (accessed on 15 July 2023).

Trump, D., (2016a). *Transcript: Trump on NATO, Turkey's Coup Attempt, and the World.* The New York Times. Available at: https://www.nytimes.com/2016/07/22/us/politics/donald-trump-foreign-policy-interview.html (accessed on 15 July 2023).

Trump, D., (2016b). *Transcript: Donald Trump's Foreign Policy Speech.* The New York Times. Available at: https://www.nytimes.com/2016/04/28/us/politics/transcript-trump-foreign-policy.html (accessed on 15 July 2023).

Trump, D. (2017). *The Inaugural Address.* The White House. Available at https://www.whitehouse.gov/briefingsstatements/the-inaugural-address/(accessed on 30 July 2023).

Tsygankov, A. P., (2005). Vladimir Putin's vision of Russia as a normal great power. *Post-Soviet Affairs, 21*(2), 132–158.

Tsygankov, A. P., (2013). *Russia's Foreign Policy: Change and Continuity in National Identity.* Rowman & Littlefield Publishers.

Tsygankov, P. A., & Tsygankov, A. P., (2004). Dilemmas and promises of Russian liberalism. *Communist and Post-Communist Studies, 37*(1), 53–70.

Tuathail, G. O., (1999). A strategic sign: The geopolitical significance of 'Bosnia' in US foreign policy. *Environment and Planning D: Society and Space, 17*(5), 515–533. https://doi.org/10.1068/d170.

Tucker, S. C., (2017). *Modern Conflict in the Greater Middle East: A Country-by-Country Guide.* ABC-CLIO.

Tunç, H., (2004). *Amerika'nın Irak Savaşı.* İstanbul: Harmoni Yayın.

Turner, S., (2009). Russia, China and a multipolar world order: The danger in the undefined. *Asian Perspective, 33*(1), 159–184.

U.S. National Archives and Records Administration, (2020). *Declaration of Independence: A Transcription. Available at:* https://www.archives.gov/founding-docs/declaration-transcript (accessed on 15 July 2023).

Ukraine Wins IMF Deal; Faces $9 Billion in Debt Payments This Year, (2014). Available at: https://www.reuters.com/article/uk-ukraine-crisis-debts-imf-idAFKBN0DH3BG20140501 (accessed on 15 July 2023).

Ulfstein, G., (2003). Terrorism and the use of force. *Security Dialogue, 34*(2), 153–167.

US Department of Defense, (2011). In: Chambliss, W. J., & Eglitis, D. S., (eds.), *Discover Sociology – 2016.* London: SAGE Publications.

US GDP As Percentage of World GDP, (1997–2021). YCharts. Available at: https://ycharts. com/indicators/us_gdp_as_a_percentage_of_world_gdp (accessed on 15 July 2023).

US Institute of Peace, (2002). *International Terrorism: Definitions, Causes, and Responses.* Available at: https://www.usip.org/sites/default/files/terrorism.pdf (accessed on 15 July 2023).

Uslubaş, F., (2005). *Küresel Terör, Afganistan, BOP, ABD; İmparatorlukların Bataklığı.* İstanbul: Toplumsal Dönüşüm Yayınları.

Üncel, A. E., & Güner, O., (2021). 17+1 cooperation: An overall assessment on China-central and eastern European countries relations. *Uluslararası İlişkiler ve Diplomasi, 4*(2), 49–67.

Varrall, M., (2020). *Behind the News: Inside China Global Television Network.* Lowy Institute. Available at: https://www.lowyinstitute.org/publications/behind-news-inside-china-global-television-network (accessed on 15 July 2023).

Viotti, P. R., & Kauppi, M. V., (2019). *International Relations Theory.* Rowman & Littlefield.

Walt, S. M., (2009). Alliances in a unipolar world. *World Politics, 61*(1), 86–120. doi: 10.1017/S0043887109000045.

Walt, S. M., (2017). *In Praise of a Transatlantic Divorce.* Foreign Policy. Available at: https://foreignpolicy.com/2017/05/30/in-praise-of-a-transatlantic-divorce-trump-merkel-europe-nato/ (accessed on 15 July 2023).

Walt, S. M., (2018a). *The Hell of Good Intentions: America's Foreign Policy Elite and the Decline of the US Primacy.* Farrar, Straus and Giroux.

Walt, S. M., (2018b). The Donald versus the blob. In: Jervis, R., Gavin, F. J., Rovner, J., Labrosse, D. N., & Fujii, G., (eds.), *Chaos in the Liberal Order: The Trump Presidency and International Politics in the Twenty-First Century,* (pp. 99–109). Columbia University Press.

Walt, S. M., (2018c). US grand strategy after the Cold War: Can realism explain it? Should realism guide it? *International Relations, 32*(1), 3–22.

Waltz, K. N., (1993). The Emerging Structure of International Politics. *International Security, 18*(2), 44–79. https://doi.org/10.2307/2539097.

Waltz, K. N., (2000). NATO expansion: A realist's view. *Contemporary Security Policy, 21*(2), 23–38. https://doi.org/10.1080/13523260008404253.

Waltz, K. N., (2010). *Theory of International Politics* (p. 121). Long Grove. Illinois: Waveland Press, Inc.

Webber, M., (2009). The Kosovo war: A recapitulation. *International Affairs, 85*(3), 447–459. doi: 0.1111/j.1468-2346.2009.00807.x.

Weber, S., & Jentleson, B. W., (2010). *The End of Arrogance: America in the Global Competition of Ideas* (pp. 377, 378). Harvard University Press.

Weiss, J., & Wallace, J., (2021). Domestic politics, China's rise, and the future of the liberal international order. *International Organization, 75*(2), 635–664.

Wendt, A. E., (1987). The agent-structure problem in international relations theory. *International Organization, 41*(3), 335–370. http://www.jstor.org/stable/2706749 (accessed on 15 July 2023).

Wendt, A. E., (1999). *A Social Theory of International Politics*. New York: Cambridge University Press.

Western, J., (2002). Sources of humanitarian intervention. *International Security, 26*(4), 112–142. doi: 10.1162/016228802753696799.

What You Need to Know About Implementing Steel and Aluminum Tariffs on Canada, Mexico, and the European Union, (2018). White House, Articles [Economy&Jobs]. Available at: https://trumpwhitehouse.archives.gov/articles/need-know-implementing-steel-aluminum-tariffs-canada-mexico-european-union/ (accessed on 15 July 2023).

White, G. M., (2004). National subjects: September 11 and pearl harbor. *American Ethnologist, 31*(3), 293–310.

Wides-Munoz, L. (2022). *U.S. announces $350 million in additional military aid to Ukraine.* Los Angeles Times. Available at: https://www.latimes.com/politics/story/2022-02-26/us-additional-military-aid-ukraine (accessed on 30 July 2023).

Wiseman, P., & McHugh D., (2022). *Economic Dangers from Russia's Invasion Ripple Across Globe.* AP News. Available at: https://apnews.com/article/russia-ukraine-vladimir-putin-coronavirus-pandemicbusiness-health-9478a9825c9abfde5f6505bd34b2998c (accessed on 15 July 2023).

Wohlforth, W., (1999). The stability of a unipolar world. *International Security, 24*(1), 5–41. doi: 10.1162/016228899560031.

Wohlforth, W., (2002). U.S. strategy in a unipolar world. In: Ikenberry, G. J., (ed.), *America Unrivaled* (pp. 98–118). Cornell University Press.

Woodward, B., (1996). *The Choice.* Simon & Schuster.

World Bank Group, (2022). *Four Decades of Poverty Reduction in China.* Washington DC International Bank for Reconstruction and Development/The World Bank.

World Economic Outlook Databases, (n.d.). International Monetary Fund. Available at: https://www.imf.org/en/Publications/WEO/weo-database/2010/April/select-country-group (accessed on 15 July 2023).

Worthington, K. J., (2019). *The Political Leadership of International Security in the Middle East* Degree of Bachelor of Arts, Fordham University. Available at: https://research.library.fordham.edu/cgi/viewcontent.cgi?article=1022&context=international_senior (accessed on 15 July 2023).

Wright, T., (2017). *The Foreign Crises Awaiting Trump.* The Atlantic. Available at: https://www.theatlantic.com/international/archive/2017/01/trump-russia-putin-north-korea-putin/513749/ (accessed on 15 July 2023).

Wu, J., (2016). The China factor in Taiwan: Impact and response. In: Schubert, G., (ed.), *Handbook of Modern Taiwan Politics and Society* (pp. 426–446). Routledge.

Yüce, S., (2022). Understanding Iraq's persistent domestic instability: A revisit to the 2003 Iraq War and the effect of the US foreign policy. *Afro Eurasian Studies, 8*(3), 249–260.

Yuri, M. Z., (2016). Trading hard hats for combat helmets: The economics of rebellion in eastern Ukraine. *Journal of Comparative Economics, 10*(43), 1–15.

Zając, J., (2016). *Poland's Security Policy* (p. 167). London: Palgrave Macmillan.

Zakaria, F., (2020). *It's Easy to Blame Trump for this Fiasco. But There is a Much Large Story.* Washington Post. Available at: https://www.washingtonpost.com/opinions/the-us-is-still-exceptional--but-now-for-its-incompetence/2020/03/26/4d6d1ade-6f9b-11ea-a3ec-70d7479d83f0_story.html (accessed on 15 July 2023).

Zapatero, J. L. R., (2004). *Statement by the President of the Government of State at the 59th Session of the United Nations General Assembly.* Available at: http://www.un.org/webcast/ga/59/statements/spaeng040921.pdf (accessed on 15 July 2023).

Zhao, L., & Kao-Jen, L., (2022). The speed and quality of China's economic growth during the COVID-19 pandemic. *The Singapore Economic Review*, 1–17. https://doi.org/10.1142/S0217590822400021.

Index

Made in the USA
Monee, IL
24 July 2024